FORGIVE

FORGIVE

WHY SHOULD I
AND HOW CAN I?

TIMOTHY KELLER

VIKING

VIKING
An imprint of Penguin Random House LLC
penguinrandomhouse.com

LIBRARY OF CONGRESS CATALOGING-IN-PUBLICATION DATA
Names: Keller, Timothy, 1950- author.
Title: Forgive : why should I and how can I? / Timothy Keller.
Description: New York : Viking, [2022] | Includes bibliographical references.
Identifiers: LCCN 2022013423 (print) | LCCN 2022013424 (ebook) |
ISBN 9780525560746 (hardcover) | ISBN 9780525560753 (ebook)
Subjects: LCSH: Forgiveness—Religious aspects--Christianity.
Classification: LCC BV4647.F55 K43 2022 (print) | LCC BV4647.F55 (ebook) |
DDC 234/.5—dc23/eng/20220803
LC record available at https://lccn.loc.gov/2022013423
LC ebook record available at https://lccn.loc.gov/2022013424

Printed in the United States of America
4th Printing

DESIGNED BY MEIGHAN CAVANAUGH

To David A. Powlison and Donald A. Carson—

Two friends and gifted Bible teachers whose scriptural insights on forgiveness served as the foundation for this book

CONTENTS

PRACTICING FORGIVENESS

THE PARABLE OF THE
UNFORGIVING SERVANT

Then Peter came up and said to him, "Lord, how often will my brother sin against me, and I forgive him? As many as seven times?" Jesus said to him, "I do not say to you seven times, but seventy-seven times.

"Therefore the kingdom of heaven may be compared to a king who wished to settle accounts with his servants. When he began to settle, one was brought to him who owed him ten thousand talents. And since he could not pay, his master ordered him to be sold, with his wife and children and all that he had, and payment to be made. So the servant fell on his knees, imploring him, 'Have patience with me, and I will pay you everything.' And out of pity for him, the master of that servant released him and forgave him the debt.

"But when that same servant went out, he found one of his fellow servants who owed him a hundred denarii, and seizing him, he began to choke him, saying, 'Pay what you owe.' So his fellow servant fell down and pleaded with him, 'Have patience with me, and I will pay you.' He refused and went and put him in prison until he should pay the debt.

"When his fellow servants saw what had taken place, they were greatly distressed, and they went and reported to their master all that had taken place. Then his master summoned him and said to him, 'You wicked servant! I forgave you all that debt because you pleaded with me. And should not you have had mercy on your fellow servant, as I had mercy on you?' And in anger his master delivered him to the jailers, until he should pay all his debt.

[And Jesus said,] "So also my heavenly Father will do to every one of you, if you do not forgive your brother from your heart." (Matthew 18:21–35, ESV)[1]

"NO FUTURE WITHOUT FORGIVENESS"

For me, forgiveness and compassion are always linked: how do we hold people accountable for wrongdoing and yet at the same time remain in touch with their humanity enough to believe in their capacity to be transformed?

—BELL HOOKS, IN CONVERSATION WITH MAYA ANGELOU[1]

The Conflict over Forgiveness

Desmond Tutu, a Black South African who grew up under apartheid, insisted that "without forgiveness there is no future" for South Africa. He rejected the Nuremburg trials model that was used in post-Nazi Germany in dealing with war crimes. That approach would have required a full trial and punishment for all accused of violent crimes under the apartheid regime. Instead Tutu devised a plan that offered amnesty and forgiveness for any perpetrators of violence—Black or white—who would come forward and publicly confess the full truth of what they had done during certain prescribed years.

While there were no civil penalties for confessors, the light of truth and knowledge made it possible for their society to move forward; there were natural consequences, moral and social, for the perpetrators. The Truth and Reconciliation Commission created opportunities for personal forgiveness to be extended and relationships to be restored. Bishop Tutu argued that the alternative to forgiveness in South Africa would have been the cycle of violence seen in the Balkans after the breakup of Yugoslavia.[2]

When Desmond Tutu died the last week of 2021, I wrote this on Twitter:

> Many argue "forgiveness culture" helps abusers escape accountability. Desmond Tutu argued that without forgiveness abusers hold us in thrall, that it was possible to pursue both forgiveness and justice at once. He rejected the Nuremberg Trial model for Truth and Reconciliation.[3]

The response, as I expected, was mixed. Many survivors of abuse warned that the requirement of forgiveness had been used against victims, imploring them to move on, get over it, and forgive. Some responders saw this as a strategy for institutions and abusers to avoid accountability. And yet most of these same voices could not deny the accomplishment of Desmond Tutu's commission. One person responded to the tweet: "Asking people to forgive and move on . . . helps abusers escape responsibility," but then added: "I know Rev Tutu did an amazing job and showed and taught true grace."

Others said that Tutu's model might modify our current cancel culture. Michael Dyson admitted that today, his call for forgiveness "might seem quaint, hokey or downright irrelevant . . . including most social justice advocates," but he urged all to pay attention to it nonetheless.[4]

The Fading of Forgiveness

The contradictory responses to Tutu's work upon his death serve as a micro-cosm of our own society's conflicted attitude toward forgiveness. In June 2020 Elizabeth Bruenig of *The New York Times* tweeted:

> There's just something unsustainable about an environment that demands constant atonement, but actively disdains the very idea of forgiveness.[5]

She was quickly inundated with upset emails and soon deleted what she had written out of concern for the distress she had caused. In an interview, however, she explained that we have a culture marked by an outraged sense of justice and the desire to make people atone for sins. "I [see] in American culture how offended people seem by the very idea of forgiveness itself. They seem to find it immoral and I think that is very disturbing."[6]

Many are finding the concept of forgiveness increasingly problematic.

After the 2014 deaths of Michael Brown in Ferguson, Missouri, and Eric Garner in New York City, a new movement for racial justice emerged, originally embodied by a new network called Black Lives Matter. But after George Floyd was killed in Minneapolis in May of 2020, the calls for changes to the systemic racism in Western societies burst the banks of any one organization. Tens of millions of people took to the streets around the world to call for change. This new movement sounded different notes than did the civil rights movement of the sixties. "This ain't your grandparents' civil rights movement,"[7] said rapper Tef Poe. He argued that it would be much angrier.

Our cultural problem with forgiveness is not confined to matters of race. The #MeToo movement also struggles with the call to forgive. Many women ask: Doesn't forgiving perpetrators only encourage abuse? The so-cial media world also seems to be a realm in which missteps and wrongful posts are never forgiven. Instead, screenshots of every foolish word you have ever said online can be circulated in perpetuity.

Even after TV personality Whoopi Goldberg apologized for offensive remarks about the Holocaust, she was still suspended and punished. Jew-ish writer Nathan Hersh found this lack of forgiveness "troubling." He found Goldberg's remarks anti-Semitic and offensive, but he cited the Jewish and biblical tradition of forgiving the person who repents. He ex-pressed concern that the culture's need to cancel even those who were willing to change would not serve to diminish bigotry. It might fuel it.[8]

"To Hell with Forgiveness Culture"

Relatives of the nine African Americans killed in Charleston, South Caro-lina, publicly said to the shooter, Dylann Roof, "I forgive you." A *Washing-ton Post* opinion piece by Stacey Patton responded that "Black America Should Stop Forgiving White Racists."[9] The expectation and admiration for Black people's forgiveness, she wrote, "is about protecting whiteness. . . . It enables white denial about the harms that racist violence creates. . . . Our constant forgiveness [only] perpetuates the cycle of attacks and abuse." Quick forgiveness, she argued, translates into the inability to hold perpetra-tors of injustice accountable for their behavior.

In September 2018 Amber Guyger, a Dallas police officer, came home from work and entered a neighboring apartment, mistakenly thinking it was her own. When she saw a Black man inside the apartment, she shot and killed him. It was Botham Jean, her unarmed neighbor, watching TV in his own home. Just after Guyger was sentenced in court to ten years in prison, the victim's brother Brandt Jean publicly forgave her and embraced her. Across the country the response to this moving scene was decidedly mixed. The Institute for Law Enforcement Administration gave Brandt the 2019 Ethical Courage Award.

But others argued that such public Black forgiveness of whites only ends up supporting white dominance. Kevin Powell wrote an article entitled "The Insanity of White Justice and Black Forgiveness: Reducing Another Tragic Loss of Black Life to a Hallmark Card Is Not Justice."[10] Lawyer and activist Preston Mitchum tweeted: "Black people are historically forced to show empathy to colonizers and made to feel bad when we don't."[11]

However, Barbara Reynolds, a septuagenarian who had marched in the civil rights protests of the 1960s, wrote a counterpoint essay to Stacey Patton's in the same newspaper. She argued that the movements led by Martin Luther King Jr. and Nelson Mandela won the high moral ground and persuaded the majority because they were marked by "the ethics of love, forgiveness and reconciliation," and they triumphed because of "the power of the spiritual approach."[12]

Reynolds concluded her article by asserting that that love and forgiveness "are missing from this movement." Forgiveness, she argued, disarms the oppressors and wins over many of their supporters, weakening the system. "If you get angry," she quotes Andrew Young as saying, "it is contagious and you end up acting as bad as the perpetrators." The current angry approach, she said, could lead to short-term gains but in the end will only divide the country rather than unify it.

And yet—don't those people frustrated with the lack of change, like Stacey Patton, have a point? Isn't it true that if a continually oppressed group of people forgive their oppressors, it may merely keep the system in place?

Sabine Birdsong blames the abuses of forgiveness not just on bad practice but on Christianity itself. A blog post with the eye-catching title "To Hell with Forgiveness Culture" argued that "we continue to believe forgiveness makes a person superior and if they can't manage something so simple, the fault lies with them." The author blames this on "a deeply in-grained religious hangover from Christianity," a mindset that "manifests itself in edicts like forgive and forget, turn the other cheek." We condemn persons who won't forgive, saying they are "'poisoning themselves,'" which is "tantamount to another Abrahamic culturally-ingrained guilt trip. In short, it is victim blaming." This serves only to help abusers who "can act with impunity . . . [because] no matter the grave depths of their actions, they can rest in smug assurance that they will be forgiven." The emphasis on forgiveness also tends to humanize perpetrators, making it harder to hold them accountable. "People love a good redemption story. This [for-giveness] narrative is nothing but a mere plot device spun to give character depth . . . [to] the perpetrator at the expense of their victims."[13]

In a follow-up the author urged that we "rewrite the outdated narra-tives of forgiveness," which idealize "the pseudo-spiritual fairy-tale of re-demption and forgiveness over the inherent right for people to not be abused."[14]

This final quote isolates the problem we feel today—the apparent con-tradiction between forgiveness and justice, the sense that we will have to choose one over the other.

But is that true?

The Indelible Need for Forgiveness

The human need for forgiveness appears to be indelible. It won't go away by denouncing it or trying to deconstruct it. The need I'm referring to is both a profound need *to grant* forgiveness and *to receive* forgiveness.

On New Year's Eve in 1843, in a Lutheran parish in Möttlingen, Ger-many, a young man came to the door of the church's pastor, Johann Blum-hardt. He unburdened himself in confession of many sins and misdeeds, both major and minor. The man experienced great relief and word of it spread. By the end of January, 35 people had come to unburden their consciences with the pastor and ask for God's forgiveness. By mid-February over 150 had done so.

This revival, chronicled in a number of places, was remarkable for the concrete changes in behavior it brought about. "Stolen goods were returned; enemies were reconciled; infidelities were confessed and broken marriages restored. Crimes, including a case of infanticide, were solved," and alcoholics found sobriety.[15] Here we see an example of how the granting of forgiveness ignited a movement toward greater justice in that town.

During Christ's early ministry, a group of four friends brought a paralyzed man to the house where Jesus was speaking in hopes of getting a healing for him. "Since they could not get him to Jesus because of the crowd, they made an opening in the roof above . . . by digging through it and then lowered the mat the man was lying on" (Mark 2:4). To everyone's shock, Jesus did not at first heal his paralysis. Instead "when Jesus saw their faith, he said to the paralyzed man, 'Son, your sins are forgiven'" (verse 5).

For a moment imagine yourself as the paralyzed man. You would have felt (and if you had a bold personality you might have said), "Uh, thanks— but isn't it obvious I have a more urgent need here?" And if you had said that, Jesus would have answered, "No, you don't."

It's likely that the man had been feeling, "If I could just walk again— then I'd be happy. I'd never complain. I'd be content." But Jesus, as it were, is saying: "Look around you at all these people—they can all walk. Are their hearts all filled with contentment? Are they all happy? If I only heal you, you will be overjoyed for a while, but then you will become like everyone else." No. What the man needed was forgiveness. Forgiveness gets down to the bottom of things—to the alienation we feel from God and from ourselves because of our wrongdoing.

Jesus was saying: "I want to show you that the deepest need of your nature is for me. Only I can bestow perfect love, new identity, endless comfort, hope, and glory. *And the doorway into all of that is to know forgiveness.*"

It's time to open that door and walk through it.

FORGIVE

CHAPTER 1

A STORY OF FORGIVENESS

WILL MUNNY: It's a hell of a thing, ain't it, killing a man. You take everythin' he's got and everythin' he's ever gonna have.

THE SCHOFIELD KID: Well, I gu-guess they had it . . . comin'.

WILL MUNNY: We all got it comin', Kid.

—UNFORGIVEN (1992)

A Story of Forgiveness Failure

Tom was a professional investor who had done well in his stock picking over the past few years. Flush with confidence, he went to a wealthy friend, Joseph, and asked for an enormous loan so he could buy large stakes in various hot stocks. He promised Joseph a great return and, based on past performance, that seemed very possible. However, he hid from Joseph a number of facts about the companies in which he was investing.

When one of the companies went into crisis and the market moved against Tom's stocks, Joseph lost millions of dollars. When Joseph saw what had happened, he wrote:

> How could you have done this to me, Tom? I trusted your word and you hid from me the level of risk to which you had me ex-

posed. You have wronged me. I demand that you pay me back, and I am going to court to see that this happens.

Tom went to see Joseph. He walked into Joseph's office, sat down, and burst into tears. "If you sue me for this amount, I will literally have nothing left! Please forgive me!"

And Joseph did forgive him. It was an astonishing act of mercy. Joseph had lost a fortune because of Tom's wrongdoing, but he forgave it.

Tom's friends were shocked when he told them of Joseph's magnanimity and generosity. But they were just as amazed when they saw the next thing Tom did. One man in their circle of friends, Harry, had just been through a bruising divorce. His wife had gotten the house and custody of the children, and Harry was living in a small rented room on very little income.

"Hey," Tom said to Harry within days of his meeting with Joseph, "I lent you five thousand dollars last year and I need it back now."

"You couldn't have asked me at a worse time," said Harry. "That's nearly all I have in savings. If I gave that to you, I'd be out on the street. Please give me more time—or, if you'd be willing, just forgive the debt altogether. That's what I most need now."

"What do you take me for?" laughed Tom. "If you don't give it to me, I'll find ways to make your life pretty uncomfortable! Pay me now or else."

One of Tom's appalled friends contacted Joseph and told him the whole story. Joseph called Tom and said: "Shouldn't you have forgiven your friend his debt as I forgave you yours? Tomorrow I'll resubmit my lawsuit against you for losing my money. We'll let the courts deal with you."

The Parable of the Unforgiving Servant

Readers may have already recognized that this is a retelling of a parable told by Jesus Christ himself. This passage (which was printed at the beginning of this volume) is perhaps the most sustained treatment of the subject of forgiveness in the New Testament. But it does not come in the form of a treatise or an essay. Instead, it is a gripping story, and a tragic one. This realistic account of life in this world shows how an act of forgiveness, even with all its healing, life-transforming potential, can still be abused in a way that brings ruin to all those around.

> Then Peter came to Jesus and asked, "Lord, how many times shall I forgive my brother or sister who sins against me? Up to seven times?" Jesus answered, "I tell you not seven times, but seventy-seven times." (Matthew 18:21–22)

The Lord had given the issue of forgiveness great prominence in his teaching. Indeed, the only rider added to the Lord's Prayer itself is Matthew 6:14–15, in which he says emphatically that if we deny forgiveness to others, God will deny forgiveness to us.

The disciples were stunned by Jesus's claim that forgiveness by God and forgiveness of others were interdependent. Peter's question shows his concern that Jesus's command could be used by an unscrupulous perpetrator to sin against others without accountability. So Peter suggests a limit. "Lord, how many times shall I forgive my brother or sister who sins against me? Up to seven times?" Peter's proposal would have seemed generous to him, for even the Talmud (b. Yoma 86b–87a) held that we have to forgive the same person only three times.[1]

Jesus refuses to grant that there is a limit to forgiveness. His startling declaration is that we must forgive "not seven times, but seventy-seven times." The term he uses is sometimes translated as meaning seventy *times* seven, or 490. But to focus on the precise number is to miss Jesus's meaning entirely. The number seven signified completeness. And that means

> this [statement by Jesus is in] the language of hyperbole, not of calculation. Those who are concerned as to whether the figure should be 77 or 490 . . . have missed the point. . . . [T]here is no limit, no place for keeping a tally of forgivenesses already used up. Peter's question was misconceived: if one is still counting . . . one is not forgiving.[2]

To make his case for this astounding claim, Jesus tells a story.

> "Therefore the kingdom of heaven may be compared to a king who wished to settle accounts with his servants. When he began to settle, one was brought to him who owed him ten thousand talents. And since he could not pay, his master ordered him to be sold, with his wife and children and all that he had, and payment to be made. So the servant fell on his knees, imploring him, 'Have patience with me, and I will pay you everything.' And out of pity for him, the master of that servant released him and forgave him the debt.
>
> "But when that same servant went out, he found one of his fellow servants who owed him a hundred denarii, and seizing him, he began to choke him, saying, 'Pay what you owe.' So his fellow servant fell down and pleaded with him, 'Have patience with me, and I will pay you.' He refused and went and put him in prison until he should pay the debt.
>
> "When his fellow servants saw what had taken place, they were greatly distressed, and they went and reported to their master all that had taken place. Then his master summoned him and

said to him, 'You wicked servant! I forgave you all that debt because you pleaded with me. And should not you have had mercy on your fellow servant, as I had mercy on you?' And in anger his master delivered him to the jailers, until he should pay all his debt.

[And Jesus said,] "So also my heavenly Father will do to every one of you, if you do not forgive your brother from your heart." (Matthew 18:23–35, ESV)

The offense. A king had a servant who owed him a debt of ten thousand talents. All scholars point out the deliberately unrealistic nature of this sum. An ordinary working man could expect to earn perhaps a single talent in a year. Translated into today's terms, in which the average working-class job earns $40,000 a year, that makes the debt $400 billion—more than the gross national products of 80 percent of the countries of the world today. Granting that this is fiction, we still need to understand Jesus's intended meaning. Why did he introduce an inconceivable number? Within the framework of the story, this could not have been a business or personal loan. No king in real life could have or would have given any servant ten thousand talents.

Some think Jesus wanted hearers to imagine a servant who was actually a wealthy governor or satrap in the kingdom and who, through epic mismanagement and malfeasance, had put the entire economy and the very kingdom in jeopardy. On the other hand, it may be that Jesus deliberately intends to point to something that rends the fabric of worldly reality. The talent was the greatest currency denomination in the empire, and ten thousand was the highest number for which the Greek language had a specific word.[3] Jesus may simply be speaking vividly of an *infinite*, immeasurable debt.

The king confronts the servant and demands that he make good on his debt, but this is something that no human being could possibly do. The customary way to handle bankruptcy in ancient cultures was to become a slave, and the king calls for his sale, although of course it could not possibly help him recoup his losses.

The request. The servant asks that the king "have patience with me, and I will pay you everything." Falling on his knees signifies deep emotion, real sorrow for wrongdoing. The offer to "pay back everything" is not just an expression of regret but an offer to make restitution. But even the most sincere effort on the part of the servant could never replace the money that the king and kingdom had lost.

The release. In response the king "released him" and "forgave him the debt," freeing him from liability and obligation. The request by the servant for "patience"—*makrothumeo*, a Greek word that literally means to be slow to boil or melt—hints at the cost of forgiveness. The older English translation for *makrothumeo* was "long-suffering." Patience is the ability to bear suffering rather than give in to it. To forgive someone's debt to you is to absorb the debt yourself. If a friend borrows your car, totals it through reckless driving, and hasn't any ability to remunerate you financially, you may say, "I forgive you," but the price of the wrong does not evaporate into the air. You either find the money to buy a new car or you go without one. Either way, forgiveness means the cost of the wrong moves from the perpetrator to you, and you bear it.

Forgiveness, then, is a form of voluntary suffering. In forgiving, rather than retaliating, you make a choice to bear the cost.

The new offense. In the next scene we see the forgiven servant meeting a second servant. This second man owes the forgiven servant the modern equivalent of a few dollars. But the forgiven servant seizes him and starts choking him! The second servant responds in exactly the same way the forgiven servant responded to the king—making the very same request. But when his fellow servant cannot immediately produce the money, the forgiven servant throws him into prison.

The verdict. When the king hears this, he summons the first servant, and he says, in effect: "How can anyone who has experienced the lavish mercy I showed you have such a cruel, ungenerous attitude toward others?" And with that he throws the first servant into prison. Jesus ends with this chilling line: "So also my heavenly Father will do to every one of you, if you do not forgive your brother *from your heart.*"

The meaning is not hard to discern. The king is God himself. We all are the servant. The ten thousand talents is the infinite debt we owe God. God created us and sustains our lives every second—so we owe him supreme love, dependence, and obedience, but we do not give this to him. There is not a person on earth who does not receive the mercy of God in some way (cf. Psalm 145). Yet the way we treat other human beings falls infinitely short of the generous mercy with which God treats us.

With that basic understanding of the parable's meaning, here's what we learn about both God's forgiveness of us and our forgiveness of others.

The Difficulty of Forgiveness

As we have seen, forgiveness is perceived as difficult and problematic in our society. The parable is more than realistic about this.

Forgiveness is difficult for us to receive. The enormous debt that the servant owes tells us that our debt to God is too large to ever make up. God's forgiveness cannot in any way be merited—it will have to be absolutely free. The servant's pathetic offer to pay the king back is as unrealistic as any effort to earn our way to heaven through good works. To say to God, "If you forgive me, I'll go to church every week, I'll try harder to be a better person!" is as futile as saying, "I'll pay back the four hundred billion dollars by sending in five dollars a month." It is also pointless to think, as the Unforgiving Servant thought, "If I loathe and abase myself and grovel, then I will be worthy of forgiveness." No amount of self-flagellation can undo the damage we've done. Our only hope is astounding, *free* grace and forgiveness from God himself.

Forgiveness is not merely difficult for us. While we have to speak carefully and reverently here, the parable points to what we will see in the rest of the Bible, namely, that God himself faces obstacles to forgiveness. The story hints at the extraordinary *costliness* of forgiveness to God. The parable does not address this directly, yet Jesus deliberately chose an unthinkably mind-numbing size debt that he knew even a great king would find impossible to forgive without destabilizing his kingdom. How forgiving us required of God measures costly even to him remains outside of the scope of this parable.[4] It is hinted at, however—and that is important.

Forgiveness is also difficult for us to grant. Perhaps the most shocking part of the story is the callousness of the forgiven servant toward others. How could he fail to be softened and transformed by the king's mercy? As listeners to the story, we can see the incongruity clearly. Yet we who live only by the mercy of God every second of our lives fail to be kind, merciful, generous, gracious, and forgiving every day. This story, then, is an arrow pointed directly at our own hearts.

The Definition of Forgiveness

Of course there is nothing more important for us than to ask: What *is* forgiveness, actually? False understandings of repentance and forgiveness, as we will see, are spiritually and socially fatal. However, this story helps us see the core definition of forgiveness. In the person of the king, God did four things—he *brought the man* before him but then took *pity on him, forgave the debt, and released him.*[5]

The king first of all had the man "brought to him" (verse 24). Then the actual debt was named. Forgiveness starts with truth telling, with exposure rather than a cover-up of excuses or half-truths.

But then the king *took pity* on him (verse 27). To have pity on somebody who has wronged you means you deliberately do the internal work of understanding the perpetrator's situation, the perpetrator's vulnerability. That is not a natural thing to do. Your heart wants to concentrate only on how bad the wrongdoer is and how much he deserves to suffer. But the king, representing God, thinks of the perpetrator not just as a villain but as a human being with his own fears and griefs.

To *cancel the debt* (verse 27) brings us to the very heart of forgiveness. When the king forgave the debt, it means he absorbed the loss himself. If I take a loan from someone and then say I can't pay it back, and the creditor forgives my debt, that means that she absorbs the loss. "But how does that work," you say, "if we're not talking about money?" Forgiveness means that, when you want to make them suffer, instead you refuse to do it. And this refusal is *hard*. It is difficult and costly, but through it you are absorbing the debt yourself. Some think that by remaining angry they are giving the wrongdoers what they deserve. But in reality you are enabling their actions to continue to hurt you. If instead, bit by bit by bit, you *grant* forgiveness in this way, eventually you'll begin to feel forgiveness.

Finally, it says that the king *let him go* (verse 27). This means the relationship between the man and the king was restored. The man was no longer a debtor and violator of the king's trust but a citizen and servant again. This part of the story will raise questions from those who have concerns about justice, but two things should be borne in mind. As we will see, forgiving and pursuing justice must go hand in hand. In fact, if you don't forgive the person, your justice seeking will likely veer into the territory of revenge.

But this parable does not descend to that level of detail. Instead it shows that anyone who truly forgives—as the king does—is open to reconciliation, to the restoration of the relationship. That, however, is dependent on the response of the one to whom forgiveness is extended. Because the servant does not respond to the king's forgiveness with genuine repentance and a changed life, the relationship with the king breaks down again.

To forgive, then, is first to name the trespass truthfully as wrong and punishable, rather than merely excusing it. Second, it is to identify with the perpetrator as a fellow sinner rather than thinking how different from you he or she is. It is to will their good. Third, it is to release the wrongdoer from liability by absorbing the debt oneself rather than seeking revenge and paying them back. Finally, it is to aim for reconciliation rather than breaking off the relationship forever. If you omit any one of these four actions, you are not engaging in real forgiveness.

The Dimensions of Forgiveness

Perhaps the most fundamental lesson of the parable is that human forgiveness must be based on an experience of divine forgiveness. A superficial reading of verse 35 ("this is how my heavenly Father will treat each of you unless you forgive . . .") has led some to interpret Jesus as saying that God's forgiveness of us depends on and is earned by our forgiveness of others.[6] But the narrative of the story does not fit that interpretation at all. The king extends forgiveness first and then says specifically that the servant's forgiveness of his fellow servant should have been based on and motivated by the king's forgiveness of him. Jesus's final sentence means that divine mercy should change our *hearts* so that we are able to forgive as God forgave us. If we will not offer others forgiveness, it shows that we did not truly repent and receive God's.

The main idea here is found in the king's words of verse 33—"Should not you have had mercy on your fellow servant, as I had mercy on you?" (ESV). Human forgiveness is dependent on divine forgiveness.

In other words, there are three basic dimensions to Christian forgiveness. First there is the vertical—God's forgiveness to us. Second there is the internal—our granting forgiveness to anyone who has wronged us. Third there is the horizontal—our offer to reconcile. The horizontal is based on the internal, and the internal is based on the vertical.

The Dimensions of Christian Forgiveness

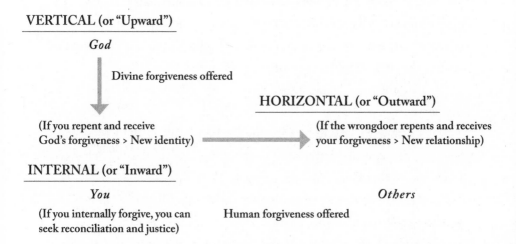

VERTICAL (or "Upward")

God

Divine forgiveness offered

HORIZONTAL (or "Outward")

(If you repent and receive
God's forgiveness > New identity)

(If the wrongdoer repents and receives
your forgiveness > New relationship)

INTERNAL (or "Inward")

You   *Others*

(If you internally forgive, you can   Human forgiveness offered
seek reconciliation and justice)

We must consciously base our forgiveness of others on God's forgiveness of us. The king's forgiveness should have made the servant a forgiver. Why didn't it? The answer, the missing link—as we will explore much further in this book—is the lack of authentic repentance on the part of the servant. Jesus's final words—that forgiveness must be from the *heart*—are crucial. The servant's expression of great emotion and sorrow turns out to have been self-pity rather than genuine contrition. And his failure to repent means there was no link between the vertical and the horizontal dimensions.

(Our) Failures of Forgiveness

We should not miss the confrontational nature of this parable. Jesus's parable about forgiveness is not a feel-good story about people receiving God's forgiveness and then eagerly spreading the love to others. Rather, it is a story about a man asking for forgiveness and then being utterly unchanged when he gets it.

Sometime after King David had taken Uriah's wife, Bathsheba, to be his own, Nathan the prophet came and told David a story about a rich man who had plenty of sheep but who, when he needed food for a party, stole the only lamb owned by a poor man. David grew angry and said the man in the story should surely die.

"*You* are the man!" said Nathan (2 Samuel 12:7), and David was cut to the heart.

This is how we should be listening to the parable of the Unforgiving Servant. The rest of Matthew 18 is about the kind of radically changed relationships that Christians should have. They should be marked by humility and service toward others rather than pride (Matthew 18:1–5), by patience and understanding regarding people's flaws (Matthew 18:6–10), and by a readiness to reconcile and heal broken relationships (Matthew 18:11–17).

Yet Jesus then wakes us up to bitter reality with this story. Most people who profess to have asked for God's forgiveness have not been transformed by it—and the place we see it is in our relationships. Jesus says that visible, unusual, evident love is a mark of his true disciples (John 13:34–35), that the unique, loving community that Christians form is one of the main ways the world will know Jesus is who he claimed to be (John 17:20–23). John drives this home repeatedly in his first epistle—it is extraordinary love that is evidence that you know God personally and not just in a formal, nominal way (1 John 2:5,10, 3:11,14,16–18, 4:7–11,16–21).

This parable is an account of forgiveness failure because *that is the usual human story*. The movement from divine forgiveness to human forgiveness is constantly being frustrated by human sin. Even in Jesus's other famous parable about forgiveness—the parable of the Prodigal Son—we see the Father's action causing offense and controversy instead of love and generosity.

Are Christian churches famous for their love and graciousness to skeptics and nonbelievers? They are not. Are you a professing Christian? If so, are you known by your friends and neighbors for being unusually loving, generous, gracious, and forgiving? If not, then hear this parable and hear Jesus saying, "*You* are the one." If we have truly grasped and received his salvation, it should change us as it did not change this man. God's mercy *must* and *will* make us merciful—if it doesn't, then we never understood or accepted God's mercy in truth.

If you believe the gospel—that you are saved by sheer grace and the free forgiveness of God—and you still hold a grudge—at the very least it shows that you are blocking the actual effect of the gospel in your life, or you're kidding yourself and perhaps you don't believe the gospel at all. Either way, spiritually speaking, to not forgive somebody is to put yourself in a kind of jail. The final act of the parable—where the Unforgiving Servant is thrown into prison—seems harsh, but it is quite realistic. The self-centeredness that grows when you stay angry at somebody, when you hold things against them, when you continue to regard them as if they're liable to you and they owe you, is a prison.

When I was a young pastor in a small town in Virginia, I came upon two people almost the same week who were locked in their own prisons of non-forgiveness. It was June and we were sponsoring a "vacation Bible school." We knocked on all the doors in the surrounding neighborhood to invite the residents to send their children for the week. One young father at the door was initially polite and said, "No, thank you." However, when I offered to come by and pick his sons up, he answered with some heat, "My father *forced* us to go to church. He *forced* religion down our throats. I will *never, ever* let my sons darken the door of any church!" I'm pretty sure he then mumbled something about how unhappy he was that there was even a church so near his house. There was nothing more to say, but it was clear that, because he was still so angry at his father, both he and his parenting were still being directed and controlled *by* his father.

Not long afterward I had a long talk with a teenage girl who was a member of my church. She too had an overbearing and difficult father, and he had embarrassed her in front of her friends. She told me that she refused to ever forgive him for that. My counterpoint went something like this: "Yes, he did you wrong, but if you don't forgive him the way Jesus forgave you, you will actually give him power over you. You will do things not because they are the best things to do but because in your heart you know your father wouldn't like them. You will *not* do other things because you know your father *would* like them. I've seen this happen with other kids. I don't want it to happen to you." To my surprise, it made perfect sense to her. "I never thought of it like that," she said.

She was able to evade the prison that the Unforgiving Servant—and many others—did not.

Growing Wings for Forgiveness

The strong and rightful condemnation of the Unforgiving Servant can distract us from the life change that the parable assumes. We don't forgive through trying harder or appeals to social benefits or self-interest. We are to meet the living God through repentance and faith, receiving not just an abstract pardon but Christ himself and a new identity as an accepted, justified, adopted, and unconditionally loved child of God. Then we are to commune with that God through the Word, prayer, and worship so that these objective realities become more and more subjectively real to our hearts and so shape the instinctive ways we respond to life.

In a hymn the eighteenth-century poet William Cowper eloquently describes this change. Cowper had obeyed the law and sought to be moral strictly for pragmatic reasons—he wanted to merit God's blessing and heaven in the afterlife. Yet he found that these reasons, which were basically negative ones of fear of punishment, were not sufficient to truly change his character. His faith was resting in his own ability to live up to moral standards, and the pressure was crushing him. When salvation by grace and forgiveness was explained to him, he put his faith in Christ truly, and it completely changed his inner motivation.

> How long beneath the Law I lay
> In bondage and distress;
> I toiled the precept to obey,
> But toiled without success.
> Then all my servile works were done
> A righteousness to raise;
> Now, freely chosen in the Son,
> I freely choose His ways.
> To see the law by Christ fulfilled
> And hear His pardoning voice,
> Changes a slave into a child,
> And duty into choice.[7]

C. S. Lewis has a classic metaphor for what Cowper has described:

> For mere [moral] improvement is not redemption. . . . It is not like teaching a horse to jump better and better but like turning a horse into a winged creature. Of course, once it has got its wings, it will soar over fences which could never have been jumped and thus beat the natural horse at its own game. But there may be a period, while the wings are just beginning to grow, when it cannot do so: and at that stage the lumps on the shoulders—no one could tell by looking at them that they are going to be wings—may even give it an awkward appearance.[8]

The parable tells us that if we are really Christ's followers, if we have grasped and experienced gospel grace, those "wings" *will* be growing. Jesus is saying, at the end of the parable, something like this: "If you hold a grudge, if you retaliate against somebody else, then even though you say you believe you're a sinner saved by grace, you don't really believe that. You're denying it in both your heart and your life, no matter what you say."[9]

Hashim Garrett is a man who grew these wings. Hashim was a fifteen-year-old, living with his mother and hanging out on the streets of Brooklyn with a gang, when he was shot six times and was left paralyzed from the waist down. For most of the next year he lay in a New York City hospital, fantasizing about revenge. He later wrote: "Revenge consumed me. All I could think about was, 'Just wait till I get better; just wait till I see this kid.'"

But when he was lying on the sidewalk immediately after his shooting, he had instinctively called out to God for help and, to his surprise, he had felt a strange tranquility. Now during his rehabilitation, a new thought struck him, namely that if he took revenge on this kid, why should God not pay *him* back for all *his* sins? "You see six months before this happened," he wrote, "I shot a kid, for no reason except that a friend told me to do it and I wanted to prove how tough I was. Six months later, I am shot by somebody because *his* friend told *him* to do it." That thought was electrifying—he could not feel superior to the perpetrator. They were both fellow sinners who deserved punishment—and needed forgiveness.

> In the end . . . I decided to forgive. I felt God had saved my life for a reason, and that I had better fulfill that purpose. . . . And I knew I could never go back out there and harm someone. I was done with that mindset and the life that goes with it. . . . I came to see that I had to let go and stop hating.[10]

The King Who Was a Servant

This parable sketches out the difficulty, definition, and dimensions of for-giveness. The only major aspect of Christian forgiveness that it hints at but does not explicitly depict is the "dynamic" of forgiveness—the basis of it all. What is it that enables God to forgive us so radically even though he is holy and just? What is it that enables us to forgive others so radically by giving us the inner resources of supernatural humility, confidence, love, and joy? It is the atoning death of Christ on the cross.

What was so incongruous about the Unforgiving Servant's attitude to-ward his fellow servants? It is this: you have a man who is a servant, living only by the mercy of the king, acting as if *he* were the king and judge. "Into prison with you!" he says to his fellow servant. How unsuitable and inappropriate. But Jesus wants us to see ourselves in the mirror of this story. When we, who live only by God's mercy, sit in judgment of others, are we not putting ourselves in God's place? If we do, we are judging one another, paying one another back and then suffering retaliation and giving it back again. We're all servants acting like kings.

What will change our hearts? The only thing that will change a ser-vant from acting like a king is getting a view of the amazing love of the King who became a servant.

We should be in the accused prisoner's dock, but we put ourselves in the judge's seat. But the Lord, who rightly sat in the universe's judgment seat, came down, put himself in the dock, and went to the cross. The Judge of all the earth was judged. He was punished for us. He took the punishment we deserve. This humbles us out of our bitterness because we know we are also sinners living only by sheer mercy. But it also exalts us out of our bitterness because we can say: "I've been justified and adopted in Jesus Christ. You've harmed me and I will confront you about it, but you can't take away my real goods, my deepest joys." Then you can forgive.

When Jesus Christ was dying on the cross he said, "Father, forgive them, for they do not know what they are doing" (Luke 23:34). He is saying that what they've done is *wrong*—and requires forgiveness—and yet he asks the Father to give it to them. Instead of screaming at his executioners, "You'll get yours," what does he say? "Father, they really don't understand the magnitude of what they're doing." Jesus was pleading for forgiveness for those who were killing him.

If he treats his executioners like that, how can you and I be cold and withdrawn—how can we be caustic and harsh with people? Jesus wouldn't talk like that even to his torturers. May God give us the grace and patience that can grow only out of a deep grasp of Christ's dying mercy for us.

LOSING AND

FINDING

FORGIVENESS

CHAPTER 2

THE FADING
OF FORGIVENESS

Why should the injured, the still bleeding, bear the onus of forgiveness?

—DELIA OWENS, *WHERE THE CRAWDADS SING*[1]

elia Owens expresses a question that more and more people are asking in our culture. How does the story of the Unforgiving Servant and its rich teaching on forgiveness address our society's anxiety and confusion regarding forgiveness?

#MeToo and the Problem of Forgiveness

In 2006 a sexual assault survivor, Tarana Burke, coined the term *MeToo* to help women who had been similarly abused speak out. Then in late 2017 the movement went viral, ignited by the revelations of Harvey Weinstein's history of sexual abuse. During the first few months of the movement, many women found the new support enabled them to come forward with stories of sexual harassment, abuse, and assault. It showed society that this behavior by men was far more pervasive than people had wanted to admit. In this movement's wake, many pointed to a host of good changes, from new workplace rules to increased support, formal and informal, for abuse victims. Inevitably the issue of forgiveness surfaced.

The actress Salma Hayek wrote that she had rationalized her silence about Weinstein's sexual harassment because "I had been proud of my capacity for forgiveness."[2] But, she said, this emphasis on forgiveness had been a cover for her "cowardice" and her unwillingness to publicly seek justice. In this she had failed to protect future victims.

Danielle Berrin asked, "Should We Forgive the Men Who Assaulted Us?" in *The New York Times*.[3] She concluded that she was not ready to forgive her assailant but held out the possibility that "restitution made publicly as well as privately" might move her to forgive. Other voices were less open. A comment on Berrin's article charged that forgiveness was an extension of patriarchy.

> Insisting that she forgive . . . plays into the sickness of patriarchal misogynistic male-supremacist religions that blame women. Forgiveness . . . heals [neither] the body or mind. . . . Let the criminal ask his gods, if there be any, for forgiveness. . . . Instead of talking about victims who must forgive, we should be talking about tattooing the words "Rapist" or "Sexual Predator" on the foreheads of the criminals—this would actually help make women and children safer.[4]

What lies behind this conflict over forgiveness? All the complaints around forgiveness assume definitions and models of it that indeed can be problematic. It is not enough, then, to simply call people to be more forgiving. The three current models of forgiveness need to be critiqued.

Pressure to Nonconditionally Forgive

In 1987 Dianna Ortiz, an American nun of the Ursuline order, went on a two-year mission to the western highlands of Guatemala to teach poor indigenous children to read and write. On November 2, 1989, she was kidnapped, tortured, and raped by members of the Guatemalan military. When it was discovered that she was not Guatemalan herself but an American citizen, the panicked captors released her with the stern directive to not tell anyone about what had happened. She was charged to be a good nun and "forgive."[5]

It wasn't just her torturers who told her to forgive. Her capture and rape was a great embarrassment to Guatemalan government officials, who had been looking the other way while right-wing forces terrorized indigenous people as a way of ostensibly fighting communism. She recalled: "I was asked by others, friends as well as strangers, not whether I was receiving any justice from my government but whether I had forgiven my torturers. . . . They wanted me to forgive, so that they could move on. I suppose, once I forgave, all would be well—for them. Christianity, it seemed, was concerned with individual forgiveness, not social justice."[6]

In another incident, Susan Waters was regularly molested by her older brother and an adult swim instructor beginning when she was seven. Her brother continued to abuse her into adolescence.[7] Later in life, she "sought help in Christian literature" and friends but to no avail. What she heard was that she should let go of her anger, should "forgive and forget," because God has forgiven and forgotten our sins. She could "only find lovely stories about reconciliation or praying for the abuser's redemption. God forgave me, so I must forgive. This just compounded my sense of guilt, buffeted by a sea of secrets."[8]

Over time she saw how often within the church the idea of forgiveness was used against victims of abuse and injustice. Abusers knew how to use the doctrine of forgiveness to bring about their quick restoration to positions of trust—from which they could abuse again. The abused who did not immediately "forgive and forget" were said to be vindictive. The call to forgive was often the way churches or Christian institutions guarded their public image and reputations rather than redressing wrongs.

"The pressure to blindly forgive," said Susan, "particularly within Church teaching, can keep people stuck and unsafe. I believe this easy grace can allow abuse to thrive within families and institutions."[9]

Where Susan uses the term *easy grace*, one could put Dietrich Bonhoeffer's famous phrase *cheap grace*. Dianna and Susan were called to forgiveness without conditions, a cheap grace whereby the power differentials between abusers and the abused remained unchanged and no justice was pursued.

Pressure to Transactionally Forgive

Another contemporary approach has been called "transactional" or "earned" forgiveness. In *Harper's Bazaar*, Jennifer Wright asked, "Should We Forgive Men Accused of Sexual Assault?" Her conclusion:

> Women have rarely been in a position to be angry before, but we've rarely been in a position where our forgiveness was not automatically assumed before. Giving it out judiciously to those who earn it, that too, is a kind of power we deserve.[10]

Here we see her describing two of the current contemporary models of forgiveness. First is her "angry" position (the no-forgiveness model) and second is the automatically assumed path (the nonconditional model). She counsels a third way—make the perpetrators "earn" forgiveness. This, she indicates, gives women "a kind of power." As a commenter on the article's website put it, the problem in the past was that we were told that forgiveness was something "that's *owed* to men rather than a thing that is *earned*."[11] This is a call for transactional, merited forgiveness.

At first glance this seems to be a good compromise between the bitterness of the no-forgiveness position and the apparent injustice of nonconditional forgiveness. However, this approach has also received strong and convincing criticism. A recent Twitter conversation I saw proves this point: "Forgiveness is completely overrated and just serves to create power imbalances. 'I forgive you' = 'I am morally superior to you' however you look at it."[12] "It is a function of what Nietzsche called the slave morality of modern bourgeois society."[13] And indeed, Nietzsche saw conditional forgiveness as punitive. He argued that Christians, who had not achieved success or power in terms set by pagan cultures, invented a new way to feel superior, that is, by being more kind and forgiving.[14]

Nietzsche, then, agrees with Jennifer Wright's statement that merited, earned forgiveness is in the end a way of exercising power over someone. But that means that it is *not* really forgiveness. It can be just another skillfully hidden way to pay people back and get control over them—a form of revenge masquerading as virtue.

The strongest and most thoughtful critic of "transactional forgiveness" is Martha C. Nussbaum of the University of Chicago. She describes how it is "vigorously championed" as "a central political and personal virtue." She outlines the basic road map. First the victim does confrontation. If the perpetrator responds with confession and apology, then the wronged person "works through" her feelings, and finally "the wronged person emerges triumphant, unburdened by angry emotion, her claims fully acknowledged, ready to bestow the grace of her non-anger."[15]

But, Nussbaum argues, the real "condition" for the forgiveness is "enough weeping, imploring, and apologizing—typically involving considerable self-abasement." If the perpetrator does enough of this, he or she is forgiven but *the abasement is the precondition for the elevation*."[16]

Her conclusion: "in its classic transactional form at any rate, forgiveness exhibits a mentality that is all too inquisitorial and disciplinary."[17] In the end it is not really forgiveness—it is a gauntlet through which the perpetrator is forced to run until he or she is wounded sufficiently.

Pressure to Not Forgive at All

Because of the shortcomings of these other culturally dominant models of forgiveness, there is pressure to not forgive at all.

One day in late November 1984, thirteen-year-old Candace Derksen called her mother and said she was on her way home from school, but she never arrived. Her parents, Wilma and Cliff, called the police, who launched the biggest civilian search in the history of their city, Winnipeg, Manitoba. Seven weeks after she disappeared, her body, with hands and feet bound, was found in a shed less than 1,500 feet from the Derksen home. The coroner determined that she had frozen to death.[18]

The day that Cliff and Wilma learned of her death they met another man whose daughter had been murdered some years earlier. It was evident as they listened to him that he had been consumed by his anger and grief and it had ruined his life. "And so we made a decision that night," Wilma wrote years later, "that we would respond differently, and we chose the path of forgiveness. . . . The next day at the press conference when a reporter asked us what we thought of the offender . . . we replied that our intention was to forgive."[19]

They met with horrified responses. When she joined Family Survivors of Homicide, Wilma was told in no uncertain terms to stop talking about forgiveness because it was wrong, both socially and emotionally. Some said that they could not have really loved Candace if they could forgive the murderer. Others said that their forgiveness was creating a more dangerous society in which violent criminals would not be held accountable. Some complained that the Derksens were making them feel guilty for not them-selves forgiving. "At times it was incredibly tough," Wilma said.[20]

A professor of psychology at one university was enlisted to train an-other university's counseling professionals so they could provide "forgive-ness therapy" to students. But when a higher-up at that university heard about the plan, the professor was called in and denied permission to do what he had been asked to do.

"Forgiveness? It victimizes!" the professor was told. Then came the ex-planation. When people are treated cruelly by others and you come along and tell them they must forgive, you have introduced a new hurt into an already-hurting heart. And might not an effort to forgive someone go along with that person's attempt to control you? In your process of forgiveness you may say, "Well, he's not such a bad person. Maybe what he did wasn't so bad after all." And so forgiveness becomes a way that people with abu-sive power maintain their power.[21]

The no-forgiveness model singles out women and minorities, telling them they should not forgive since they have historically been given so little advantage or opportunity. Other opponents argue that forgiveness is inherently opposed to the pursuit of justice and accountability for perpe-trators.

As we can see in the experiences of Dianna Ortiz and Susan Waters, the opponents of forgiveness have a point. Forgiveness—conceived as au-tomatic, nonconditional, and expected—*has* been a way for women and minorities to be controlled. But transactional forgiveness can be a barrier to public justice. The victim may triumph over his or her anger if the per-petrator does sufficient obeisance, but is it really the right of the victim to be the only one who determines what the wrongdoer deserves? And is it the right of the victim to declare the person absolved?

Others who advise the no-forgiveness model appeal not to mental health and self-respect but to moral appropriateness. In the twentieth cen-tury the human race has perpetrated the Holocaust, the rape of Nanking,

South Africa's apartheid regime, the Armenian genocide, the "ethnic cleansings" of the Balkans, and the killing fields of Cambodia. In a 2006 interview, Holocaust survivor Elie Wiesel was asked if he forgave the Nazis. He responded: "Who am I to forgive? I am not God. . . . No, I cannot forgive."[22] Many today think he's right. It seems morally inappropriate to forgive evil.

Models of Forgiveness

So we see three approaches to forgiveness that have emerged in our secular society:

Cheap grace. The nonconditional-forgiveness model, in which all the emphasis is on the victim being therapeutically liberated from anger. Confrontation with the perpetrator may be involved, but only if and to the degree it helps with the victim's inner healing, which is the only real concern.

Little grace. The transactional-forgiveness model, in which all the emphasis is on the perpetrator meriting forgiveness. The victim gives up anger only if the wrongdoer earns it through extensive acts of repentance and reparation.

No grace. The no-forgiveness model, in which forgiveness is abandoned completely in favor of the pursuit of justice for the victim.

What these models have in common is the lack of any vertical dimension. They all contrast with the *costly grace* model of forgiveness assumed in the Bible, which has both a horizontal and vertical dimension to it.

Before proceeding to examine this biblical model in later chapters, it is important to recognize the background beliefs and assumptions in our culture that support these three approaches to forgiveness.

The Therapeutic Culture

Our culture has taken a strongly inward turn. While other cultures have stressed the importance of community and the need to forge a personal identity that negotiates and aligns with the common good, modernity has stressed looking inward to forge our own identity based on our desires, and then moving outward to demand that society honor our individual interests.

Modern therapy was designed to defend individuals against any community or outward influence that foisted guilt-producing standards on them. Freud took an "analytic" approach—one of deconstruction—of any moral norms or beliefs that created anxiety or shame. Individual authenticity came to mean liberation from any norms that you do not choose or create yourself.

An actress's recent interview in an issue of *Global Heroes* magazine distributed with *The Wall Street Journal* perfectly exemplifies the therapeutic turn. When asked, "What is one good choice that everyone can make to improve the world around them?" She answered: "Question everything. . . . Look for your own truth, LIVE your own truth, instead of repeating anyone else's." She elaborated: "What's crucial to me is to make my audience . . . question . . . [their] old beliefs."[23] She counsels her fans to "every day . . . ask 'what do I need today?'" and then go and get it. It "could mean therapy, a change in your diet, a divorce, a yoga retreat, or (yes, sometimes) a medication. . . . The only person who can walk through that door is you. Isn't that empowering?" All the emphasis is on the individual extricating him- or herself from the bonds of tradition, duty, and obligation to community in order to pursue his or her personal aspirations and desires.

Some years ago a Christian was auditing a class at Harvard in "systems of counseling." The professor artfully explored a case study in which a patient was enabled to see in himself great hidden hostility toward his mother. Making the mechanisms visible to him—of his inner anger and of the various sorts of denial he used—helped him a great deal. When the Christian student asked how the therapist could then go on and help the patient forgive his mother, the professor responded that the therapist should not do that. "[The client] will have to learn to live with [his hostility] and hopefully not be driven by it."

Interestingly, some secular students in the class lined up on the Christian's side. They asked why forgiveness was so problematic, and the professor responded, "Don't force your values . . . about forgiveness onto the patient." The point of therapy, in his view, was to support the patient against the world and not impose a moral burden or "value" of forgiveness on him, which would in a sense force him back into relationships that he did not want.[24]

L. Gregory Jones sees the therapeutic turn and what he calls "the church's psychological captivity in Western culture" as perhaps the greatest reason that we have such "impoverished contemporary understandings and practices of forgiveness in modern Western culture. . . . If all that matters is individual autonomy, then forgiveness and reconciliation—which are designed to foster and maintain community—are of little importance."[25]

Today, Jones argues, forgiveness is either discouraged as imposing a moral burden on the person (the no-forgiveness model) or, at best, offered as a way of helping yourself acquire more peaceful inner feelings (the nonconditional-forgiveness model), of "healing ourselves of our hate."[26] In contrast, Jones argues, the church is to be a foretaste of the future world of love and perfect community under the lordship of Jesus.[27] Our sin inclines us to behavior that regularly weakens and breaks relationships, but through the Spirit we are given the ability to realize—partially, never fully in this life—something of the beauty and joy of those future relationships through practices and disciplines of forgiveness and reconciliation now.

But the resources for healing relationships and strengthening community are being eliminated by therapeutic culture.

A New Shame-and-Honor Culture

The second influence impoverishing the modern practice of forgiveness is a new, inverted shame-and-honor culture that some have called a new secular religion.

Bradley Campbell and Jason Manning have discussed this new culture both in an academic paper and later in a book.[28] Their argument is that, while Western culture had shifted from originally being an honor culture like the rest of the world to being what they call a "dignity" culture, now a new kind of shame culture is emerging. This new culture is like the older honor cultures but with a new twist that borrows from the therapeutic.

Modern culture teaches us that our primary concern is to demand respect and affirmation of our own identity. In this it mirrors the desire for respect and honor that drove pagan cultures centuries ago. People today are encouraged to respond with outrage to even the slightest offense, as was true in the older societies.

However, the difference today is this: Modern therapy sees individuals as being oppressed and controlled by society's expectations, roles, and structures. Greater honor and moral virtue are assigned to people the more they have been victimized and subjugated by society or others in power. The further *down* the existing social ladder one is, the greater honor is possible. Ironically, then, we have developed "a shame and honor culture of victimhood."

Campbell and Manning's critique is that this new reverse honor culture—also called "cancel culture"—ends up valuing not strength but fragility and creates a society of constant good-versus-evil conflict over the smallest issues as people compete for status as victims or as defenders of victims. It atrophies our ability to lovingly overlook slights (cf. 1 Peter 4:8, "love covers a multitude of sins" [ESV]). But most of all, it sweeps away the very concept of forgiveness and reconciliation. Forgiveness is seen now as radically unjust and impractical, as short-circuiting the ability of victims to gain honor and virtue as others rise to defend them.[29] And so this culture is littered with enormous numbers of broken and now irreparable relationships.

As several others have argued well, this has turned politics into a new kind of religion, but one without any means of acquiring redemption or forgiveness.[30] Rather than seeing others as mistaken, they are now regarded as evil, the heretics. "The heretic must not be looked at, let alone engaged."[31]

Some claim that this new secular religion was inevitable because Western culture, with its relativism about moral truth, leaves people feeling morally empty and isolated and leads inevitably to social fragmentation. As Émile Durkheim argued, no culture can create solidarity without a "conscience collective." That is: a set of shared moral norms that bind us together and are grounded in something sacred—a set of values that are incommensurable, to be held and defended whatever the cost, not to be questioned.[32] Durkheim saw that religion had always been the ordinary way that a conscience collective was formed, and recognized the difficulties secular cultures had to ground their moral beliefs in something strong and unquestionable enough to unite people.[33]

The sacralizing of secular, progressive values into a kind of religion, then, is not a surprise. Because the Western ideas of human rights, universal benevolence of the poor, and social justice have deep roots in biblical religion, Christians can often be allies with secular people who are working for racial and economic justice.[34] However, if we root our moral norms in the biblical God, that means grounding ourselves in not only a holy and just God but also a merciful and forgiving one. Respectful interaction with opponents and forgiveness of wrongdoers is part of the church's faith.

But these traits are not part of either the ancient or the modern shame-and-honor cultures. In such a secular religion, deviation from norms is simply unforgiveable.

Social media has only accelerated this movement toward a graceless culture. As Alan Jacobs has written:

> When a society rejects the Christian account of who we are, it doesn't become less moralistic but far more so, because it retains an inchoate sense of justice but has no means of offering and receiving forgiveness. The great moral crisis of our time is not, as many of my fellow Christians believe, sexual licentiousness, but rather *vindictiveness*. Social media serve as crack for moralists: there's no high like the high you get from punishing malefactors. But like every addiction, this one suffers from the inexorable law of diminishing returns. The mania for punishment will therefore get worse before it gets better.[35]

In summary, the new shame-and-honor culture either produces a heavily inquisitorial, merited-forgiveness approach or leads people to abandon forgiveness altogether.

No Future without Forgiveness

The cheap-grace model of forgiveness focuses strictly on inner emotional healing for the victim, on "getting past it and moving on," but then ends up letting the perpetrator off the hook. The little-grace and no-grace models basically seek revenge, which can lead to endless cycles of retaliation and vengeance, back and forth, between the victim and the wrongdoer. What all these secular models lack is the transformed motivation that the vertical dimension brings. The experience of divine forgiveness brings profound healing. It is grounded in a faith-sight of Jesus's costly sacrifice for our forgiveness. That reminds us that we are sinners in need of mercy like everyone else, yet it also fills the cup of our hearts with his love and affirmation. This makes it possible for us to forgive the perpetrator and then go speak to him or her, seeking justice and reconciliation if possible. Now, however, we do not do it for our sake—but for justice's sake, for God's sake, for the perpetrator's sake, and for future victims' sake. The motivation is radically changed.

Our society cannot live without forgiveness. When it is absent, the results are horrifying. Uncountable numbers of shooting deaths in our urban areas are revenge attacks between gangs or even family members. So many of the so-named mass shootings are attacks by gunmen who have nursed grudges. A man who had a falling-out with the members of his carpool methodically shot and killed six of them. As he died from his wounds inflicted by the police, he calmly explained why he had a grudge against each of them and expressed regret that he hadn't murdered the last one.[36]

There have been an enormous number of lesser-known genocides that are the product of historical grievances and resentments with the resulting cycles of retaliation that last for generations—such as the Holodomar ("terror famine") of Ukraine, the Anfal campaign against the Kurds, and the massacres of the Igbos in Nigeria and the Hutus in Burundi and Rwanda.

During the strife in the Balkans after the breakup of the former Yugoslavia, a Serbian soldier was captured by the Kosovo Liberation Army. He was interviewed on TV by a journalist and freely admitted that his military unit had been killing ethnic Albanians. However, he said, "You must understand . . . it was our revenge!"[37] The Kosovo Liberation Army itself was also guilty of violence against ethnic Serbs and Roma for the same reason. As one Albanian put it, it was the "understandable desire for revenge."[38]

These examples are the merest tip of the tip of the iceberg of submerged anger and resentment beneath the surface of the human race. They bear compelling testimony to the truth observed by Thackeray—(to paraphrase him) "revenge may be wicked, but it is absolutely, overwhelmingly natural."[39] It is indeed too natural a part of human nature to have such an easy solution. There is no "structural," political solution. If we are going to be saved from ourselves and learn to forgive, we will need powerful inward resources and helps.

We have from Hannah Arendt, Martin Luther King Jr., and Desmond Tutu—people representing groups who were egregiously oppressed in the twentieth century—ringing, insistent calls to forgive. Arendt, a Jewish political philosopher writing after the Holocaust, said:

> Without being forgiven, released from the consequences of what we have done, our capacity to act would, as it were, be confined to one single deed from which we could never recover; we would remain the victims of its consequences forever, not unlike the sorcerer's apprentice who lacked the magic formula to break the spell.[40]

Martin Luther King Jr. wrote: "He who is devoid of the power to forgive is devoid of the power of love. . . . We can never say, 'I will forgive you, but I won't have anything further to do with you.' Forgiveness means reconciliation, and coming together again."[41] These thinkers make a compelling case that to be a healthy society—one in which broken relationships can be regenerated—we must learn forgiveness.

Arendt, King, and Tutu represent times in history in which horrendous, systemic oppression had to be met with both truth and love, both justice and forgiveness. But these "big forgivenesses" should not obscure our urgent need for learning how to do small forgivenesses every day. We are awash in slights, letdowns, and inadvertent hurts, let alone the many deliberate ways people wrong us in small ways every day. No one can live unless he or she learns when to forgive silently, when to bring the matter up, and how to forgive even if the other person is reluctant to admit his or her fault. We can't love without forgiveness, but we can't live without it either.

Communities of Forgiveness

The need for forgiveness is clear and the calls for it are eloquent. But is it achievable?

In October of 2006 a gunman took hostages in a one-room Amish schoolhouse at Nickel Mines, Pennsylvania. He shot ten children age seven to thirteen, five of whom died, and then committed suicide. Within hours members of the Amish community visited both the killer's immediate family and his parents, each time expressing sympathy for their loss. The Amish uniformly expressed forgiveness of the murderer and his family. The forgiveness and love shown toward the shooter and his family amazed many. Numerous voices called Americans to emulate the Amish and become more forgiving.

However, four years later a group of scholars wrote about the incident, and their conclusion was that simple appeals to be more forgiving will go unheeded in our culture.[42] They argued that our secular society can no longer produce people who can handle suffering without retaliation the way the Amish did. Americans are committed to self-realization and self-assertion and have a profound sense of entitlement. They believe that their happiness, interests, and needs always come first.[43]

The Amish, however, have as one of their core values "self-renunciation," with forgiveness being one form of it. It is giving up your right to pay back the person for what they did to you—in sharp contrast to American culture, which pits self-fulfillment against self-sacrifice, and which will produce revenge or withdrawal as a response to any mistreatment. "Most of us have [therefore] been formed by a culture that nourishes revenge and mocks grace," the authors conclude.[44] In such a culture, forgiveness is seen as self-hating, and revenge and anger are considered authentic.

For the Amish, however, the ability to forgive is based on two factors—one of form and one of vision.

First, the Amish constitute a genuine community, one in which relationships take precedence over individual self-interest. The Amish are part of the Anabaptist tradition, and many of their communities today still hold to and teach the Dordrecht Confession of Faith (1632), a Mennonite and Anabaptist statement of faith. Candidates for baptism are often given this confession to study and then to affirm on the day of initiation. True to the tradition, the Dordrecht Confession has an entire article dedicated to countering revenge.[45] That article reads:

> We believe and confess that the Lord Christ has forbidden and set aside to His disciples and followers all revenge and retaliation, and commanded them to render to no one evil for evil, or cursing for cursing, but to put the sword into the sheath, or, as the prophets have predicted, to beat the swords into ploughshares. (Matthew 5:39,44; Romans 12:14; 1 Peter 3:9; Isaiah 2:4; Micah 4:3; Zechariah 9:8,9)
>
> From this we understand that therefore, and according to His example, we must not inflict pain, harm, or sorrow upon any one, but seek the highest welfare and salvation of all men, and even, if necessity require it, flee for the Lord's sake from one city or country into another, and suffer the spoiling of our goods; that we must not harm anyone, and, when we are smitten, rather turn the other cheek also, than take revenge or retaliate. (Matthew 5:39)

And, moreover, that we must pray for our enemies, feed and refresh them whenever they are hungry or thirsty, and thus convince them by well-doing, and overcome all ignorance. (Romans 12:19,20)[46]

This strong communal rejection of revenge was not an abstract theological principle. It is "the Lord Christ" who forbids revenge. And they are not merely to refrain from retaliation but to seek the highest welfare of even those who have hurt them. Why? They are to act *according to His example*." At the heart of their faith and culture, the Amish Christians worship a man dying for his enemies. Through communal practices this self-sacrificing figure is depicted, praised, sung, believed, and celebrated constantly. For Jesus to give his life and to forgive his tormentors was an act of enormous love and spiritual strength, and one of surpassing beauty. It is burned into the hearts and imaginations of every member of the community.

The apostle Peter saw this beauty with his own eyes and summarized it vividly:

When they hurled their insults at him, he did not retaliate; when he suffered, he made no threats. Instead, he entrusted himself to him who judges justly. "He himself bore our sins" in his body on the cross, so that we might die to sins and live for righteousness; "by his wounds you have been healed." . . . Do not repay evil with evil or insult with insult. On the contrary, repay evil with blessing, because to this you were called so that you may inherit a blessing. (1 Peter 2:23–24; 3:9)

This is the kind of community that produces forgiveness and the healing of relationships. How will we establish other such communities in the future?

CHAPTER 3

THE HISTORY OF
FORGIVENESS

Resentment is like drinking poison and then waiting for the other person to die.

—CARRIE FISHER[1]

T he loss of forgiveness in our culture is indeed disturbing—but that raises a question. Where did our understanding of it come from? How can we maintain or recapture it?

Hannah Arendt gives her own answer: "The discoverer of the role of forgiveness in the realm of human affairs was Jesus of Nazareth. The fact that he made this discovery in a religious context and articulated it in religious language is no reason to take it any less seriously in a strictly secular sense."[2] She suggests we go to the teachings of Jesus, the author of the world's understanding of forgiveness.

The Absence of Forgiveness

Arendt's thesis assumes that ancient cultures, even the most admirable and sophisticated, did not value forgiveness. Much modern scholarship confirms this.

Classicist David Konstan writes: "The modern concept of forgiveness, in the full or rich sense of the term, did not exist in classical antiquity, that is, in Greece and Rome [the chief influences on Western civilization], or at all events it played no role whatever in the ethical thinking of those societies."[3] Charles L. Griswold, in perhaps the most respected contemporary philosophical treatment of forgiveness, says, "It is surprising and illuminating that forgiveness is not seen as a virtue by the ancient Greek philosophers."[4]

This does not mean that the Greeks did not sometimes recognize the virtue of pity—but this falls far short of our modern understanding of forgiveness. The "cardinal virtues" were wisdom, justice, courage, and self-control, all of which tend to exclude or at least discourage the tender emotions of mercy and affection. The ancients "pictured the gods as human, endowing them with such passions as jealousy, spite, and vengeance, and therefore could not grasp the sublime idea of a free and gracious forgiveness."[5]

The Iliad of Homer is an epic whose plot is driven almost completely by the pursuit of blood justice and vengeance. It speaks of "that gall of anger that swarms like smoke inside of a man's heart and becomes a thing sweeter to him by far than the dripping of honey."[6] It climaxes in the return of Achilles in books 21 and 22 to battle the Trojans after the death of his friend Patroclus. Only after he both kills Hector and desecrates his body does Achilles listen to King Priam, Hector's father, who risks his life by coming alone to Achilles's tent by night and pleading for his son's body. He asks Achilles to pity him (*eleison*) by remembering his own father (book 24, 503–5). Achilles at last shows sympathy and returns the body to Priam for a proper burial.

However, this Greek term *eleison* (pity) and another—*sungnome*, to be lenient in judgment—denote only a less severe punishment or judgment out of compassion or fellow feeling. By contrast, the key biblical term for forgiveness is *aphiemi*, which means to legally acquit or to cancel a debt, not just to lessen the penalty. There is no indication that Achilles has forgiven Hector or the Trojans or their king for their deeds against the Greeks and against him.[7]

Likewise, there is no prominence at all to forgiveness in ancient Greek philosophy. Aristotle uses the term *pardon*, but only when "someone does a wrong action because of conditions of a sort that overstrain human nature, and that no one can endure."[8] *Sungnome* (pardon) for the Greeks is not forgiving but excusing. It is saying not "This is wrongdoing and I forgive it" but "This couldn't have been avoided." To excuse is to not hold the doer responsible for the action because of extenuating circumstances, even if the action in itself was wrong. To excuse is to tie an action "to a fault with which one can sympathize and whose expression is unintentional."[9]

This is "making allowances" rather than forgiveness. Rather than saying, "I forgive you," Aristotle is saying, "I excuse you." It is a striking contrast with Matthew 6:12, where Jesus tells his disciples to pray, "Forgive us . . . as we . . . have forgiven" using the word *aphiemi*, which means to acquit legally or to release a debt. So though Aristotle counts "generosity" or "magnanimity" as a virtue that entails making allowances and pardoning people, he is not speaking of what we call forgiveness today.

The Reasons for the Absence

Griswold cites two reasons that forgiveness was not seen as a great good in classical antiquity.

To begin with, virtuous persons will not themselves be in need of forgiveness because they are people of moral excellence. Only "inferior people" need forgiveness, and why should the virtuous grant it? Aristotle argues that persons of excellence should respond to those who wrong them not with forgiveness (which assigns perpetrators too much importance) but instead with contempt. To be virtuous is to "be above resenting the actions of *hoi polloi*."[10] Look down on them until what they have done becomes inconsequential to you. Resentment should be beneath the virtuous person, as are the wrongdoers themselves.

What is obviously missing here is the Christian idea that even morally good persons are flawed, imperfect sinners needing forgiveness. Griswold writes that forgiveness only fits within

> an outlook that emphasizes the notion of a common and irremediably finite and fallible human nature. . . . Forgiveness is a virtue against the background of a narrative about human nature . . . that accepts imperfection as our lot . . . our vulnerability to each other; our mortality . . . the pervasiveness of suffering. . . . These are part and parcel of our imperfection.[11]

Similarly, the Greeks had no concept of the equal dignity of all people regardless of race, culture, or moral character. Griswold writes: "The idea of the inherent dignity of persons seems missing from this . . . aristocratic scheme. The . . . scheme within which forgiveness has its place recognizes . . . our standing to demand respectful treatment from one another."[12]

THE HISTORY OF FORGIVENESS

The second reason forgiveness was ignored in classical thought is because of the Greeks' view of the universe itself. They believed that the universe was fundamentally impersonal. While the common people understood the world as governed simply by fate, philosophers argued that behind the universe was the *logos*—a rational (but still impersonal) transcendent principle that ordered the universe and history. In either case the cosmos was unyielding and certainly unforgiving. Within this universe there was a pantheon of gods, but as one scholar has put it, after reading all the ancient stories and accounts of them, "Greek gods [not only] do not command us to forgive . . . they are not conspicuously forgiving. . . . Because the Greeks lacked a divine or messianic example of unconditional forgiveness, they did not feel a religious compulsion to forgive other persons."[13]

After examining Aristotle, Griswold goes on to look at Plato and the Stoics and finds that they give even less attention to the idea of pardoning, let alone of forgiveness. One reason is that forgiveness and reconciliation entail sympathy for another's point of view and while, as we have seen in *The Iliad*, the concept of sympathy often played a role in ancient literature, it was ignored in ancient moral philosophy.[14] Griswold concludes that ancient philosophy was "perfectionistic," that is, it required moralistic near perfection and showed no sympathy at all for those who could not muster it. He concludes that in these ancient cultures "forgiveness is not a virtue because the perfected [moral] soul is almost immune from receiving injury or from doing injury."[15]

The Coming of Christianity

From the very beginning, the Christian church was remarkable for its emphasis on and practice of forgiveness and nonretaliation. Larry Hurtado surveys the field of recent historical studies and concludes that Christianity was the most persecuted religion in the first three centuries within the Roman empire. There was a high social cost to being a Christian (rejection by relatives and neighbors, loss of income or job, harassment and violence), and in many cases there were political/judicial costs, the most extreme being execution.[16] Despite this, Christianity grew rapidly. Why? When historian Kenneth Scott Latourette sought to answer the question, he named many factors, but he included this:

> It is important, too, to remind ourselves again that the church did not seek retaliation against its persecutors. In the Christian writings of the period there is little or nothing of bitterness or of a desire for revenge against those who were hounding the faithful. . . . So far as we are aware no imprecatory prayers were offered against them.[17]

The third-century Christian bishop Cyprian preached a sermon that has come down to us entitled *De bono patientiae* ("On the Good of Patience"). He notes that believers not only face the personal crises of finances and sickness and death that all people face but also experience loss of land, prison, sword, beasts, fire, and execution for being Christian.[18] But despite this, Christians must not take revenge. Cyprian candidly acknowledges that, because of the recent wave of persecutions, some Christians "either because of the weight of their pressing injuries or because of resentment toward those who attack them . . . wish to be revenged quickly."[19] But, Cyprian says, Christians do not do that, nor do they need to do that.

They should not do it because Jesus both modeled and taught us to love our enemies, to turn the other cheek, but, Cyprian adds with great impact, Christians are to "wait and to endure with a strong patience the day of future vengeance."[20] Jesus came the first time as suffering servant, and we are to follow him in this, but in his Second Coming he will be the Judge to right all wrongs, and we are to wait for that with a hope that gives us endurance. The sermon is noteworthy for how it calls Christians to non-retaliation, patience, and love for enemies and yet does not do so by diminishing the injustice of what has been done to them.

To understand the impact of Christianity on Western culture, consider how Dr. C. John Sommerville, an English history scholar who taught at the University of Florida, used to illustrate it to his students. "When the Anglo-Saxons in England adopted Christianity," he writes, they did not understand "what they were buying into." Like the Greeks and Romans before them, "the values . . . [they] had always found self-evident were . . . the concept of honor, which means earning and insisting on respect from others" through shows of strength, even sometimes of brutal strength.[21] People who had earned higher social honor were worthy of regard, but people without social honor—slaves, women, cowards—were not. By contrast, the values self-evident to the Christian missionaries who won the pagan European tribes to Christ included service, forgiveness, and "charity, meaning wanting the best for others" based on the idea that every human being as created in the image of God had a dignity and should be given neighbor-love.

A Thought Experiment

To show students the difference, Sommerville asked them: Imagine seeing a fragile old lady coming down the street toward you at night in the dark with a big purse under her arm. It is obvious that you would be able to grab that purse and get whatever is in it without her even seeing who you are—so there is no chance of your being punished for it. Would you do it?

The ancient Anglo-Saxon warrior would not do it. It would be beneath him. An older person was worthy of respect for her age, and she was also a woman—to rob her would besmirch his honor in his own eyes. And if anyone else saw what he did, he would lose honor in their eyes as well. "In other words," Sommerville writes, if you were an Anglo-Saxon, "you would be thinking entirely of yourself, of your honor or reputation, not of the little old lady."[22]

What, however, if instead you thought of how terrible, vulnerable, and traumatized she would feel if someone mugged her? You also realize that other people might be dependent on her money. Stealing the purse could spread suffering to others. So you don't do it. Why? "You are taking others into consideration and wanting the best for them."[23] An ethical system in a shame-and-honor culture is a self-regarding and self-actualizing ethic, but an ethical system that draws on Christian beliefs is an "other-regarding" ethic based on a commitment to the good of others for *their* sake, not yours.

Obviously, in a self-actualizing culture forgiveness makes little sense. If you are wronged, you can get your honor back only by shaming and revenging yourself on the other. Sommerville writes: "With honor goes a concentration on pride rather than humility, dominance rather than service . . . glory rather than modesty, loyalty [to one's tribe and people] rather than respect for all, generosity [only] to one's friends rather than equality," and revenge rather than forgiveness. However, within the Christian worldview forgiveness is a sign not of inner weakness but of the greatest moral virtue and strength. Sommerville adds that whenever he puts these contrasting values—between pagan honor cultures and Christian dignity culture—on a board, students instantly see how deeply their moral orientation has been shaped by Christianity, even if they reject its doctrines and faith.[24]

However, even the casual observer will note that the West never became anything like a thoroughly Christian culture. To the Anglo-Saxons the very idea of forgiveness sounded dangerous. Surely social order was based on respect for strength. Didn't people have to know that if they wronged you they would be pursued and avenged? So Western countries allowed Christianity to have only so much influence. "They twisted Christianity into something that could preach the Crusades—which were [conducted] to protect God's honor. A medieval division of labor left women and serfs and monks to specialize in the charitable virtues."[25] To mention another example—dueling, an obvious holdover from shame-and-honor culture, did not die out until the early nineteenth century.[26]

Nevertheless, the Christian love ethic was a revolutionary idea which made Europe very slowly and imperfectly into the first culture which professed the equal dignity and rights of every individual, in contrast to the more corporate shame-and-honor cultures which assigned greater status to "higher" classes and families. While in an honor culture people had to earn honor or be despised, in a Christian-inspired culture, all individuals were assumed to have dignity that they didn't need to earn. In dignity cultures we turned away from personal aggression and violence and turned to courts or administrative bodies to solve disputes.

So Hannah Arendt was right. Her argument was that even though Jesus spoke of forgiveness "in a religious context" there was no reason not to take forgiveness seriously "in a secular context."[27] But Nicholas Wolterstorff hastens to add an important caveat to Arendt's admonition:

> But what we have seen is that . . . there are frameworks of thought within which forgiveness can find no home. Forgiveness entered the world along with the recognition of divine and human worth . . . of rights, of duty, of guilt. It cannot occur where those are not recognized.[28]

Is this what is happening today? Many think that it is.

The Persistence of Forgiveness

Is it possible that the concept of forgiveness in our culture could just melt away, confronted by a new and different emphasis on justice and honor rather than on love and mercy? I don't think so. While the theological and cultural resources for it are diminishing in society, forgiveness will not disappear. There remains a powerful human intuition about its importance and power even in a secular culture that eliminates the vertical relationship with God. That intuition is explained by the strange and wonderful brief verses in Ecclesiastes 3. It comes from "eternity in the heart."

> I have seen the burden God has laid on the human race. He has
> made everything beautiful in its time. He has also set eternity in
> the human heart; yet no one can fathom what God has done from
> beginning to end. (verses 10–11)

The word translated in the New International Version as "eternity" denotes endlessness or timelessness. It means that we sense a reality that exists outside of time and we long for it. We long for life and love without parting, for final triumph over evil, for many things that this world cannot give. "Unlike the animals, immersed in time, we long to see [the events and facts of life] in their full context, for we [unavoidably] know something of eternity."[29] If this world is all there is—and if nature has always just been a pattern of the strong eating the weak—then why does evil bother us at all? Why do we feel so deeply that there are real moral absolutes when we tell ourselves they cannot exist? Why do we feel that when others violate these absolutes they deserve punishment, but when *we* violate them we desire forgiveness?

The answer of the book of Ecclesiastes is that we cannot escape our knowledge of God and eternity. We may, with our intellects, deny that there is anything except this world "under the sun." We may say that there is no meaning in life, no moral absolutes, no soul. Yet then we cannot live this way—we simply do not, in our heart of hearts, believe that life "under the sun" is all there is.

It is often pointed out that one of the main themes in Mozart's operas is forgiveness. In *Abduction from the Seraglio*, two men seek to break their lovers free from a harem but are apprehended. The police chief is eager to punish them, but the benevolent pasha offers the couples a pardon. In *Idomeneo* the god Neptune offers forgiveness to the main characters at the end. In *Così fan tutti*, two women who are unfaithful to their fiancés are forgiven. But by far the most famous depiction of forgiveness in Mozart is the ending of *The Marriage of Figaro*.

Figaro, a domestic servant, is engaged to Susanna, a maid. Together they work for Count Almaviva and his wife, Countess Rosina. The Count is an unhappy and irritable man and is attracted to Susanna. He pursues her, to the sadness of the Countess.

In the final act, Susanna and the Countess switch clothing, hoping to deceive the Count and trick him into falling back in love with his wife. He begins to woo "Susanna," who is actually his spouse. Then the Count sees Figaro being intimate with the woman he thinks is the Countess (in reality Susanna), and he is outraged. Both Susanna (still disguised as the Countess) and Figaro beg the Count for forgiveness, but he refuses.

Finally the Count sees the ring that "Susanna" (actually the Countess) is wearing and realizes that he was trying to seduce his own wife. He suddenly sees himself through the eyes of others and recognizes the destructiveness and evil of his behavior. Stricken, he lifts his wife to her feet and then kneels before her. Now stripped of all his self-justifications and self-pity, and no longer blaming others for his actions, he sings, "Contessa, *perdono!*" My lady, forgive me. The Countess responds, "Yes," and all around sing, "Then let us all be happy!"

What makes this scene so famous, however, is the music itself. Generations of listeners have sensed that somehow the music is not merely beautiful and memorable, but that it conveys the unique sweetness and beauty of forgiveness and its almost supernatural power to wipe slates clean, lift burdens, re-create relationships, and change identity. Many have claimed that if listeners of the music hear it with penitence, it provides a kind of absolution. On hearing the words of forgiveness, the Count's inner darkness finally lifts.

But the power of this scene and music does not make a lot of sense from a secular point of view, the one that denies any vertical or transcendent dimension to it. This is what Ian Power sensed when he wrote about the Count's aria, "Contessa, perdono": "Why does this Mozart piece make me cry even though it's stupid and probably evil?"[30] Power, a teacher of music at the University of Baltimore, writes that the story of Figaro emerges from an oppressive, stratified slave society. The opera doesn't address any of the crushing inequities of that society—indeed it celebrates and supports them. And the very idea that some people have the power to judge and forgive others morally is part of that traditional structure of oppression. Power believes this but incongruously finds the scene incredibly moving nonetheless.

> The problem that poses [for] me is that it [the final scene] is really stupid. . . . [It's] a rich as***le apologizing to his wife for trying really hard to cheat on her only to fail at it, and the wife telling him that it's all chill because she's a better person, followed by the crowd around them singing "Let's move on" for twenty minutes. So why does it make me cry?

Power tries out the answer that great, skillful music simply works directly on the emotions. "Is it the heartbreakingly simple three-part harmony? Those Deceptive Cadences? The way the chorus sneaks into the

THE HISTORY OF FORGIVENESS

intimate texture like the leaves of a forest coming into focus? The way the strings reset the harmony in the most unassuming way possible . . . ?" But Power rightly rejects this. "I don't believe that music has a context-less power to affect emotion. . . . There must yet be something about its semantics that gets to me." "Sad" or "happy" or "thoughtful" or "bittersweet" music is named as such because we connect it to actual lived experiences. It is meaningful because there is something meaningful about those human experiences.

But then if, as Power believes, the actions of the scene just "prop up feudalistic oppression" and are a snapshot of "the slavery and horror that propped (props) up that culture"—why would those actions be moving to him?

In the end, he can only say: "This is how we investigate affect: by admitting that it is real, whether or not it 'should' be." In some ways, Power is following in the footsteps of the character Salieri in the play and movie *Amadeus*. Despite his hatred of Mozart, Salieri was astounded by the piece.

> I heard the music of true forgiveness, filling the theater, conferring on all who sat there perfect absolution. God was singing through this little man to all the world. *Unstoppable.*[31]

As Yale sociologist Philip Gorski argues, the secular assumption that all things must have a material cause makes morality either the product of our evolutionary biology or the construction of our culture, which is always designed to support the people in power. Either way, morality is relative—there are no absolutes.[32] In such a worldview, confession and forgiveness are always something of a sham: Who is to say what a sin is? Why should I feel guilty for something I want to do? Who are you to declare whether I am forgiven or not?

Ian Power was intellectually consistent with his worldview when he judged the action of forgiveness in "Contessa, perdono" as "stupid or even evil," and yet he could not shake the feeling that it was wonderful none-theless. Just as Leonard Bernstein—secular man though he was—found Beethoven's music making him feel that "heaven" and "God" were real,[33] so Power found Mozart's music making him sense that forgiveness was real.

And it is.

CHAPTER 4

THE BOOK OF FORGIVENESS

> And he passed in front of Moses, proclaiming, "The Lord, the Lord, the compassionate and gracious God, slow to anger, abounding in love and faithfulness, maintaining love to thousands, and forgiving wickedness, rebellion and sin. Yet he does not leave the guilty unpunished; he punishes the children and their children for the sin of the parents to the third and fourth generation."
>
> —EXODUS 34:6–7

To begin to recover forgiveness we need to look at the wellspring. As Hannah Arendt said, that source is the Bible in general and the teaching of Jesus in particular. In fact, it can be said that forgiveness is at the heart of the Christian message and is all throughout the Bible.

Denial of the Claim

There are critics who insist that the Bible does not stress forgiveness. One author writes: "The . . . puzzling thing is the infrequency of references to 'forgiveness' in the New Testament, which is surprising of course given how theologians insist that forgiveness is central to Christianity."[1] Harvard biblical scholar Krister Stendahl says that the most common Greek words for forgiveness (*aphesis* and *apheiemi*) are "spectacularly absent" from the Pauline epistles.[2] All this is meant to promote the revisionist idea that forgiveness is not as present in the Bible as is commonly thought.

However, just because one of the words denoting forgiveness is not in a passage does not mean the idea is not present, and when Paul *does* use the term, he shows its importance to all his thought. In verses like Colossians 1:14 for example the word is able to summarize the essence of what Christ has accomplished for us and given to us. Jesus has rescued us from darkness, transferred us into God's kingdom, all to give us "the forgiveness of sins."

And in the gospels, Jesus's declaration that he can forgive sins created an enormous controversy but was essential to his claim to being God himself (Matthew 9:2–6; Mark 2:7–10). Jesus says his blood is poured out "for the forgiveness of sins" (Matthew 26:28). And as we have seen, forgiveness of others is the one petition of the Lord's Prayer that Jesus repeats, underscores, and emphasizes (Matthew 6:14–15).

So regardless of the number of word usages, the concept of forgiveness is central to the meaning of the Bible—both Old and New Testaments—and the faith of Christians.

In the Hebrew Scriptures there are three root words that convey forgiveness. *Kpr* means to cover sin and is used constantly in connection with the animal sacrifices. *Slh* is a word that means to pardon, or to stop blaming someone, and it is also connected to the sacrifices. It shows that forgiveness requires some kind of atonement—some sort of payment—to be made. *Ns* means to lift or bear away, a picture of sin being removed far from us (cf. Psalm 103:12). This last one is used to speak of human forgiveness as well as divine (cf. 1 Samuel 25:28; Genesis 50:17).

The concept of forgiveness, then, is often present in Scripture when specific words for it are not used. A careful reading will recognize it in nearly all the main accounts in the book of Genesis.

Forgiveness in the Books of Moses

Adam and Eve were told in Genesis 2:17 that, literally, "in the day" they ate of the tree of the knowledge of good and evil they would "surely die" (ESV). When they actually do eat of the tree, however, they continued to live. Augustine explains:

> If it be asked what death God threatened man with [in Genesis 2:17], whether bodily or spiritual or the second death, we answer: It was all. He comprehends therein, not only the first . . . death, wheresoever the soul loses God, nor the second . . . death—eternal, and following after all . . . but all.[3]

Adam and Eve lost their relationship with God, experiencing what Augustine calls "spiritual death"—alienation from God (hiding among the trees), alienation from each other (the covering fig leaves). Yet on the day of their sin, God did not strike Adam and Eve with both bodily and eternal death, which, according to his own decree, they deserved. Why not? It was his grace and mercy, the divine attributes that are the ground of all forgiveness.

The same thing happens when Cain murders his brother Abel. Rather than repenting for the crime, Cain complains that now others will find him and kill him for what he has done (Genesis 4:13–14). In an astonishing move, God puts a "mark" or tattoo on Cain—"not a stigma but a safe-conduct"[4]—that in some undisclosed way protected him so he could live out a normal life span. As one commentator observed, "it is the utmost that mercy can do for the unrepentant."[5]

When Abraham has his faith "counted . . . to him as righteousness" (Genesis 15:6, ESV), it means he has been forgiven fully for his sins, as Paul makes clear in Romans 4:1–16, though the word *forgiveness*, again, does not explicitly appear in the Genesis text.

The Noahic flood narrative seems at first glance to be one merely of divine judgment on sin. But before the deluge, when God saw "that the wickedness of man was great in the earth" (Genesis 6:5, ESV), the text tells us "it grieved him to his heart" (Genesis 6:6, ESV). The Hebrew word indicates a combination of both anger and sorrow—and here in the earliest pages of the Bible we get a remarkable insight into God's stance toward sin.

God is not merely sad nor merely angry—because he is not merely holy nor merely loving. He is angry over the offense and violation of sin but mourning over its effects, over what it is doing to the creation and the human race he loves. It is important for our purposes to see that, among other ways of describing it, the Bible shows us the *grievousness* of sin to God. Derek Kidner looks at Genesis 6:6 and puts it in its starkest terms: "Already God suffers on man's account"—a foreshadowing of God's voluntary suffering for sin on the cross.[6]

Because God finds sin not merely infuriating but grievous, we glimpse in the being of God that there is not only an insistence on punishment for evil and injustice but also love, even for his fallen people. It is this apparent tension between God's holiness and his love—between the necessity that sin be punished and the desire for sinners to be delivered—that becomes the basis for the forgiveness that God appoints, achieves, and offers to us. It is one that equally honors justice and mercy.

The idea that sin is grievous to God also has profound practical implications for people who want to change their lives and habits. If you say, "I must stop doing this thing, because it will get me into trouble," then you are not really sorry for the sin itself but for the *consequences* or results of the sin. You are not sorry primarily because it grieved God but because it grieved you or others. This means that as soon as your sinful habit stops causing trouble for you, you will stop causing trouble to it. But if you recognize and feel poignantly what your sin is doing to God, you will have a deeper and more permanent motivation to turn away from the sin itself.

The first time forgiveness is explicitly mentioned in Genesis, and therefore in the Bible, is in the story of Joseph. Joseph's brothers ask him to forgive them for selling him into slavery (Genesis 50:17). The Hebrew word used is *nasah*, one with the sense of sending sin away so that the forgiver no longer counts it against the perpetrator. While Joseph does not say, literally, "I forgive you," he nevertheless responds by rejecting vengeance and pledges love to them—a crucial element in forgiveness.

Once we move out of Genesis, we see more frequent references to forgiveness. Moses prays for and receives God's forgiveness for the people (Exodus 32:32, 34:9; Numbers 14:19–20). Most obvious is that the entire system of worship at the tabernacle is established to provide forgiveness. The animal sacrifices are for the forgiveness of sin (Leviticus 4:20,26,31,35, 5:10,13,16,18; Numbers 15:25,26,28). When Solomon builds the temple to replace the tabernacle, he prays that, through the temple, God will hear his people and forgive them. The theme of forgiveness dominates Solomon's prayers and understanding of the temple (1 Kings 8:30,34,36,39,50; 2 Chronicles 6:21,25,27,30,39). At the heart of all the Old Testament worship, then, is forgiveness. Without it, there can be no relationship with God at all.

Forgiveness in the Psalms

The Psalms are perhaps the premier Old Testament expression of both the character of God's forgiveness and the means for its reception. The so-called penitential psalms (Psalms 6, 32, 38, 51, 102, 130, and 143) each outline how to approach God with repentance in order to receive his forgiveness. Yet the cries for pardon are not confined to the confessional psalms. They punctuate the Bible's prayer book throughout (Psalms 19:12, 25:11,18, 65:3, 78:38, 85:2, 99:8, 103:3).

Psalm 130, one of the penitential psalms, can serve as a case study.

> Out of the depths I cry to you, O Lord! O Lord, hear my voice! Let your ears be attentive to the voice of my pleas for mercy! If you, O Lord, should mark iniquities, O Lord, who could stand? But with you there is forgiveness, that you may be feared. I wait for the Lord, my soul waits, and in his word I hope; my soul waits for the Lord more than watchmen for the morning, more than watchmen for the morning. O Israel, hope in the Lord! For with the Lord there is steadfast love, and with him is plentiful redemption. And he will redeem Israel from all his iniquities. (Psalm 130:1–8, ESV)

The metaphor of "depths" pictures the speaker drowning or deep under the sea, or possibly deep in a pit. What sort of depths are these? Not until verse 3 are we told directly, but there is already a hint when the psalmist says that his cry is a cry for "mercy." The average person trapped in a deep pit would not be calling out for mercy—but simply for rescue—so these are depths of guilt and shame. The psalm writer is asking for "forgiveness" (verse 4). The entire prayer teaches us several things about the Old Testament view of forgiveness.

It teaches us about the *universal need* for forgiveness. The psalmist poses a rhetorical question: If the Lord should "mark iniquities"—i.e., keep a record of our sins and wrongdoings—"who could stand?" The answer is, obviously, no one. Compare this verse with Psalms 1:5 and 5:5. To "stand" spiritually means to be acceptable to God in general, or to stand "in the judgment." So the teaching is not simply that everyone sins. That would be no news to anyone. Rather, the teaching is that everyone, therefore, is spiritually alienated from God. No one is good enough to enter the holy presence of God. When Paul taught that "there is no one righteous, not even one" (Romans 3:10), he quoted Psalm 14:2–3, where David says: "The Lord looks down from heaven on all mankind to see if there are any who understand, any who seek God. [But] all have turned away . . . there is no one who does good, not even one." This verse in Psalm 130 was quoted effectively by Paul in Romans 3:10–18 to prove that the world is not divided into the "good" people who are going to heaven and the "bad" people who are not. Everyone is lost. No one will pass the test of basic goodness and decency on Judgment Day. Because of our sin—no one can "stand."

It teaches us about the *problem* of forgiveness. What makes forgiveness difficult is that sins create a "record"—a residue of liability or obligation. For example, if someone steals something from you or wrongs you in some significant way and is caught, he might say, "Well, that happened last week. That was all in the past." You, however, would feel very strongly that the sin against you created a continuing debt, liability, or obligation that does not pass away with time. The person who wronged you continues to *owe* you. Sins create a record; they do not just pass into the air and vanish. The psalmist, then, is saying that our sins create a record with God that will have to be "paid up" on Judgment Day. We will all be lost and condemned. We will all perish in the "payments due" of the record of our sins.

This psalm teaches us about the *fact* of God's forgiveness. The psalmist does not say, "There *might* be forgiveness with you," but rather "There *is* forgiveness with you." He is saying: "Even though there is a record of sins that would condemn everyone, yet you find a way to forgive." Yet he is astonished by this fact! He finds God's forgiveness shocking and inexplicable. How God accomplishes redemption is a complete mystery to the writer, even though it is not for us who know about Christ's death on the cross (cf. Romans 3:25–26). One Old Testament scholar writes: "[This] reveals how slight, on the whole, was the assurance of atonement at this stage [in history]. A Christian could have looked to the fullness of the ransom rather than [hoping for] the mildness of the reckoning. By the end of the psalm, the writer is doing just this . . . but the basis for the redemption . . . is still unrevealed to him."[7]

This verse also teaches us something of the *inward result* of God's forgiveness. In one of the most striking statements, the psalmist says that forgiveness, pardon, and grace lead to an increase in "fear" of the Lord. What does this mean? The "fear of the Lord" is one of the most basic concepts that the Old Testament uses to describe godly character. When God speaks well of Job, he says: "Have you considered my servant Job? There is no one on earth like him . . . a man who fears God and shuns evil" (Job 1:8). The term is used repeatedly in the Bible, and when contemporary readers see it, they almost always think of someone who is trembling and afraid. It is basically read as a negative. But this verse sheds new light on what it means. There are other verses that indicate this—for example, Proverbs 28:14 ("Happy is the man that feareth alway," KJV) and Psalm 19:9 ("The fear of the Lord is clean, enduring forever," ESV). But this verse gives us the clearest view of what the fear of the Lord really is.

The term *fear*, certainly, must refer at least to a sense of being humbled and overwhelmed by something. But now we see that the fear of the Lord is not a matter of mere fright. "Servile fear would have been diminished, not increased, by forgiveness. . . . The true sense of the 'fear of the Lord' in the Old Testament . . . implies relationship."[8] So this term would be best defined as "joyful awe and wonder before the transcendent greatness of who God is." The fear of God means to be affected deeply by who God is and what he did.

It is especially interesting to realize that this "fear" is paradoxical. The more we experience grace and forgiveness and love, the more we leave ourselves behind—it is then that we bow to him in amazed, wondering submission to his greatness. When we *really* understand that we are forgiven,

it does not lead to "loose living" or independence but to respectful surrender to his sovereignty. Of course, the psalmist's joyful fear could not be as
great as ours is. John Newton wrote about it:

> Let us love and sing and wonder;
> Let us praise the Savior's name.
> He has hushed the Law's loud thunder;
> He has quenched Mt. Sinai's flame
> He has washed us in his blood,
> He has brought us nigh to God.
>
> Let us wonder!
> Grace and justice
> Join and point to mercy's store.
> When in grace through Christ our trust is,
> Justice smiles and asks no more.
> He who washed us in his blood
> has secured our way to God.

The result of God's forgiveness is a paradoxical confidence and humility. Since it is unmerited love, we are both built up and awed into the dust.

We also learn in Psalm 130 of the ultimate *goal* of divine forgiveness.
The psalmist says that he is waiting for *the Lord*. He is not, ultimately,
seeking just reprieve or exemption from punishment. Rather, his goal is
God himself. His "soul" watches for the reappearance of his Lord. He longs
for fellowship and connection. Forgiveness in the fullest sense, biblically,
is not simply asking for a pardon or remission—it is always after *restored
relationship*. The goal is never merely therapeutic—a release from inward
pain. It is after, first, a restoration of our relationship with God, and second,
a deepening of fellowship with him. Here—to "wait" in repentance is to
repent and wait until the soul "sees" God again.

There are at least three ways we can "wait" for God's forgiveness: (1) We wait *expectantly*. The image of watchmen waiting for the morning (verse 6) is significant. No matter how long the night seems, morning comes. Always. This means that God will return to a repentant soul. Always. (2) We wait *obediently*. The psalmist says that he puts his hope "in his word" (verse 5). That means he takes the promises, summonses, and commands of the Scripture and follows them completely. You "wait" for God by simply obeying fully, no matter how you feel. (3) We wait *in community*. In verses 7–8 he begins to speak to the rest of his people, speaking about the "*full* redemption" (verse 7) available for "*all* their sins" (verse 8). What is he doing? He is praising God to and with fellow believers. He is practicing corporate spirituality rather than just individual spirituality. He is ministering to others.

Finally, we get only a hint of the *basis* for or the *cause* of God's forgiveness. The psalmist says, "He *himself* will redeem Israel from all their sins" (verse 8). Somehow, God himself will actually come and provide the payment for sin. We know how that happened! Zechariah, father of John the Baptist, sang about the Christ: "Praise be to the Lord, the God of Israel, because he has come to his people and redeemed them" (Luke 1:68).

While the New Testament gives us much more information about human-to-human forgiveness, the penitential psalms are unsurpassed in the Bible for instruction on how to seek and receive divine forgiveness. It is reported that, as Saint Augustine lay dying, he had these psalms put up on the wall near his bed. He then lay in bed reading, weeping, and praying them—especially Psalm 51—as he died.[9]

Forgiveness in the Prophets

The last part of the Old Testament consists of the "major" and "minor" prophets, and here again divine forgiveness is prominent. The main role of the prophets was to bring God's "covenant lawsuit" against his people. One way to understand the four parts of the Old Testament is like this. The Pentateuch describes the covenant made between God and his people, including its provision of forgiveness. The wisdom literature gives detailed explanation of how the covenant should have played itself out in the lives of the people, both in daily practice (e.g., Proverbs) and in the inward matters of the heart and of worship (e.g., Psalms). The historical books, however, tell the sad story of decline, of the people's long-term failure to keep their word and covenant. Finally, the prophets, representing God, come like lawyers from a wronged party, explaining the consequences that will come from the people's unfaithfulness to the covenant but also speaking of a future redemption and a new covenant that will be greater and bring more blessing.

Pentateuch	The covenant made	Forgiveness provided
Wisdom	The covenant lived	Forgiveness received
Historical books	The covenant broken	Forgiveness rejected
Prophets	The consequences and the covenant renewed	Forgiveness provided anew

The prophets' main burden was to tell the people that because of their faithlessness to the covenant, the consequences would be severe. There would be social decline and decay as well as military defeat, colonization by foreign powers, and exile. And yet God will remain a forgiving God and the punishment will only pave the way for a greater redemption, because he cannot forget his love for his people (Hosea 11:8). A remnant of his people will repent (Isaiah 4:3, 6:13, 7:3ff.) and will live by faith (Habakkuk 2:4; Isaiah 7:9, 28:16, 30:15). And he will make a new covenant with them, forgiving all their sins and giving them a new heart and spirit that will finally change them so they can walk with God in obedience and love (Jeremiah 24:7, 31:31ff., 32:37ff.; Ezekiel 11:19ff., 36:24ff.). The people of God will not only be more holy and committed to obeying him ("I will put my law in their minds and write it on their hearts," Jeremiah 31:33) but will also experience a thorough forgiveness ("I will forgive their wickedness and will remember their sins no more," Jeremiah 31:34).

How will all this be accomplished? No prophet tells us more about this future than Isaiah. It will be through the Messiah, who is both a King (Isaiah 11) and a suffering servant (Isaiah 52:13–53:12). This servant not only will give salvation to Israel but will also bring in the Gentiles (Isaiah 42:1). Our sins will not be remembered (Isaiah 43:25). He will establish the new heavens and new earth, the new Jerusalem in which all peoples will be forgiven (Isaiah 33:24).

There is nothing more astonishing than to realize that even the prophets, called by God to tell Israel about their sin and the coming judgments, could not avoid also speaking in the most moving way about God's grace and mercy. The message of the prophets, then, is that no amount of human evil and recalcitrance can ultimately stop God's forgiveness from finding its way to us.

Forgiveness in the Gospels

When we come to the New Testament gospels, we discover an even greater emphasis and a clearer focus on forgiveness, and not just divine (what we have been calling vertical) forgiveness, to which the Old Testament gives almost exclusive attention. We also receive instruction on human forgiveness and how it can bring about reconciliation and the healing of community. And finally, we get an explanation beyond the symbolic animal sacrifices for the basis for forgiveness—*how* God can forgive. That basis immeasurably deepens our understanding of the costliness of God's grace and mercy.

In New Testament Greek there are two main words that are used to convey the idea of forgiveness. *Charizomai* contains the term *charis* or "grace" and means to deal with someone in a gifting, gracious manner rather than in a strictly calculating way. Forgiveness is therefore not something that is earned or merited. Like any other gift, it is given out of grace and love at the expense of the giver. Paul prefers to use this word.

The other word is *aphesis*, which means "remission"—"to release someone from a legal . . . obligation or debt."[10] This is the word most often used in the New Testament (approximately forty times).[11] It is the most common word for forgiveness used in the gospels as well as in James and the epistles of John. The concept of remission hints that forgiveness always brings a cost. When a debt is canceled by the creditor, it means that the creditor, rather than the debtor, pays or absorbs the debt. Forgiveness, then, entails the perpetrator's punishment or debt being borne by another.

At the beginning of the New Testament gospels, the focus is already on forgiveness. The promise to Joseph in Matthew 1:21 was that the coming Messiah would save his people from their sins; the promise to Zechariah in Luke 1:77 was that Christ would give us "the knowledge of salvation through the forgiveness of . . . sins." Jesus's immediate forerunner, John the Baptist, preached "a baptism of repentance for the forgiveness of sins" (Mark 1:4).

When Jesus himself came preaching and teaching, he declared repeatedly that we can know God's forgiveness and then, in turn, forgive those who wrong us. As we have seen, this is at the heart of the Lord's Prayer. "Forgive us our debts, as we forgive our debtors" (Matthew 6:12, KJV).

Jesus adds: "For if you forgive other people when they sin against you, your heavenly Father will also forgive you. But if you do not forgive others their sins, your Father will not forgive your sins" (Matthew 6:14–15). Despite the first impression, Jesus is not saying that God's forgiveness is based on or earned by our forgiveness of others. Not only do the Greek words for forgiveness not convey this, but the master parable of the Unforgiving Servant (Matthew 18:23–35) makes it clear that it is God's forgiveness of us that provides the basis—the motivation and the power—for our forgiveness of others. As we saw in chapter 1, this parable gives us an extensive framework by which we can understand the two dimensions—divine and human—of all Christian forgiveness.

When Jesus forgives sins, he bears testimony not only to his deity but also to the life-transforming experience of forgiveness. When forgiving a woman, he says:

> Therefore, I tell you, her many sins have been forgiven—as her great love has shown. But whoever has been forgiven little loves little. (Luke 7:47)

The two-dimensional framework is here again confirmed. The sign that you have been forgiven is a heightened capacity for love, for gift giving, and for forgiving others. A lack of any sense of being forgiven leads to a lesser ability—or an inability—to extend grace or grant forgiveness to others.

The Basis for Forgiveness

As the gospels begin with declarations of forgiveness of sins, so they end with them. On the cross Jesus prays for the forgiveness of his enemies (Luke 23:34), and after his resurrection he charges his disciples to go and show the world how to have their sins forgiven (Luke 24:47; John 20:23).[12]

Most significantly of all, at the end of his life Jesus gives the church the sacrament of the Lord's Supper, with the cup being "my blood of the covenant, which is poured out for many for the forgiveness of sins" (Matthew 26:28). Here finally is an answer to all the questions raised in the Old Testament, especially since God revealed himself to Moses in Exodus 34:7 saying that he was the God who is both "forgiving wickedness" and yet at the same time "does not leave the guilty unpunished." How is that possible? Doesn't forgiving people *mean* they go unpunished? How could he punish every sin and yet forgive us? The animal sacrifices seemed to point to some solution (Leviticus 17:11), but it was partial. Such sacrifices were costly, but they had to be offered over and over again.

The night before he died, Jesus gave us the answer to all the riddles. The basis—the objective means of forgiveness—is Jesus Christ's atoning death on the cross. His blood "poured out," signifying his death, is what makes it possible for us to be forgiven. Paul provides his own summary: "He forgave us all our sins, having canceled the charge of our legal indebtedness, which stood against us and condemned us; he has taken it away, nailing it to the cross" (Colossians 2:13–14). The writer of Hebrews speaks perhaps the most clearly of all: "Day after day every priest stands and performs his religious duties; again and again he offers the same sacrifices, which can never take away sins. But when this priest had offered for all time one sacrifice for sins, he sat down at the right hand of God" (Hebrews 10:11–12).

In short, on the cross Jesus satisfied both the justice and love of God in the most wise, wonderful, and glorious way—which is the burden of the next chapter.[13]

C. S. Lewis's short and overlooked essay "On Forgiveness" tells how, as a young Christian, he came to realize that when he asked God to forgive him he was really asking God to excuse him:

> But there is all the difference in the world between forgiving and excusing. Forgiveness says, "Yes, you have done this thing, but I accept your apology; I will never hold it against you and everything between us two will be exactly what it was before." But

excusing says, "I see that you couldn't help it or didn't mean it; you weren't really to blame."[14]

He argues that many of us who recite in church the Apostles' Creed, "I believe . . . in the forgiveness of sins," do not really. We think instead that "God will not take us to Himself again" unless some case can be made out that we really weren't that guilty. But that is not forgiveness. "Real forgiveness means looking steadily at the sin, the sin that is . . . without any excuse . . . and seeing it in all its horror, dirt, meanness, and malice, and nevertheless being wholly reconciled to the man who has done it."[15]

This is extremely difficult if not impossible for human beings to do unaided, but in the gospel we have that aid, in supernatural proportions. Lewis explains:

> But to forgive the incessant provocations of daily life . . . how can we do it? Only I think by remembering where we stand . . . *To be a Christian means to forgive the inexcusable, because God has forgiven the inexcusable in you.*[16]

UNDERSTANDING

FORGIVENESS

CHAPTER 5

THE GOD OF LOVE
AND FURY

For God so loved the world that he gave his one and only Son,
that whoever believes in him shall not perish but have eternal life.
For God did not send his Son into the world to condemn the
world, but to save the world through him. Whoever believes in
him is not condemned, but whoever does not believe stands condemned already because they have not believed in the name of
God's one and only Son.

—JOHN 3:16–18

The key to Christian forgiveness is the cross. It is the foundation of
forgiveness because it not only makes it possible for God to forgive us without compromising his justice but it also provides both
motivation and model for our own forgiveness to those who wrong us. To
understand how we—as angry, wronged persons—can forgive, we must see
how God, the ultimate wronged person, can forgive. The way he does this
is the cross.

The Old Testament Background

The many Old Testament calls for forgiveness left open a major, unresolved question. Knowing what we know about God's holiness and justice, how is forgiveness even possible?

Heinrich Heine was reputed to have said as he died, "God will forgive me; that's his job." But the clear message of the Old Testament is that God's forgiveness cannot be taken for granted. The God of the universe will show himself holy in righteousness (Isaiah 5:16). When God descends on the mountain, it becomes holy and cannot be touched; if humans get too close they will die (Exodus 19:23–24). "Holiness is perfection, not only in a moral sense but the comprehensive sense . . . religious, ethical . . . internal, external."[1] It is the holiness of God that moves him to punish sin (Leviticus 11:44–45, 19:2, 20:7; 1 Kings 9:3–7). Directly related to holiness is God's righteousness or justice. He is always just (Genesis 18:25; Psalms 119:137, 129:4), and he will not let the unjust and evildoers go unpunished (Nehemiah 1:3ff; Exodus 20:7; Ezekiel 7:4,9, 8:18, 9:10). God's wrath is not lost temper but his holiness released judicially against evil (Psalms 6:1, 38:1; Jeremiah 10:24).

Nothing is clearer in the Old Testament than that God will do justice and that he cannot shrug, wink at, or ignore any sin or evil. Herman Bavinck argues against the "shallow idea that forgiving is natural for God."[2] While "the Old Testament knows nothing of a forgiveness wrung from an unwilling God or purchased by a bribe," at the same time God's "forgiveness is not [a given] . . . something in the nature of things. Passages which speak of the Lord as not pardoning offences abound (Deuteronomy 29:20; 2 Kings 24:4; Jeremiah 5:7; Lamentations 3:42). Where forgiveness is obtained it is something to be . . . regarded with awe and wonder."[3]

Yet despite the clear and unyielding righteousness of God, the Old Testament is nonetheless filled with claims and promises that God is a forgiving God (Numbers 14:18–20; 1 Samuel 25:28; 1 Kings 8:30–33; Psalms 25:11, 32:1–2,5,51, 103:3, 130:4, 143:2). When Isaiah meets the thrice-holy God, high and lifted up, and in agony confesses his radical sinfulness, God immediately offers him forgiveness of sins (Isaiah 6:7). So the Old Testament teaches that God forgives and that it is an astonishing, inexplicable gift.

At the heart of the Old Testament revelation, then, is this seeming paradox, which is put most starkly by Exodus 34:6–7 and Numbers 14:18–20. In Numbers 14 we read: "The Lord is slow to anger, abounding in love and forgiving sin and rebellion. Yet he does not leave the guilty unpunished" (verse 18). And God declares his name to Moses on Mount Sinai like this:

> And he passed in front of Moses, proclaiming, "The Lord, the Lord, the compassionate and gracious God, slow to anger, abounding in love and faithfulness, maintaining love to thousands, and forgiving wickedness, rebellion and sin. Yet he does not leave the guilty unpunished. (Exodus 34:6–7)

The Hebrew is even more emphatic. It says, literally, that in no way will he treat the guilty as if they were innocent.

The tension is great. Which is it? Is he a loving God who forgives the guilty or is he a just God who punishes the guilty? He is both—but how is that possible? The true answer is not revealed until the New Testament. God is *both* a God of love *and* of wrath, and it is at the cross that we see how these are not in conflict but working together to save the world.

Our Concept of God

John 3:16 is arguably the most famous single verse in the Bible. It is a "feel-good" verse—but only when taken out of context. In the very next verse the text speaks of "condemnation," and a bit later, in John 3:36, that word is starkly defined: "Whoever believes in the Son has eternal life, but whoever rejects the Son will not see life, for God's wrath remains on them."

Modern people struggle with the idea of a wrathful God who condemns, yet the Bible here puts condemnation in proximity to the most famous verse on love. In other words, the Bible never sees God's love and anger as being opposed to each other. Indeed, the Bible tells us that in God, not only are they not in tension but they are meaningless apart from each other and indeed they establish each other.[4]

He's both love and fury. It's not that he's a split personality—being loving on alternate days and wrathful in between. The reason his wrath and love cohere is because they are not like ours—they are perfectly holy and good. When we get angry, it is usually because the things we love most are threatened. But because of sin, often those ultimate loves include our public image, our ego, or some cherished plan that we think will finally deliver life satisfaction. When these things are threatened, we get angry and often harm people and destroy things.

When we see all the references to God's wrath in the Bible, we instinctively imagine God's anger must be like ours, and so we recoil. However, his anger is *not* wounded pride as ours is. God only gets angry at the evil destroying the things he loves—his creation and the human race he made for his own glory and for our happiness.

God is not just a God of love or a God of wrath. He is both, and if your concept of God can't include both, it will distort your view of reality in general and of forgiveness in particular.

If you see only a loving God who never says no, or if you only see an angry God who never says yes, it will distort your life. It will affect how you view and live your life in general. It will shape how you make your decisions, how you regard other people, how you think about yourself, how you relate to the world around you. Perhaps it is too simplistic (but not by much) to say that if you believe only in a God of love, you will live like a spoiled child, but if you believe only in a God of wrath, you will live like an abused child.

God's love and his fury are nowhere seen together as they are on the cross, where they both are satisfied and meet and coincide. It is understanding and rejoicing in Christ's work on the cross that keeps us from living as a spoiled or as an abused child.

The Wrath of God Expresses Love

The idea that there are absolute moral standards, regardless of what people believe, that are right, and that God will punish those who violate them is now in eclipse among the elites of Western civilization, and it is repugnant to many. Yet look! The law of God as summed up by Jesus (Matthew 22:36–40) is the command to love properly, proportionately, completely. Any failure to do so destroys the creation, other people, and your own heart—all things God made and loves. So God's wrath on disobedience to his law is both a call to love and an expression of his love.

C. S. Lewis famously wrote about the impossibility of instilling an ethic of love without a God of wrath who both models loving behavior and punishes unloving behavior. He describes modern moral education's efforts to develop character in students who have been taught moral relativism. "In a sort of ghastly simplicity we remove the organ and demand the function. We make men without chests and expect of them virtue and enterprise. We laugh at honor and are shocked to find traitors in our midst.

We castrate and bid the geldings be fruitful."[5] If all moral values are relative and social constructs, then how can you make the case that we all *ought* to treat others with love and not exploit them? How will you motivate people to make the sacrifices necessary to do justice if you tell them that there is no redeeming, divine love behind the universe? Will you appeal to their self-interest by saying, "The world will work better this way"— what is that but an appeal to selfishness? If that's the only way to justify a moral claim, why can't they opt to be selfish in a way practical to them?

The idea of a personal yet infinite God of love is unique to Christianity. Where did we get the original idea that God was a loving God? Did we just read the newspaper and see the state of the world and say: "Oh, it's so obvious God is a God of love"? No. It doesn't come from there. Did we read the history of humankind and say, "Oh, it's so clear from reading history that God is a God of love"?

Did we get it from reading the works of the other religions? Do you see in them the concept of a God who is a loving, personal shepherd and ally, an intimate Father, brother, bridegroom? No, it doesn't come from there.

Bavinck, in his *Reformed Dogmatics*, points out that many Eastern religions teach that any inequality we experience in this life is due to "thoughts, words, and deeds that [we] have entertained, uttered, and committed in a previous life," so that "in the moral world the unbreakable law of *karma* prevails. There is no forgiveness, only retribution."[6] No, it doesn't come from those religions.

Did we get the idea that God is love by looking at nature and its beauty? This seems more promising until we look more deeply. Think of modern evolutionary theory, which is absolutely brutal so that only the "fittest" survive. "Nature knows no forgiveness and does not in the least take account of self-humiliation and confession of wrongdoing."[7] Annie Dillard, in *Pilgrim at Tinker Creek*, won a Pulitzer for her depiction of the violence of nature that could be observed at the small creek near her mountain home.[8] No, it doesn't come from there.

The concept of a loving God came from the Bible, and it was considered very odd and strange. Human society could understand a God who was mainly a God of wrath, who demanded deference or he would simply smite people, but it couldn't really understand a loving, merciful God who makes us all in his image and then forgives people who have done wrong. It didn't like the idea of the love ethic: *Turn the other cheek. Treat every person (even the weakest) as if they were infinitely valuable.* As we saw earlier, when the ancient pagans first learned of the Christian understanding of mercy and forgiveness, they were offended and thought it dangerously unworkable. But the Christian view prevailed in many places and it changed the world.

A friend of mine who was a PhD student at Yale once told me that modern people think about slavery and say, "How could people have ever accepted such a monstrosity?" My friend said, "That's not the way historians think. They ask: 'Considering the fact it was universally believed by all societies that we had the right to attack and enslave weaker people, and since everybody had always done it, the real historical question is, Why did it occur to anybody that it was wrong? Who ever first had that idea?'" He then answered his own question, pointing out that the first voices in the fourth, seventeenth, eighteenth, and nineteenth centuries who called for the abolition of slavery were all Christian. And the Christians who called for this justice believed there was a God of love who demanded that we love our neighbors—*all* our neighbors—as ourselves.

The wrath of God is an expression of a loving God rightfully demanding love from human beings toward one another and toward him.

The Love of God Expresses Wrath

The anger of God is ultimately about love, so the love of God will often express itself in anger. In her book *Hope Has Its Reasons*, Rebecca Manley Pippert asks: "Think of how we feel when we see someone we love ravaged by unwise actions or relationships. . . . Do we respond with benign tolerance . . . ?" She speaks of watching two talented friends of hers sinking deep into destruction through drug abuse. She says, "I feel fury when I am with them. [I want] to say, 'Can't you see? Don't you know what you are doing to yourself? You become less and less yourself every time I see you!'"

"Real love," she says, "stands against the deception, the lie, the sin that destroys. Anger and love are inseparably bound in human experience," she writes. "And if I, a flawed, [narcissistic], and sinful woman can feel this much pain and anger over someone's condition, how much more a morally perfect God who made them? Anger isn't the opposite of love. Hate is—and the final form of hate is indifference."[9] So even in us flawed human beings, love and anger are not opposed to one another but can be interdependent.

We see this everywhere in the Bible. On the one hand the Bible speaks in the strongest terms of God's opposition to sin and evil. But then on the other hand, the Lord weeps over sin. His "heart [is] filled with pain" over it (Genesis 6:6).[10] He weeps over Israel's sin, speaking of his inner compassion (Hosea 11:8). Jesus weeps over sinful Jerusalem (Luke 19:41–44). This is neither harshness nor a compromise with sin.

The Bible does not reveal a God simply of fury or a God simply of love but a God of love and fury, because this is a holy God. Holy love. Holy wrath. It means his settled opposition to evil is working itself out in your life. He has set up the universe so that if you move against God's law, you move against yourself. You can get away *with* your sins, but you can never get away *from* your sins. And he did this out of love.

God in All His Glory Is Revealed on the Cross

Nevertheless, because in this world—and in our hearts—love and anger are at odds with each other, we need more help in understanding God. We tend to veer into a kind of "conservative" religion that is harsh and rooted in a severe God or a "liberal" religion that is relativistic and sees God as simply accepting. How can we escape either of the distortions?

If the real God is a God of both love and fury, then God's reality is supremely revealed on the cross. That is where we must go to heal our understanding and receive an undivided heart.

Horatius Bonar (1808–1889) was a Free Church of Scotland minister who wrote over 140 hymns on many themes. He had, it was said, "poetry in his soul," but his heart was most engaged over how the cross saves us.[11] In one of his books he writes:

> God is a Father; but He is no less a Judge. Shall the Judge give way to the Father or the Father give way to the Judge? . . . Shall He sink His love to the sinner in His hatred of the sin, or His hatred of the sin in His love to the sinner? God has sworn that He has no pleasure in the death of the sinner (Ezekiel 33:11); yet He has also sworn that the soul that sinneth, it shall die (Ezekiel 18:4). Which of the two oaths shall be kept? Shall the one give way to the other?

Bonar piles up these pairs of juxtaposed biblical truths and verses, all of which are but versions and echoes of that seeming "contradiction" posed in Exodus 34:7: "forgiving iniquity . . . but who will by no means clear the guilty" (ESV). Bonar writes in summary: "Law and love . . . One cannot give way to the other. Both must stand, else the pillars of the universe will be shaken."[12] In many ways, it is this tension that drives the plot of the entire Bible. But the resolution is not merely the death of Christ but his voluntary death as the second person of the triune God, as a substitute in our place. The classic summary of the doctrine, in unsurpassed brevity and clarity, is by John Stott in *The Cross of Christ*:

> The concept of substitution may be said, then, to lie at the heart of both sin and salvation. For the essence of sin is man substituting himself for God, while the essence of salvation is God substituting himself for man. Man asserts himself against God and puts himself where only God deserves to be; God sacrifices himself for man and puts himself where only man deserves to be. Man claims prerogatives which belong to God alone; God accepts penalties which belong to man alone.[13]

Paul himself says that the "shedding of . . . blood" (Romans 3:25) made it possible for God to be both "just, and the justifier of" those who believe (Romans 3:26, KJV). Just, yet forgiving.

> Both love and law have triumphed. The one has not given way to the other. Each has kept its ground; nay, each [is] . . . honored and glorified. Never has there been love like this love of God— so large, so lofty, so intense, so self-sacrificing. [Yet] never has the law been seen so pure, so broad, so glorious, so inexorable.
>
> There has been no *compromise*. Law and love have both had their full scope. Not one jot or tittle has been surrendered to the full; the one in all its severity, the other in all its tenderness. Love has never been more truly love, and the law has never been more truly law, than in this conjunction of the two.[14]

When Paul meditates on this, he often breaks into doxology: "Oh, the . . . riches and wisdom and knowledge of God! How unsearchable are his judgments and how inscrutable his ways! . . . For from him and through him and to him are all things" (Romans 11:33,36, ESV).

The cross does not merely provide a temporary respite from condemnation. We are told that Christ stands before the Father as our legal representative, our advocate (1 John 2:2; Hebrews 7:25; Romans 8:33–34). What this means is that the law, once our enemy, which demanded our punishment, now becomes our friend, demanding our acceptance. How so? The law has been perfectly fulfilled in our substitute, and so now it would be *unjust* for God to turn on us! For God to punish us for any sin would be to exact two payments for the same debt (since Jesus has already paid it). Now Jesus stands before the Father, in a sense, demanding not mercy but justice for us. We have both his law and his love *for* us. We could not be more secure.

John writes: "If we confess our sins, he is faithful and just and will forgive us our sins" (1 John 1:9). Notice that John does not merely say God forgives because he is merciful—though that, of course, is true. God's acceptance of us is now also a matter of justice. He has already received full payment for my debts, and it would be unjust to demand a second payment. As hymn writer Augustus Toplady put it:

If thou my pardon hast secured,
And freely in my room endured
The whole of wrath divine,
Payment God cannot twice demand,
First from my bleeding surety's hand
And then again from mine.[15]

Bonar concludes:

[On the cross] in that combination of the judicial and the paternal . . . law has become the source and vehicle of love . . . so that . . . love is the fulfilling of the law. The law that was against the sinner has come to be upon the sinner's side.[16]

An Abusive God?

In the cross, God's wrath and his love now blaze for you and not against you. Both are equally, interactively, mutually shining forth for you. If you don't grasp the substitutionary atonement of Jesus Christ theologically and existentially—done *for you, in your place*—you will be, spiritually speaking, like a spoiled or neglected child. Two questions can assess whether this truth is being grasped and appropriated.

When something happens that reveals your sins more clearly than you have ever wanted to see or admit, does it move you away from God or closer to him? If it makes you want to stay away from God and prayer and church—that shows you don't understand what Jesus did for you. If you grasped it, your inner dialogue with God would sound more like this: "Lord, I knew before that you died for me and accepted me, but I didn't know I was this foolish and sinful—so I now realize your love is greater than I thought. Your mercy is more free and undeserved than I thought!" If you understand the cross, then the discovery of new depths of weakness, fault, and evil in your life drives you closer to him and not further away.

There are many people who struggle with feelings of inadequacy and shame. They seem to have an inner voice that is always calling them a fool, an idiot, or a failure. They may be walking down the street and the voice comes and says, "You expect people to love you? You call yourself a Christian? Look at what you did." How do you deal with it? The neglected child tries excuses. Do you argue with the voice: "Well, I had a bad day" or "Yes, that wasn't good—but if you had *my* mother. . . ."? Or do you go read a book that tells you that no one has the right to make you feel guilty about anything. None of this works. The voice continues.

But if you truly understand and rejoice in what Jesus did for you on the cross, you can say to the voice—or to anyone who speaks to you like that—"Even if I hadn't done this thing I'm feeling guilty about, that wouldn't serve to make me acceptable to God. I can't do it—no one can! But Jesus can and he has. He has done it at infinite cost to himself. Now I am in him—Jesus *is* my wisdom, righteousness, sanctification, and redemption."

If you have a God who is nothing but wrath, and if you have little understanding of what happened on the cross, you'll be a driven person. You'll try hard to be moral. You'll try hard to be good, but you will always feel unworthy. It will be hard to grow into a loving person, because fear cannot awaken love. Only love can awaken and grow more love.

When the voice of conscience (or maybe of Satan himself) comes and says, "You wretch, begone! Retreat in shame," you must remember the cross and hear Jesus say, "My love, come here. I bore the blame."

A Remote and Detached God?

Here is another question to a different kind of person. You may have been raised with what today is called an enlightened view of God. That is, either you don't believe in God or you have a God who can't say no or confront you. You don't believe in the parts of the Bible that you find outdated. So if you do believe, your God is a supportive spirit of love and life, at best an assistant on your road to the goals you have chosen. You live as you see fit.

We know how damaging it is when children have either remote or absent parents who are not involved, who never cross their children's wills or discipline them. In the short run, the children love it. They can do what they want! But eventually they feel like orphans and, essentially, they are. The irony is that parents who never set down rules or discipline their children—who "spoil" them—are failing to love them. Children who are cursed with parents like that experience an emotional vertigo the rest of their lives. They don't know where the limits are, where the boundaries are.

When it comes to God, many people are like this. They are "spiritual but not religious." They want a God who does not condemn anything. They want a God who inspires them but does not lay down rules they have to obey. They look to career success or to romance and sex for affirmation, for confirmation that they are okay, but it never seems to satisfy. They are moral relativists if someone tells them how to live but moral absolutists when they are telling someone else how they ought to behave—and they sense the incoherence but they don't know what to do about it.

But if you truly understand and rejoice in what Jesus did for you on the cross, then you are free from the guilt and shame that moralistic religions can bring, yet you also feel bound to live in a way that pleases the one who died for you—and *such obedience is not a burden but a delight*. You want to bring joy to the one who brought you so much joy. As Cowper summarized it: "To see the law by Christ fulfilled . . . transforms a slave into a child and duty into choice."[17] He was looking at Saint Paul's passage in Romans 8:

> For those who are led by the Spirit of God are the children of God. The Spirit you received does not make you slaves, so that you live in fear again; rather, the Spirit you received brought about your adoption to sonship. And by him we cry, "*Abba*, Father." The Spirit himself testifies with our spirit that we are God's children. (Romans 8:14–16)

Only a grasp of what Jesus did on the cross—the doctrine of substitutionary atonement—can prevent these spiritual distortions we have been describing. Only this doctrine keeps us from thinking God is mainly holy with some love or mainly loving with some holiness—but instead is both holy and loving equally, interdependently. Only this view of God makes the spoiled or the neglected into the healthy and the loved.

Only this view of God and the cross enables us to practice human forgiveness, giving equal weight to justice *and* mercy. Without this doctrine the vertical, divine dimension atrophies and human forgiveness becomes a mere hunt either for emotional freedom or for a kind of revenge.

The doctrine of the cross is wonderful, unique, life-changing, and liberating. As the writer to the Hebrews exclaimed: "How shall we escape, if we neglect so great a salvation?" (Hebrews 2:3, KJV).

CHAPTER 6

JUSTICE AND LOVE, HONOR AND ABUSE

Though justice be thy plea, consider this: that in the course of
justice none of us should see salvation. We do pray for mercy, and
that same prayer doth teach us all to render the deeds of mercy.

—WILLIAM SHAKESPEARE[1]

od is a God of both wrath and love—and both are fulfilled at
once on the cross. How wonderful that justice and love are perfectly integrated in the being of God! Yet in our society and in
our hearts, the two seem to be locked in a deadly conflict.

God's Justice and Love Change a Culture of Shame and Honor

Ancient societies were shame-and-honor cultures based not on equal human dignity but on a hierarchy of honor and social status. In such a culture, taking vengeance was absolutely necessary to maintain one's honor. A
man who did not take revenge was not worthy of respect. In such a culture
neither justice nor love were important.

Careful calculations of just penalties took a back seat, as it were, to the right of aggrieved parties for the "satisfaction of honor" and vengeance. And it is not surprising that there are no exhortations to "love those who wrong you" in pre-Christian antiquity.

It is true that in general the Stoics counseled people to not take actions of revenge, but a closer look at their reasoning is revealing. The way to overcome bitterness and to pay back without the messiness of revenge was to despise the wrongdoers ("Don't let anything *he* says bother you"). This dismissiveness was actually a way of punishing and yet freeing oneself from excessive anger. "Resignation, not forgiveness, was the Stoic means of dealing with intransigent people or difficult circumstances."[2] Anger was diminished not by doing either justice or love but by detaching the heart.

The Bible, however, laid down principles that would undermine honor culture. The book of Proverbs teaches:

> It is to one's honor to avoid strife, but every fool is quick to quarrel. (Proverbs 20:3)
>   Pride brings a person low, but the lowly in spirit gain honor. (Proverbs 29:23)

Here we are given a revolutionary principle that flew in the face of pagan society—it is most honorable to not always be worried about one's honor. In most cultures the quickest to strike back were the people with the greatest honor. But Proverbs says the quickest to do so are actually the most foolish. Teaching about *foolishness* in biblical wisdom literature is very rich, but suffice it to say here that, biblically, fools are destructively self-regarding out of an inner emptiness and insecurity. The Bible says the persons most quick to defend themselves are the weakest, not the strongest.

The most deeply countercultural verse is Proverbs 29:23 that declares—

it is pride that brings people low and only humility and self-renunciation ultimately that gain honor and respect. Nothing could have been more counterintuitive to the ancient cultures of both East and West. The strongest, it is implied, do not lash out in anger but proceed with complete self-control to do both justice and love.

The Hebrew Scriptures alone provided antiquity with a view of a God who was infinitely glorious and greater than us, before whom only the deepest humility is appropriate.

God's Justice and Love Create a Community of Reconciliation

Revolutionary words about love of neighbor are buried deep in the ceremonial regulations of the book of Leviticus in a famous text. Jesus himself quotes and expounds on Leviticus 19:17–18 and, as one scholar put it, "the sentiment underlying this aphorism was unique in the ancient world, and represents one of the Old Testament's most outstanding moral precepts."[3]

> You shall not hate your brother in your heart, but you shall reason
> frankly with your neighbor, lest you incur sin because of him. You
> shall not take vengeance or bear a grudge against the sons of your
> own people, but you shall love your neighbor as yourself: I am the
> Lord. (Leviticus 19:17–18, ESV)

These two verses explain how God wanted the covenant community of believers to conduct themselves when one person wronged another.[4]

Three things are forbidden. We are not to *seek revenge*, to pay the person back in kind. It is not enough, however, to simply refrain from certain actions. We are also not to *hate* in our hearts, a translation of a Hebrew word that means literally to "decrease status," to hold the person who wronged us in contempt and slight regard. Nor are we to *bear a grudge*. Even if negative feelings initially are unavoidable, we are not to sustain them over time.

Yet there are two things believers in conflicts *must* do—we are both to rebuke *and* to love the person who wronged us.

The rebuke is to be frank, a word that means to pointedly show the other person their error. The text adds, intriguingly, "so you will not share in their guilt." This indicates that we will share in a perpetrator's guilt *if we fail to confront him and do not seek to stop his behavior*. In other words, God holds us responsible, even if we were the victim in the first place, if we then fail to pursue justice where it is called for.

The command to not hold a grudge is a clear command to forgive. Yet we see a remarkably nuanced approach to forgiveness. We are to forgive and to confront wrongdoers about their sin. Justice and mercy are seamlessly combined.[5]

Why should we do this? The answer is easy to miss in the Leviticus 19:18 text. After the brief exhortation comes the simple declaration—"I am the Lord." Leviticus is well known for laying down ethical regulations followed by the statement "I am the Lord." The meaning of this is crucial to grasp. Justice and love *must* be combined in us because they are combined in the Lord. Justice and love *can* be combined because they are combined in the Lord and he will help us.

Another Old Testament text hints that if we don't *combine* love and justice in our dealings with others, we will ultimately do neither. Proverbs 24:29 is a portrait of the inner psychological structure of resentment.

> Do not say, "I'll do to them as they have done to me; I'll pay them back for what they did." (Proverbs 24:29)

The heart dresses vengeance up as if it were justice: "It will be perfectly fair and just—I will simply hurt them just as they did me." But that is seldom what happens. Cain resented the favor Abel found with God and because he could not master his resentment, it led to murder (cf. Genesis 4:6–7). Your angry heart may begin by saying, "I'll hurt them only as much as they hurt me," but quickly it may become, "Well, since they did it first, they deserve *more* than what they did to me." Soon the mask of supposed justice falls away and the face of revenge is revealed.

The implications are already obvious. It is not enough to forgive perpetrators—you must also point out the injustice they have done. On the other hand, it is also not enough to just seek justice. If you don't forgive, then you will go beyond justice into vengeance and so not free yourself from what they have done. The priest Henri Nouwen wrote: "By not forgiving, I chain myself to a desire to get even, thereby losing my freedom. A forgiven person forgives. This is what we proclaim when we pray 'and forgive us our trespasses as we forgive those who have trespassed against us.' This lifelong struggle lies at the heart of the Christian life."[6]

There are, then, two ways to pursue justice—out of vengeance and out of love. You can do it to satisfy your anger and desire to see the wrongdoer suffer, but this serves to harden your heart and make you more capable of hurting people yourself in the future. In addition, it allows the perpetrator to continue to have some control over you. But you can also pursue justice—as the Leviticus verses hint—out of love. It's our job to help perpetrators see their wrongdoing out of love for them (Galatians 6:1), love for potential future victims, love for the human community, and love for God. The only way this is possible is if you forgive as you are seeking justice.

The New Testament gives us more insights about the combination of justice and love, but I will save most of them for the next chapters. Yet one is important to consider here. Christians seeking justice must be guided by the cross.

We know that God has *not* given us what we deserve. It is Jesus who received the full penalty for our sins. The punishment we deserve for our sinful lives falls on him so that the reward he deserves for his perfect and beautiful life can be credited to us. This classic understanding of the doctrine of justification by faith not works is a kind of two-edged sword. On the one side, we see how supremely concerned God is to uphold justice. He did not wave a hand at the human race and say, "Oh, I forgive you for all the evil you have done! Let's move on." He took justice so seriously that the second person of the Trinity took on a human nature, lived the life of a servant, and died on the cross, paying the debt to justice himself. Therefore we too must be passionate for justice!

And yet, on the other side, the doctrine of justification also reminds us that *we* have done wrong, that we are perpetrators of injustice whom God has forgiven. So while being deeply committed to justice, we do not go out into the world with a condescending attitude toward the unjust. We do not demonize or deal harshly or high-handedly with anyone created in God's image. We pursue justice tirelessly yet with humility.

God's Justice and Love Applied to Abuse

Rachael Denhollander is a former gymnast who was sexually assaulted multiple times by USA Gymnastics physician Larry Nassar. In 2018 she broke through the wall of official denial and was the first woman to publicly accuse him, which led eventually to hundreds of other women treated by Nassar to come forward with their own stories of abuse and assault.

Denhollander is a Christian, yet in her work as an advocate she often saw churches "routinely mishandling sexual assault allegations—counseling victims to forgive and forget, not listening when alarm bells were sounded about someone's behavior, and even, many victims alleged, interfering with or being negative toward criminal investigations."[7] She learned of women being told to forgive and to not report husbands who were abusing their daughters. At the bottom of so much of this was the churches' "teaching on concepts like unity, forgiveness, and grace that resulted in abusers being 'forgiven' while victims were silenced by being characterized as 'bitter.'"[8]

This kind of behavior has led many victims and advocates to reject forgiveness, especially in cases of abuse, and to go so far as to blame abuse in the church on the Christian doctrine of the atonement itself. The teaching that the Son of God died on the cross to satisfy divine wrath against sin is characterized as a form of "divine child abuse." The doctrine of substitutionary atonement is blamed on Anselm's famous work *Cur deus homo?* and has been criticized as a "gateway drug to right-wing extremism" because it acclimatizes us to a violent God.[9] Some, therefore, argue that the classic idea of God the "Father, punishing his Son for an offence he has not even committed . . . makes a mockery of Jesus' own teaching to love your enemies"[10] and leads necessarily to a culture of abuse.

A podcast series, *The Rise and Fall of Mars Hill*, sparked widespread discussion in late 2021.[11] Mars Hill Church in Seattle was a large evangelical megachurch that under pastor Mark Driscoll broke apart and disappeared almost overnight. Many critics of Mars Hill charged that it was evangelical theology itself that was to blame for the authoritarian, toxic ethos that developed there. One writer claimed that because "retributive, penal substitution was . . . abusive theology," it fueled "abusive ethics" in the congregation and does so across the country today. The idea that God judges people for their sins, he argued, is intrinsically hierarchical, and it fosters church cultures that are also obsessed with hierarchy and power.[12]

Many abuse victims and advocates have turned away from traditional religion and Christianity in particular in order to fight against oppression. But Denhollander, a calm but fierce defender of abuse victims, has not.

In her memoir *What Is a Girl Worth?* she recounts her extensive inner wrestling after she became aware of what had been done to her by Larry Nassar. "I did want to forgive Larry," she writes, "but I didn't want my forgiveness to be used as an excuse to act as if something terrible wasn't really that bad. Prominent [Christian] teachers had implied, 'You haven't really forgiven and trusted until you can be thankful for the evil done to you.' *Is that really what forgiveness means?* It wasn't right, but I'd heard it from authority figures so often that I felt alone in my grief."[13]

She admits that she considered "removing God from the picture" the way so many others had done. What about the secular path? Wouldn't that remove the guilt over struggling to forgive? Wouldn't it make her pursuit of justice uninhibited by all sorts of religious hang-ups? Wouldn't it be a kind of liberation to be herself and follow her own understanding of right and wrong and justice rather than having religious authority figures dictating these things to her?

But, she writes, "I'd mentally been down that path many times and it didn't fix the problem. If truth's parameters were established by people alone, I had no way to define evil, or even justice for that matter. . . . Removing God didn't fix the problem of evil. It actually made it worse." She "grappled with the critiques of the Christian faith," and her circumstances seemed to make her ripe for leaving it. But "no matter where I looked, I was confronted with things I couldn't explain without God." And while she had huge unanswered questions, she realized she had "more real answers through my faith than I had without it."[14]

In fact, Larry Nassar himself became a reason for Rachael to remain a Christian.

> Every other religion . . . outside of Christianity, relied on some form of doing enough good things to outweigh the bad, as if life were just a balancing scale, and the damage from evil would go away if someone did enough charity work, said the right prayers, or took enough pilgrimages. But that's not justice. I knew Larry had helped create an autism foundation, which was great, but that good deed didn't stop my nightmares. The evil he did was there. The damage was done. Nothing could make that wrong disappear.[15]

The Cross, Justice, and Love

In 2018 Rachael and her husband, Jacob, a PhD student at Southern Baptist Theological Seminary, presented a paper to the Evangelical Theological Society entitled "Justice: The Foundation of a Christian Approach to Abuse."[16] It begins by forthrightly confronting evangelicals for the frequent charges of sexual abuse occurring in their churches and for how often "those communities sided with the abuser, protecting them, returning them to positions of leadership and respect quickly and quietly, shielding them from consequences and traumatizing their victims in the process." Rachael and Jacob assert that while sometimes this practice is based on "outright corruption," more often the church mishandles situations "as a result of poor theology and misinformation about the dynamics of abuse."

To remedy this "poor theology," Rachael and Jacob point to a classic doctrine—the substitutionary atonement, how on the cross Jesus took the penalty for our sins so we could be forgiven. They believe a right grasp of the doctrine can provide "both comfort and vindication for victims" and also serve "as an over-arching guiding principle for Christian communities as they seek to . . . act . . . righteously in the face of abuse." They draw several principles from the doctrine of substitutionary atonement.

First, "a victim's sense of injustice and desire for vindication is upheld at the cross—injustice and unrighteousness are real and God hates them." Jesus bore the divine wrath against sin on the cross. The Denhollanders quote Fleming Rutledge:

> It makes many people queasy nowadays to talk about the wrath of God, but there can be no turning away from this prominent biblical theme. Oppressed peoples around the world have been empowered by the scriptural picture of a God who is angered by injustice and unrighteousness.[17]

It is at the cross where we see that sin and evil are no trivial things. The cross shows God's commitment to justice, and the Denhollanders argue that means that we *should* pursue justice here on earth. Nevertheless the pursuit of this-world justice will always disappoint. "Under the worst circumstances courts are an instrument of perpetuating injustice. And even under the best outcomes, it fails to achieve the restoration of what was damaged or broken . . . [but our] confidence can rest in the perfect justice of God." We console ourselves that, while no justice on earth is complete, and while full reparations and restitution here are impossible, we know that ultimately God will put all things right.

Second, the cross shows that God is committed to both justice and forgiveness; there is no pitting of one against the other. When Jesus died on the cross, it meant that in a single stroke justice was done on sin and the door for forgiveness opened. God "couples his forgiveness with the satisfaction of the requirements of justice."[18] We must pursue both together as well. This leads to the question of how the cross could be equally committed to both.

The answer is forthcoming only if we invoke the doctrine of the Trinity. Christians do not believe that there are three gods. Rather there is one God who exists in three persons—but all the fullness of the divine being resides in each. The Father is not the Son, but the Father and the Spirit are in the Son (John 14:11,20; Matthew 11:27). And therefore it is wildly inaccurate to say that on the cross the Father abused the Son. Miroslav Volf writes: "The Father would be abusing the Son [on the cross] . . . if Christ were a third party, beyond God who was wronged and humanity who wronged God. But he isn't. . . . 'In Christ,' wrote the apostle Paul, 'God was reconciling the world to himself' (2 Corinthians 5:19)."[19]

Volf adds: "Not: Christ was reconciling an angry God to a sinful world. [A typical conservative Christian error.] Not: Christ was reconciling a sinful world to a loving God. [A typical liberal Christian error.] Rather: God in Christc was 'reconciling the world to himself.'" The doctrine of the Trinity means that on the cross, as John Stott puts it, we see the "self-substitution of God."[20] God himself comes and takes the punishment and pays the debt that we should have paid.

The Denhollanders write: "A banker cannot be said to have forgiven a loan if a third party pays the loan on behalf of another; however, when the banker himself pays the loan on behalf of another, this is *both* satisfaction [of justice] *and* forgiveness [in a single stroke]."[21] At the cross, "the reality of evil and need for justice is upheld. Either divine punishment will be meted out on the individual who has done the wrong, or it is taken up by God upon himself."[22]

Third, "the example of God at the cross inverts power dynamics at play in oppression and abuse." This point is so crucial I will quote it at length:

> The devastating impact of abuse, in large part, is due to the fact that abuse upends the concepts necessary to function as a relational person. Abusers[23] frequently use grooming techniques, utilizing gifts, innocent touch, or manifestations of kindness to condition a victim and prepare them for abuse. More often than not, perpetrators are individuals who are perceived as safe and trustworthy, or even believed to be sacrificially caring for the victim. Concepts of trust, safety, security, love, compassion and care are all twisted by a perpetrator and wielded like weapons to facilitate violation at the deepest level. Every concept we as humans rely on to have healthy relationships with each other, becomes distorted and unsafe—redefined to be tools used to facilitate harm. In fact, the reason most abusers engage in sexual abuse is not simply about sexual release; they enjoy the imbalance in power and control that they are able to demonstrate.
>
> It is critical that survivors are able to define, understand, and relearn these foundational concepts. Failure to recognize harm-

ful abuse and manipulation of power can lead to survivors continually reentering abusive relationships, at times becoming abusers themselves, and nearly always being unable to interact relationally with the world around them.

The cross stands in stark opposition to the behavior of an abuser, providing the ultimate example of each of these concepts that abuse destroys. In the incarnation, at the cross, the Son sets aside his divine prerogatives—the strong becomes weak. . . . At the cross, God acts for others—to overcome evil, uphold justice, free the enslaved, and restore creation. God himself perfectly identifies with the victim because he himself has willingly subjected himself to injustice. The cross is the ultimate repudiation of the idea that power is to be wielded for the benefit and pleasure of those who possess it. In the cross, victims have the framework and foundation for beginning to properly define and understand concepts which were twisted, subverted and manipulated during their abuse, and begin to heal the damage which was done.[24]

Finally, the only possibility of healed relationships is if both justice and forgiveness are pursued concomitantly, using the model of the cross. The cross shows the victim his or her own need for forgiveness, and that makes it easier to extend it to others. The cross helps Christians in "refraining from viewing criminals and abusers as 'other' or fundamentally different from ourselves—for evil lies in our hearts as well."[25] This humbling prevents us from going beyond a desire for justice, a restoration that protects future victims, to vengefulness and a desire for the perpetrator's permanent destruction.

On the other hand, the best chance the perpetrator has to see his or her sin and self-deception and to change is if he or she is confronted with consequences.

The temporal nature of human justice serves as a picture of God's final justice. It presents the abuser an opportunity to come face to face with the reality and severity of his sin. It is a call to the abuser to repent; to side with both God and their victim and condemn the evil they have perpetrated. It is only in this scenario that the possibility of reconstructing a relationship is possible. . . . Truly repentant abusers who have come to side with God and their victims do not use their repentance as an excuse to escape human justice or make demands of their victims; true repentance involves acknowledging the harm they have done and the rightness of punishment.[26]

Rachael Denhollander put this nuanced biblical theology to work in the courtroom. There she looked at Larry Nassar and said:

I pray you experience the soul-crushing weight of guilt so that you may someday experience true repentance and true forgiveness from God, which you need far more than forgiveness from me, though I extend that to you as well.[27]

Another abuse survivor also gives testimony to the power of the cross. Mez McConnell was physically and emotionally abused by a stepmother for years.[28] In an article he writes:

As a survivor of childhood abuse, I have to be wary of how it has affected my entire life, particularly my thought life. I view new people with suspicion. I view power plays with suspicion. I detest bullying. I worry about manipulators. I lack basic trust. I think of people as guilty until they prove otherwise. I view every stranger as a potential abuser. And it's not good. . . .

That's why the cross grounds me. . . . That's why [the doctrine of substitutionary atonement] fills my pain with joy, hope, and some sort of meaning. . . . At the cross, God acts for the weak, the oppressed, and the abused. To overcome evil. To uphold justice. To free the enslaved. God Himself perfectly identifies with all the victims of vile manipulation and power plays. The cross is the greatest demonstration of that we have ever seen or ever will see.[29]

The Lamb of God

The justice and love of God can be seen in one of the most famous stories of the Bible—the Exodus.

God calls the Egyptians to release the Israelites from slavery but they refuse. After numerous warnings, God determines to bring judgment against Egypt for its oppression and enslavement of human beings, a great evil (Revelation 18:13). He sends out the destroying angel. The punishment of justice is that the firstborn son—the hope and strength of ancient families, who passed their estate down to their oldest boy—will die in every household. However, God directs the Israelites to observe the Passover. They are to slay and eat a lamb, to put its blood on the doorposts of their houses, and not leave their homes for any reason. This reveals two remarkable truths.

It means, first, that the "angel that brings death" (Exodus 12:23, CEV), the bearer of the wrath of God on evil and sin, did not go only to the homes of the Egyptians. The divine wrath on sin is no respecter of persons. It came to *every* home in Egypt because every home deserved it. There is no hierarchy here between the "good" Israelites and the "bad" Egyptians. It is as if God was saying to Israel, "You are the oppressed; they are the oppressor. You worship the true God; they worship idols. Yet if tonight I were to judge you by my righteous standards, you would not pass the test either. All fall short of the glory of God. All are sinners. You are as lost and as in need of grace salvation as the Egyptians." It is the radical truth on which Paul bases the gospel of sheer grace, namely, that "there is no one righteous, not even one" (Romans 3:10).

It means, second, that *substitution* is the way to satisfy justice and love together. Every firstborn son in every Hebrew home should have looked at the table and seen the lamb on the plate and said, "The only reason I'm not dead is because this lamb is." As we have seen, all sin incurs a debt, and that debt never vanishes—it is paid for one way or another. Someone always pays—either someone substitutes for you so you can be forgiven or you pay your own penalty. It never goes away on its own.

When you put these two truths together—the sinfulness of all people and therefore our universal need for a substitute—it becomes clear that the Passover pointed beyond itself. The New Testament articulates what any thoughtful observer must have felt: that the blood of animals could never atone for sins (Hebrews 10:4). The lamb can't possibly be the substitute we need. So where do we look?

Jesus Christ, on the night when he was betrayed, celebrated the Passover meal with his disciples. They expected to hear him say what the presider at Passover usually said: "This is the bread of our affliction. Our ancestors suffered in the wilderness so we could be free." Instead, he got up and said, "This is my broken body." In other words, "This is the bread of *my* affliction. It's *my* suffering that's going to be the ultimate liberation for you." There may have been a roasted lamb on the table, but the true Lamb of God was *at* the table.

This is the reason why John the Baptist looked at Jesus and said, "Behold the Lamb of God, which taketh away the sin of the world" (John 1:29, KJV). He was saying, "I see at last! Our firstborn sons were not saved because of the death of some little animals. Our firstborns were saved because God was willing to give up *his* firstborn." John 19:33 points out

Jesus's bones were not broken. Why? Because the Passover lamb could not have broken bones. It had to be without spot or blemish.

Jesus cried out on the cross that he was forsaken (Matthew 27:46). Since he was, by all accounts, the best man who ever lived, why would he have been forsaken? He was forsaken *in our place*. He was our substitute.

If you stopped an Israelite in the desert of Sinai and asked, "What are you doing and where are you going?" he would have said, "I was an alien in a foreign land under penalty of death, but I took shelter under the blood of the lamb, and was saved. Now I've been brought out of slavery, and even though I am in a wilderness, God is with me and he's taking me to the Promised Land."

Do you realize that's exactly what a Christian says? All the purposes of God to redeem us came to fulfillment on the day Jesus Christ became the Lamb of God who takes away the sins of the world.

CHAPTER 7

THE BASICS OF FORGIVENESS

> At the sight of men's sins . . . always decide to use humble love. If
> you resolve to do that, once and for all, you can subdue the whole
> world. Loving humility is marvelously strong, the strongest of all
> things, and there is nothing else like it.
>
> —FYODOR DOSTOYEVSKY[1]

The Christian understanding of forgiveness is rich and multidimensional, and it has quite literally changed the world. However,
to practice it we must begin to look at its basic components. There
is no better starting point than Jesus's two pairs of directives to his disciples on how to respond to wrongdoing.

Jesus's Two Forgiveness Directives

Jesus gives two directives regarding forgiveness that at first sight appear
contradictory. Taken together they are crucial for understanding how forgiveness actually works. In Mark 11:25 he said, "And when you stand
praying, if you hold anything against anyone, forgive them, so that your
Father in heaven may forgive you your sins."

It was customary to pray standing up (1 Kings 8:14,22; Nehemiah 9:4;

Psalm 134:1; Luke 18:11,13). If you are praying and you realize or remember that you are holding something against someone, you must forgive them on the spot. Scholars point out that "forgive them" (*aphiete*) is in the present tense of the imperative for the strongest possible emphasis.[2]

Jesus adds, "so that your Father in heaven may forgive you your sins," (Mark 11:25). Again we should remember that this cannot mean that God's forgiveness is merited by ours. Rather, it means that to be unforgiving reveals that you have failed to understand and accept God's unmerited grace yourself. Perhaps you thought that your contrition and reparations before God earned his favor. You may have made your remorse and shame into a kind of "good work" that (you thought) put God in your debt. The telltale sign that you have done something like this, rather than actually receiving God's unmerited forgiveness and mercy, is the inability to forgive others. The humility that comes from admitting your lostness *and* the joy that comes from knowing your acceptance in Christ are simply absent.

Without the humility that sees yourself as equally deserving of condemnation, and without the joy of knowing your standing in Christ's love, it will be impossible to give up your desire for revenge. "Therefore, to be forgiven and not forgiving, to have obtained mercy and not be merciful, is in reality to have failed to experience God's gracious acceptance and makes a mockery out of prayer as understood in vv 22–24."[3] Jesus's point: if you realize you have not forgiven someone, do it right away.

This text taken alone would support what we have called the "cheap grace" model of forgiveness, which puts all the emphasis on the wronged person banishing their anger and with no provision for change in the perpetrator.

But this call to forgive on the spot—as you are praying—seems to contradict another statement by Jesus in Luke:

> "If your brother or sister sins against you, rebuke them; and if they repent, forgive them. Even if they sin against you seven times in a

day and seven times come back to you saying 'I repent,' you must forgive them." (Luke 17:3–4)

There are two responsibilities set forth here. First, if someone sins *against you*—rebuke them. This does not say that we must correct any sin we see anyone doing. Galatians 6:1 and 1 Thessalonians 5:14 give some direction here (more about this later), but this verse is not speaking of sin in general. Jesus says if someone sins against *you*, you are to "rebuke," a word that means to confront. But if they repent, your second responsibility is to forgive.

From this text we learn, first, that the responsibilities to confront and to forgive are equally laid on us. The reality of human temperament is that few can sustain such a balance without the help of the Holy Spirit. People are prone to be either more ready to confront and challenge than to forgive or more ready to forgive and forget than to challenge. We also learn here that the repentance Jesus speaks of might happen "seven times in a day." We should not think that Jesus is saying that this is a likely scenario. But what he is saying is that we should not require the perpetrator's repentance to be a long, drawn-out, self-flagellating affair. We should not forgive slowly or begrudgingly.

Finally we learn that the goal of forgiveness is primarily neither inner healing nor payback to the offender. Certainly forgiveness *can* bring inner healing and *can* be part of the pursuit of justice. But the ultimate purpose of forgiveness is the restoration of community. "[Forgiveness's] purpose here is not to humiliate, defeat, or drive out sinners, but to correct and restore them. It is often easier to turn a blind eye to sin in the community. The admonition of fellow believers requires the church to function as a body in the costly work of reconciliation."[4]

Reading Luke 17 apart from Mark 11:25 has led many to believe that no forgiveness is necessary until there is full repentance and restitution by the offender. However, Mark 11:25 is emphatic: "Forgive, if you have *anything* against *anyone*" (ESV). It does not say "unless they don't repent." On the other hand, Mark 11:25 can give the impression that forgiveness is something that happens completely in one's heart and can be completed in an instant.

The Anglican Articles of Religion includes Article XX: "It is not lawful for the Church to . . . expound one place of Scripture, that it be repugnant to another."[5] On the basis of this time-honored principle of biblical interpretation, how do we read these two texts so that we don't allow one of them to be the absolute standard and relativize and minimize the force of the other?

The answer is that forgiveness can have two meanings that overlap. "Sometimes the forgiveness of which the New Testament speaks presupposes repentance on the part of the offender and sometimes not."[6] Luke 17:3–4 is an example of the first, while Mark 11:25 is an example of the latter. When Stephen died praying, "Lord, do not hold this sin against them" (Acts 7:60), it is clear that there was no repentance from the wrongdoers, since they were stoning and killing him as he spoke. Yet Stephen forgave them.

Inward and Outward Forgiveness

How can these two directives both be true? The answer is that the word *forgiveness* is being used in two somewhat different ways. In Mark 11 "forgive them" means inwardly being willing to not avenge oneself. In Luke 17 "forgive them" means "reconcile to them." There is, then, a kind of forgiveness that ends up being inward only and another kind that issues outwardly toward a possible restored relationship (cf. Matthew 5:24—"be reconciled to your brother," ESV; Matthew 18:15—"If your brother sins against you, go and tell him his fault, between you and him alone. If he listens to you, you have gained your brother," ESV). The victim of the wrongdoing in either case must forgive inwardly, while reconciliation depends on whether the perpetrator recognizes his wrongdoing and repents or does not. Some have called one of these "attitudinal forgiveness" and the other "reconciled forgiveness."[7]

These are not two kinds of forgiveness but two aspects or stages of it. One could say that the first must always happen, and the second may happen but is not always possible. Attitudinal forgiveness can occur without reconciliation, but reconciliation cannot happen unless attitudinal forgiveness has already occurred. If the victim in Luke 17 has not personally forgiven, why would they be open to reconciliation? For a victim to be open to reconciling, they must have already done some kind of forgiveness in their heart. An unwillingness to repent on the part of the perpetrator is no excuse for ongoing bitterness, something that the Bible says will inevitably poison the soul (Hebrews 12:15).

We learn two important lessons from these two directives.

First, Christian forgiveness is never simply individualistic—concerned only with inner healing of the heart. It is at least that, but it is much more. God's concern is for the outer and social healing of the community as well. Inward attitudinal forgiveness wants and seeks reconciliation even if the offender does not. So forgiveness is never only about the inner peace of the victim, as important as that is. The secular therapeutic models of forgiveness leave this concern out.

Second, Christian forgiveness never undermines the pursuit of justice but promotes it. Why? Inward forgiveness changes the attitude of the heart from a desire for the wrongdoer's pain to a desire for his or her good. That is the essence of inward forgiveness, and it means going from antipathy to love. Love is genuinely willing someone's good, putting one's happiness "into" the happiness of others, so that their thriving brings you joy. Love, then, is the essence of granting forgiveness. The secular merited forgiveness model leaves love out.

But that is also the essence of doing justice! *Why* should a Christian seek justice? Because injustice grieves the God we love, it mars the creation we love, it harms people we love, and it even harms the wrongdoer, whom we should love and not hate. *What* is seeking justice? It is to speak the truth in love and to not shield people from the consequences of their actions.

> What this suggests . . . is that moral indignation, even moral outrage, may on occasion be proof of love—love for the victim, love for the church of God, love for the truth, love for God and his glory. Not to be outraged [and to not seek justice] may in such cases be evidence not of gentleness and love but *of a failure of love.*[8]

This calls for discernment and heart searching. Passion for justice and moral outrage can easily be a function of our ego, a desire to be right and have the high moral ground and feel virtuous, or a desire for revenge against people we do not like. To be morally outraged out of love for God, his creation, people, and even the offender is rare—but required.

And since doing justice is at its essence loving your neighbors enough to want them to be freed from the evil at work in their hearts, then it is possible to pursue both justice and forgiveness, to renounce revenge and still pursue justice for the good of all, not for your own emotional satisfaction.

So discerning these two aspects of forgiveness is pastorally crucial, enabling us to navigate many common situations that frustrate efforts to forgive.

What if the offender has broken the law, as is the case in abuse and assault in the workplace or within relationships or against children? We can forgive a person in our hearts and still insist that the person pay the penalty for criminal action.

What if the offenders refuse to meet with you or listen to you or continue to try to attack you? You are not handcuffed by their action. You can still forgive and keep their evil from dominating your life and memory and behavior.

What if the person who wronged you is dead, as is often the case when dealing with the abuse of a parent or family member? Again, you are not helpless. While reconciliation is the most desirable and healing outcome, if it is not possible to be reconciled, there is a way to keep your heart from being so damaged that you cannot grow or enjoy life.

Steven McDonald was an NYPD officer who in 1986, while on duty in Central Park, was shot three times at point-blank range by a fifteen-year-old boy. Amazingly, he lived, but he was paralyzed from the neck down. "About six months after I was shot," he later wrote, his wife "gave birth to a baby boy. We named him Conor. To me, Conor's birth was like a message from God that I should live and live differently. . . . I prayed that I would be changed, that the person I was would be replaced by something new."[9]

The first answer to his prayer was a desire to forgive the young man, Shavod, now in prison, who had shot him. Steven began by writing him. "At first he didn't answer my letters," but then, to his surprise, Shavod wrote back and even called from prison to apologize for what had happened. Steven thought a reconciliation had been achieved, but "eventually the exchange fizzled out." Shavod went silent. After he was released from prison in 1995, he died in a motorcycle accident three days later. Many felt that Steven's efforts to reconcile with his attacker had been wasted. But though Steven had not been able to effect any real change or a new relationship, his efforts had helped him become even more free from bitterness. He began to see a bigger picture that helped him understand Shavod:

> I was the system that let landlords charge rent for squalid apart-
> ments in broken-down tenements; I was the city agency that fixed

up poor neighborhoods and drove the residents out, through gen-
trification, regardless of whether they were law-abiding solid citi-
zens, or pushers and criminals; I was the Irish cop who showed up
at domestic disputes and left without doing anything, because
no law had been broken. To Shavod Jones, I was the enemy. . . .
And I couldn't blame him. Society—his family, the social agencies
responsible for him, the people who'd made it impossible for his
parents to be together—had failed him way before he had met me
in Central Park.[10]

Steven McDonald had forgiven internally even though he was not able
to get his wrongdoer to change. Yet even his largely failed effort to reconcile aided the renewal of his heart and was a witness to the world. Here,
then, we can see the power of the half-truths of the popular secular models of forgiveness. Both the therapeutic and the merited-transactional
model are partly right but overall wrong. The first puts all the stress on
the inward attitude, and the second puts all the emphasis on the repentance of the perpetrator. But not only is seeking both required by Jesus's
teaching, they are interdependent, as the case study of Steven McDonald
illustrates. These models, which are secular in their origin, are nonetheless quite prevalent within the church, including the evangelical church.
David Powlison wrote:

> Seeing that our forgiveness of others has two interconnected parts
> helps us navigate the opposite messages that one often hears in
> Christian circles. Some in the church teach, "If you forgive from
> the heart, then you don't need to go to the person." Others teach,
> "Unless the other person asks for forgiveness, you don't need to
> forgive." Each focuses on a half-truth—and draws a false conclu-
> sion. When you put together both halves of what Jesus did and
> taught on forgiveness, you get a coherent truth.[11]

Jesus's Two Directives on Loving Enemies

The end of Matthew chapter 5 is often called the "high point" of the Sermon on the Mount. Certainly it is the most radical part. In verse 20 he speaks about a "righteousness"—a way of life—that greatly exceeds that of the scribes and Pharisees. This is at first a puzzling statement. The Pharisees were fastidious in their detailed obedience to the law—indeed, they added many regulations and rules to the Mosaic law that had been revealed by God. Elsewhere Jesus critiques their legalism. How, then, can he talk about *exceeding* their righteousness? The end of chapter 5 explains what this new way of life looks like. Indeed it goes beyond anything in the Old Testament, let alone the philosophies and ethics of pagan antiquity. Jesus lays out a life of love that includes enemies and "evil persons," not just friends and "good persons."

Jesus says:

> "You have heard that it was said, 'Eye for eye, and tooth for tooth.' But I tell you, do not resist an evil person. If anyone slaps you on the right cheek, turn to them the other cheek also. And if anyone wants to sue you and take your shirt, hand over your coat as well. If anyone forces you to go one mile, go with them two miles. Give to the one who asks you, and do not turn away from the one who wants to borrow from you." (Matthew 5:38–42)

As nearly all scholars and commentators point out, Jesus is not overturning the *lex talionis* ("an eye for an eye") as it was originally given in Exodus 21:24, Leviticus 24:19–20, and Deuteronomy 19:21. "[The rule] was given, as the OT context shows, to provide the nation's judicial system with a ready formula of punishment, not least because it would decisively terminate vendettas."[12] In other words, the *lex talionis* was a rule of thumb for judges deciding legal cases and the limits of restitution; it was not given as warrant for revenge in personal relationships, which Leviticus 19:17–18 expressly forbids. Evidently, however, by Jesus's time, this rule of thumb had become just that—a way people responded to any wrongdoing.

Jesus, however, lays down a startling principle—"do not resist [*anthistemi*] an evil person," (Matthew 5:39). Is Jesus saying that we must let any evil person do anything they wish to us? Even before we look at his examples in the following verses, we know we cannot read this phrase that way. Jesus does not say not to oppose evil—nor does the rest of the New Testament. God's face is against those who do evil (1 Peter 3:12). We are to resist the devil (James 4:7; 1 John 2:13–14). We are to expel an evil person from our midst rather than tolerating them (1 Corinthians 5:13; Revelation 2:2). We are told to wrestle against evil (Ephesians 6:12). All this means Jesus is not saying that we should simply allow evil to have its way with us.

So what *is* Jesus saying? As John Stott points out:

> The first clue to a correct understanding of his teaching is to recognize that the words *tō ponērō* ("the evil") are here masculine not neuter. . . . Jesus does not deny that [there] is evil. . . . What he does not allow is that we retaliate.[13]

Jesus is not telling us to allow evil to have its way. But we are to overcome evil with good (Romans 12:18ff.), without simply destroying the evildoer. The four illustrations Jesus gives support this view.

The first is a slap on the right cheek. Since most people are right-handed, this refers to a blow with the back of the hand, the ancient Near Eastern way to lodge an insult. We are talking here about something that is designed not to physically injure us but to humiliate. Christians are not to respond that way.

Secondly, when incurring a debt, a garment ("your shirt") could be offered as collateral. Jesus says here, if you are sued, rather than responding resentfully and doing all you can to resist the creditor, do everything to square things with him or her, even voluntarily offering another garment.[14]

The third and fourth cases are even clearer. "If anyone forces you to go one mile, go with them two miles. Give to the one who asks you, and do not turn away from the one who wants to borrow from you," (Matthew 5:41–42). The word *forced* is better translated as "conscripted" (Greek, *angareuo*)—an older word would be *impressment*. By law, Roman legions could conscript civilians without their consent to carry military equipment for a distance of up to a Roman mile. While infuriating, again, this was perfectly legal, and Jesus counsels his disciples to take a stance not of begrudging, spiteful helpfulness to the soldiers before you. The final example is someone needing a loan, and the Mosaic law already commanded Israelites to loan and give to those in need (Exodus 22:25; Leviticus 25:37; Deuteronomy 23:19) with a generous spirit (cf. Deuteronomy 15:7–11; Psalms 37:26, 112:5).

Jesus's teaching, then, is not that we should allow evil to have its way. In Matthew 18:15–18 Jesus commands us to confront those who have wronged us. Paul opposes and therefore resists Peter publicly when he is in serious error (Galatians 2:11ff.). The Bible is filled with exhortations to correct and rebuke (e.g., Galatians 6:1). The New Testament explains that governments were appointed by God to punish evil (Romans 13:1–8; 1 Peter 2:14).

But while resisting evil, Christians are not to target the wrongdoers to hurt them or their reputations just in order to pay them back. In every one of Jesus's case studies he calls believers to not respond to wrongdoing with fury, hurt pride, and vengefulness.[15]

As one Christian writer reflected on these verses: "[This] is a very spiritual teaching. . . . I must be right in my attitude towards myself and the spirit of self-defense that immediately rises when any wrong is done to me. I must also deal with the desire for revenge and the spirit of retaliation that is so characteristic of the natural self."[16]

The Revolution

Jesus's final paragraph is even more revolutionary:

> You have heard that it was said, "You shall love your neighbor and hate your enemy." But I say to you, Love your enemies and pray for those who persecute you, so that you may be sons of your Father who is in heaven. For he makes his sun rise on the evil and on the good, and sends rain on the just and on the unjust. For if you love those who love you, what reward do you have? Do not even the tax collectors do the same? And if you greet only your brothers, what more are you doing than others? Do not even the Gentiles do the same? You therefore must be perfect, as your heavenly Father is perfect. (Matthew 5:43–48, ESV)

As noted before, Leviticus 19:17–18 was unique in the ancient world. And yet in a number of ways it stopped short of commanding listeners to love their enemies. First, it did not specifically use the term for "enemy." Also, Leviticus 19:17 makes it clear that the instructions on no vengeance referred to "a fellow Israelite," which was taken to mean that the rule against revenge applied only within the believing, covenant community.

Jesus begins by showing that this was how Leviticus 19:17–18 was interpreted. "You have heard that it was said" that you should "love your neighbor" (a quote of Leviticus 19:18) "and hate your enemy." People, of course, interpreted the word *neighbor* to mean only your own people—your own nation and religion. Outsiders were not covered—they were not considered neighbors. The directive to love one's neighbor applied only to those of the same race and religion in that thinking.

But now Jesus says that is *not* the way to read the command to "love your neighbor." Elsewhere, in the parable of the Good Samaritan (Luke 10:25–37), he teaches that one's neighbor is anyone at all. The "good neighbor" of the parable gives costly and risky help to a man of a different religion and different nationality. Here in the Sermon on the Mount, however, Jesus makes this explicit.

He makes clear that Christians are to show love rather than hate to all people, even those of other religions and races. He explicitly tells his disciples not to only greet "brothers," their own people. Since the traditional greeting was often an embrace and the word *shalom*, a word that means full flourishing and peace, Jesus is saying that we cannot confine our commitment to the good of others to our own tribe and people, not even to the community of Christian believers. We are to open our arms and hearts to the "Other"—those religiously, racially, morally, and politically different from us. And we are to will their *shalom*. So Jesus "introduces a concept of undiscriminating love."[17]

"To love those who do not love you is not offered as a piece of pragmatic wisdom, but as a reflection of the character of God himself (v. 45) who gives a fruitful earth, through rain and sun, to all people regardless of the motives or character."[18] In the final verses, Jesus says that this principle will set apart his disciples from all others. The normal human life is self-interested and transactional; you "love those who love you." We give affirmation to people we admire and whose affirmation we desire. Our love relationships are often modeled on economic relationships. We invest where we know we will make a profit. We give love if we know it means we will get love that will build us up. We will not love others who do not love us back or will not give us an affirmation we value.

Behind the rhetorical questions of verses 45–47 are two assumptions. One is that Christians *should* live lives of love that are visibly "different, special, extraordinary," and distinct from the rest of society.[19] The other is that they *can* do this because "we love because he first loved us" (1 John 4:19). This is the higher righteousness of verse 17. It is a whole new way of living life, one based not on honor and pride and strength but on respect, grace, humility, and forgiveness.

The simple phrase "love your enemies" exploded like a bombshell and changed the course of human life. It has been debated furiously in innumerable ways. Does it mean we cannot have a police force? No. Does it mean pacifism? Certainly it means warfare only in highly selective situations. But the main question is how this is to work itself out in personal relationships. The most common Christian approach—along with its transformative possibilities—is illustrated by this classic account.

Tom Skinner was an African American evangelist who was born and raised on the streets of New York.[20] He was converted, and in his memoir *Black and Free* wrote: "Second Corinthians 5:17 is true. If any man is 'in Christ' he is a new creature. If I had not been reached by Jesus Christ I would either be dead, in prison, or graduated to a higher form of hoodlumism. . . . Jesus Christ is alive in me. My life has new meaning and purpose because of him. The tremendous work that the Spirit of God had done in my life in transforming me soon became evident to me. He took the bigotry, hate, and violence out of my life."[21] He relates an incident that happened several weeks after his conversion:

> In a football game several weeks later my new-found Christian love met another test. I played left guard on the team. It was my job on end runs or off tackle plays to run interference when the halfback took the ball. So when the quarterback called an end run play, I pulled out and blocked the defensive end, knocking him out of play. The halfback went through and scored.
>
> We were getting up from the ground to head back to the huddle. . . . The kid that I happened to block got up and was furious. He jumped in front of me and slammed me in the stomach. As I bent over from the blow he hacked me across the back.

I hit the ground as he kicked me, shouting, "You dirty black ****!
I'll teach you a thing or two!"

Under normal circumstances the old Tom Skinner would have
jumped up and pulverized this white boy. But instead I got up
from the ground . . . and I said to him, "You know, because of
Jesus Christ, I love you anyway." . . .

The kid threw his helmet down to the ground, ran off the
field, and couldn't play for the rest of the game. When the game
was over he met me in the locker room and said to me, "Tom,
you've done more to knock prejudice out of me by telling me that
you loved me than you would have if you'd socked my jaw in."[22]

It is important to note that despite Skinner's deep internalization of
Jesus's command to love his enemies, he became a social critic and an ar-
dent proponent of racial justice inside and outside the church. There was,
in Skinner's mind, no conflict between loving forgiveness and the pursuit
of justice. He was right.

PRACTICING

FORGIVENESS

CHAPTER 8

OUR NEED FOR
FORGIVENESS

I'm so guilty
I'm so far gone and you're the only one who can save me
—ADELE, "MY LITTLE LOVE" (SONG TO HER SON ABOUT
HIS PARENTS' DIVORCE) FROM THE ALBUM *30*

The first irreplaceable dimension of Christian forgiveness is what we have called the "vertical"—it is recognizing both our need for and our reception of forgiveness from God. Christians believe that an experience of God's forgiveness is a uniquely powerful motivation—as well as the instructive pattern—for the extension of it to others. Because this is fundamental to the granting of forgiveness to others, we will take two chapters to explore it.

Faith in Jesus Christ and his gospel gives us a way to understand our profound, ineradicable need for God's removal of our guilt and shame. It also gives us resources available only to believers, resources necessary for both receiving forgiveness from God and giving it to others.

Understanding Guilt and Shame

Wilfred McClay has written of "The Strange Persistence of Guilt."[1] If Christians begin to talk about the importance of God's forgiveness, some will say that to do so is to live in the past. Yes, they say, in the late nineteenth and early twentieth centuries people were still mourning the decline of faith and struggling with guilt, but that was just a holdover. Friedrich Nietzsche, in *On the Genealogy of Morals* (1887), argued that as more and more people rejected religion and God, the older moral reflexes that those beliefs had created—and in particular the experience of guilt and shame—would melt away.

Then there is the work of Sigmund Freud, and while much of his psychoanalytic framework has been rejected today as being not sufficiently science based, his basic idea of therapy has entered the fabric of the culture and is stronger than ever. Human beings, Freudianism taught, are crushed under guilt and shame imposed through "interdictions"—condemning judgments imposed on people by families, tribes, religions, and other oppressive, life-suffocating cultural institutions. Freud sought to "demoralize" guilt by treating it as strictly subjective, as not being grounded in objective moral realities at all. Freedom comes by being "analytical"—by defusing and deconstructing and thereby weakening the power of these social interdictions. We must come to see that our guilty inner feelings are really just impositions upon us by those who want to keep us under their power and influence.

A third thinker whose work undermined the idea of inner guilt and shame was Karl Marx. While Marx's work was not, like Nietzsche's and Freud's, directly or largely concerned with guilt, he gave both of the other thinkers the tools to deconstruct any moral claims as "really just" the creation of one's social location. Moral claims are all, in Marx's view, ways that those in power keep their power and keep the class structure that benefits them in place.

So with these prominent philosophers and thinkers having become so dominant, and with the secularization of Western society continuing at an increasing pace, surely, as Nietzsche predicted, the experience of guilt and shame would diminish across society and continue only, if at all, among isolated pockets of very religious people.

It is clear that this has not happened. Over the last two decades, books on healing shame and guilt by John Bradshaw, Brené Brown, and other authors have been read and listened to by millions. And other terms—low self-esteem, feelings of inadequacy, poor body image, self-loathing, self-harm—map directly onto what has traditionally been called guilt and shame.[2] Why has Nietzsche's guilt-free society not come about?

McClay shows that secular society has not been able to shed guilt and shame even though it has relativized the concept of moral truth. Secular people are in a strange position of feeling like sinners without having a name for it. There is a "pervasive need to find innocence through moral absolution and somehow discharge one's moral burden, [yet] the fact [is] that the conventional means of finding that absolution—or even of keeping the range of one's responsibility for one's sins within some kind of reasonable boundaries—are no longer generally available."[3]

McClay argues convincingly that our new reverse shame-and-honor culture, in which the victims and marginalized have the greater honor, is a response to this need for sinners to discharge their guilt without admitting they are sinners. "Making a claim to the status of certified victim, or identifying with victims . . . offers itself as a substitute means by which the moral burden of sin can be shifted, and one's innocence affirmed."[4] McClay is sympathetic, and so should we be. What he calls this new "moral economy"—this new solution to the problem of guilt apart from God and confession—is "not something as simple as hypocrisy that we are seeing.

Instead, it is a story of people working out their [self-] salvation in fear and trembling."[5]

Guilt Unlocated, Unplacated

Franz Kafka saw all this coming long ago. In his book *The Trial*, Josef K. is living a normal life, and on his thirtieth birthday he's arrested. He is indicted and put under house arrest and interrogated and given hearing after hearing, but he never learns what he's accused of. At first he thinks it's all a mistake and he can easily clear it up. But as time goes on, he begins to look at his life and he realizes that there were bad things he did that just might be the reason for all this. He begins to doubt himself. But he cannot get to the bottom of it. Does he deserve to be arrested or not? Is he guilty or not?

In the end, he never finds out. His jail warden brings him outside and stabs him to death. And the story ends. Many college students who are required to read *The Trial* find it frustrating in the extreme. It seems to be a dark, hard-to-follow story that in the end has no resolution. There seems to be no point. But as John Updike wrote, "Kafka epitomizes . . . the modern mind-set: a sensation of anxiety and shame whose center cannot be located and therefore cannot be placated."[6]

Modern culture has done everything to say: "We don't believe in God. We don't believe in heaven. We don't believe in hell. We don't believe in moral categories." Kafka says it hasn't helped. If anything, it has made it worse—because our guilt now can't be eradicated. We can say, "I don't believe in sin, I don't believe in guilt," and yet there's a voice in us that calls us cowards, calls us fools, makes us ashamed, makes us say we're not living up. There's something going on. What is it? Secular culture has no definitive answer.

The Condition of Nakedness

The Bible provides a far better explanation of why we feel as we do:

> Then the eyes of both of them were opened, and they realized they were naked; so they sewed fig leaves together and made coverings for themselves. Then the man and his wife heard the sound of the Lord God as he was walking in the garden in the cool of the day, and they hid from the Lord God among the trees of the garden. But the Lord God called to the man, "Where are you?" He answered, "I heard you in the garden, and I was afraid because I was naked; so I hid." (Genesis 3:7–10)

In this famous account, Adam and Eve sin and immediately experience shame and guilt, vividly depicted as a feeling of *nakedness*. They feel exposed and vulnerable and must immediately cover up and hide the truth of who they have become from God and from each other. They sense in the depths of their being that there is something wrong with them, something they cannot justify. Now they are desperate to cover up, to control what others see of them, and to hide the truth of who they are even from themselves.

Jean-Paul Sartre, in his book *Being and Nothingness*, has a chapter called "The Look" in which, consciously or not, he adopts the biblical metaphor of nakedness and exposure to convey the indelible sense of shame and guilt with which we live. He envisions a situation in which he is in a room and he's looking through a keyhole at somebody. He sees them and all they are doing, but they do not even know he is looking at them. He likes it! It gives him a sense of power—they can't cover and control what he sees of them, but he is covered and safe.

Then suddenly he hears a noise in the hallway through another door, and he suddenly realizes somebody is looking at *him* through the keyhole. He is traumatized and outraged, and he cannot bear it. Why? Because his unviewed viewing is being viewed by an unviewed viewer. He loved *being* the unviewed viewer, but he cannot bear to be the *object* of an unviewed viewer. It's like being stark naked in a room of clothed people.

Sartre is saying that the human condition needs a spiritual covering. We cannot bear to have people get an unfiltered, out-of-our-control look at who we really are. We are not proud of who we are "in the raw," and so we desperately look for ways to cover up and to curate a flawless image. But Instagram is not enough!

The Inadequacy of Fig Leaves

We cannot bear to lose control of what people know about us. We need to filter it, spin it, explain it. To have people actually see the unvarnished, un-processed self, the self without any makeup on, is intolerable. Sartre goes on in that chapter and later in the book to make an ingenious argument against belief in God. There's nothing more dehumanizing than being the object of an unviewed viewer, and if there were a God he would be that very thing. So even if he exists, I need to oppose and defy God, in the name of being a full human being.

But Sartre doesn't ask *why* human beings can't bear to be viewed by the unviewed viewer. If we had nothing to hide, there would be no fear—but we have *much* to hide. Nakedness is a deep sense that there's something wrong with me, something imperfect *about* me. There's something inad-equate about me—I'm not what I ought to be. That's the reason we cannot bear to let somebody else see us as we really are. Imagine if every thought you've had for the last forty-eight hours could be captured and put out over the internet. What if people saw how foolish so many of your thoughts were, how petty, how scared, how obsessed? You couldn't bear it. We spend all our lives finding ways to cover up that deep, radical sense of inadequacy.

Why do so many people work themselves to death to be successful? Why do some people have no boundaries—are not able to say no to anyone? Why do others stay unattached, not allowing any real friendships or committed romantic relationships to develop? Why are some people *rescuers* who are always trying to save people in crisis?

Why do some live in a perpetual victim mode, spending all their time blaming others for harming them? Why do others engage in abusive behavior, living a life based on the principle "Do unto others before they get a chance to do unto you"?

Why do some work so hard to promote relativism? They say, "No one can make me feel guilty—I define my own moral values!" Why do others become highly religious and moralistic and then turn to condemn everyone with the wrong beliefs?

Why do so many seek out noncommitted sexual encounters on Tinder or Grindr when some voice inside tells them this isn't wise or right?

Why do so many love to spread slander and gossip about others? Why do we want to believe that all people in leadership are really on the take, that all institutions are corrupt?

Why all these things? These are fig leaves. Your perfectionism is a fig leaf. Your work is a fig leaf. Your holding on to your youth is a fig leaf. Your desperate need for approval is a fig leaf. We are like Lady Macbeth running around saying, "Out, damned spot! All the perfumes of Arabia will not sweeten this little hand." We know there's something foul and we are looking for perfume. These are desperate efforts to deal with the sense of unacceptability—of unlovability—we all have.

But fig leaves don't work. Imagine for a moment trying to make do with an actual garment of fig leaves for clothing. Such a garment would be always falling apart. And so it does.

I have pastored two churches in my career—one in a blue-collar small town in the South for nine years, and one in the middle of Manhattan for twenty-eight years. In both ministries I had a pair of parallel pastoral cases that helped me understand this profound psychological-spiritual issue of fig leaves.

In the first church I counseled two women in almost identical situations. They were each mothers of single children—each had a teenage son who was doing poorly in school and getting into trouble with the law. Both rightly blamed their husbands for being too detached from parenting their sons. I gave both women the same advice, namely, to forgive their husbands. But one woman was able to forgive and communicate with her spouse in a winsome way and see changes in his life and in her son's. The other woman could not forgive, could not communicate except in harsh, alienating ways, and their family fell apart. The difference? The second woman had made her mothering into her main spiritual covering. If her son went off the rails, she did not have sorrow and grief merely about him. It was about her. It meant that her spiritual strategy—of covering her sense of inadequacy and unacceptability with being a successful mother—had fallen apart. Despite her Christian profession, she had not learned to rely on Jesus and his work for eliminating that deep sense of shame and sinfulness.

In my second church I counseled two young men who had moved to New York City to pursue acting careers. Both of them failed to break into the field and get good parts. One man simply accepted the disappointment with tears but moved on to other things. The second man could not accept his failure. A successful acting career was his strategy for a spiritual covering, and now his fig-leaf garment was falling apart. Despite good counsel from many sources, he spiraled down into depression and addiction.

If we are not willing to hear the Bible's teaching about where this sense of "nakedness" comes from—and if we don't recognize the fig leaves in our own lives—we will be trapped.[7] We may spend all our time on the internet trying to expose other people for their sins, thereby achieving a small sense of power and control, as well as a biological dopamine response, which makes us feel good temporarily. Or we may move along to some other desperate effort to cover ourselves or, as some say, to "patch up a righteousness" (cf. Genesis 3:7 with Philippians 3:9–10), to find ways to not let anybody, including ourselves, know how weak we really are.

Three Resources

There are three spiritual resources that Christianity gives us that are crucial both for receiving God's forgiveness and for extending it to others. The first two are seen in the famous epilogue to the story of Joseph and his coat of many colors:

> When Joseph's brothers saw that their father [Jacob] was dead, they said, "What if Joseph holds a grudge against us and pays us back for all the wrongs we did to him?" So they sent word to Joseph, saying, "Your father left these instructions before he died: 'This is what you are to say to Joseph: I ask you to forgive your brothers the sins and the wrongs they committed in treating you so badly.' Now please forgive the sins of the servants of the God of your father." When their message came to him, Joseph wept. His brothers then came and threw themselves down before him. "We are your slaves," they said. But Joseph said to them, "Don't be afraid. Am I in the place of God? You intended to harm me, but God intended it for good to accomplish what is now being done, the saving of many lives. So then, don't be afraid. I will provide for you and your children." And he reassured them and spoke kindly to them. (Genesis 50:15–21)

Joseph's words and actions here are the climax of a long and important story. It begins with Jacob, who poisoned his family's life through the same favoritism that he had experienced so painfully from his father, Isaac. Jacob showed obvious favoritism to the children of his wife Rachel—to Joseph and Benjamin—rather than to his other ten sons. This not only began to turn Joseph into a spoiled, self-involved youth but also embittered the other sons, making them capable of cruelty. They sold Joseph into slavery and lied to their father, making it look like he had been killed by a wild animal.

In Egypt Joseph was humbled and changed and began to look to God for his strength. He rose up to be the steward of a wealthy man's home, but through the subterfuge of his master's wife, he was put in prison. There again he looked to God rather than despairing, and eventually he was released and revealed his divinely granted insight into the future to Pharoah. He became the leading governing authority in Egypt next to the king himself.

After all this, Joseph's brothers come to Egypt and stand before him, in order to buy food from him to survive the severe famine. They don't recognize Joseph because it has been twenty years, but he recognizes them.

He does not at first reveal himself to them. Instead, he accuses them of being spies, testing them. Through a long process, the brothers show real repentance, and Judah even offers to be enslaved in order to save his family. At that point, Joseph looks around at all the others besides his brothers and cries, "Leave us." All leave but the brothers, and with tears he says, "I am Joseph!"

And when the truth sinks in, that this powerful man is the boy they betrayed decades ago, they are "terrified" and speechless (Genesis 45:3). Over the months and years they had begun to believe that God was going to punish them for what they had done, and now indeed, it seemed their judgment had finally come upon them. They were falling into the pit they had dug for Joseph. They waited for the word of condemnation.

But it never came.

Instead there was overwhelming tenderness, kindness, and affection.

Joseph kisses his brothers and weeps over them (Genesis 45:15). Old Testament commentator Derek Kidner concludes: "Just how well-judged was [Joseph's] policy can be seen in the growth of quite new attitudes in his brothers, as the alternating sun and frost broke them open to God."[8]

Humility and Joy

The fascinating epilogue to the Joseph story comes after Jacob's death. The sons doubt whether Joseph has really forgiven them—they believe he simply refrained from revenge for his father's sake. When Joseph sees this doubt, he weeps. He's weeping because they still don't believe how much he loves them.

When we become Christians, we often walk the same path. At the beginning of the relationship, we accept God's forgiveness in Christ. But it won't be long before we live in ways that reveal that our hearts still doubt his love. It shows up in myriad ways—the way we try to earn our self-worth through our overwork, the way we continually beat ourselves up internally over our failures, the way we fail to forgive because the reality of God's forgiveness is faint to us.

I don't think it's a stretch to say that Jesus is grieved when we act like that, just as Joseph was grieved when he got his brothers' message. Joseph's classic answer is something of a recap of all we have been learning in this chapter (Genesis 50:19–21). Joseph restates his forgiveness but does so in a remarkably God-centered way. He grounds his "horizontal" forgiveness of his brothers firmly in the vertical forgiveness of God. If you are having any trouble forgiving, here's how it's done.

First he says, "Am I in the place of God?" *Joseph had enough humility to forgive.* If you are having trouble forgiving, you're forgetting you're a sinner, not God. Joseph says, "The only way I could stay mad at you is if I considered myself worthy to be your judge. But I am not."

We must tread carefully here, because the Bible shows that God wants us to cry out to him when we are hurt. The Psalms are full of such emotional reality and of cries for justice. Nevertheless, anyone who remains bitter has said, "I'm in the place of God. I have the right to judge."

Second, he says, "You intended to harm me, but God intended it for good." *Joseph had enough joy to forgive.* Notice he says, literally in the Hebrew, "You meant it for *evil*." He doesn't forgive by glossing over things, saying, "Well, what you did wasn't so bad." No, he says, "What you did was evil." He speaks truth: "I realize in spite of your evil deed, I have a God who loves me, who has lifted me up, who has worked all things out for my good."

Evil people can do some very evil things, and again, we must be careful not to do anything to short-circuit the rightful laments and expressions of pain that the prayers of the Bible show are healthy and justified. Again, however, we must not get stuck there. If you know like Joseph that God is working out his plan for good in all things (Romans 8:28), then you can look at the perpetrator and say, "You cannot ultimately harm me. You can't take me out from under God's care and love."

Lastly, Joseph says, "'So then, don't be afraid. I will provide for you and your children.' And he reassured them and spoke kindly to them." This is the action step. *Joseph repays evil with good.* Forgiveness is often (or perhaps usually) granted before it's felt inside. When you forgive somebody, you're not saying, "All my anger is gone." What you're saying when you forgive is "I'm now going to treat you the way God treated me. I remember your sins no more. That doesn't mean I can't actually recall them. It means I'm not going to act on the basis of them. They're not the controlling reality in my life." What is the controlling reality? The grace of God and the way in which, out of love, he controls history.

Joseph was a remarkable man. And perhaps you are saying, "Ah! Back then there were saints. But this is beyond me. I can't do that." The problem with that reasoning is you forget that you have what Joseph did not. Joseph did not know about Jesus.

The cross, the ultimate example of God bringing good out of evil, will make you much humbler than Joseph was, because you see more than Joseph just how bad we are. Joseph didn't realize God would actually have to die to save him. On the other hand, it'll make you more confident than Joseph was. When you see what Jesus Christ was willing to do for you, how much more assurance do you want that God means everything for your good? If we have access to resources for greater humility than Joseph and even greater assurance because we are in Christ, then, if anything, we ought to be even better at forgiving and reconciling with those around us.

Christ's Costly Love

So Christians have a humility and a joy that makes forgiveness possible. There's one more thing that Christianity gives us as a resource. I'm talking about an understanding of the *costliness* of Jesus's saving love.

> Then he said to them, "My soul is overwhelmed with sorrow to the point of death. Stay here and keep watch with me." Going a little farther, he fell with his face to the ground and prayed, "My Father, if it is possible, may this cup be taken from me. Yet not as I will, but as you will." (Matthew 26:38–39)
>
> About three in the afternoon Jesus cried out in a loud voice, *"Eli, Eli, lema sabachthani?"* (which means "My God, my God, why have you forsaken me?"). (Matthew 27:46)

There are many people who understandably recoil from the idea of hell and eternal judgment. But there are ramifications that come from such a rejection. One we have already mentioned above. How will justice ever be done for all the evil and corruption and violence that has happened in history? Justice will never be done if there is not a divine Judgment Day. If there is no Judgment Day, what hope is there for the world?

But there is another serious implication of the rejection of a God of wrath. It minimizes what Jesus did for us. After worship service once, years ago, a woman came up to me and told me how narrow she thought my whole sermon was. I said, "Why?" She said, "Well, because of this whole idea that you have to believe Jesus died. I believe in a God of pure love who loves everybody no matter what. Jesus didn't have to die. He just loves everyone."

As gently as possible I asked, "What did it cost your God to love you?" She said, "I guess nothing." I answered that if you don't believe in a just God who must punish sin, you don't have a sense of what it *cost* Jesus to love us. He had to somehow take that infinite, eternal punishment in his own being, in our place.

That is why in the garden of Gethsemane the divine Son of God could say that he was overwhelmed to the point of death, that he felt already he was being crushed. That is why on the cross Jesus did not cry out, "My hands, my hands!" or "My feet, my feet!" or "My head, my head!" He certainly could have. His body had nails and thorns penetrating it. He was slowly, excruciatingly dying of blood loss and asphyxiation. Yet instead he cried, "My God, my God, why have you forsaken me?" It was the spiritual separation from God that was the ultimate agony.

Someone says, "Oh, God just loves everyone." But such a God is not as loving as the God of the Bible, who because he was holy *and* loving gave us grace. Because he's loving, there's free, free, free, free grace for us. But because he's holy, it was *costly* grace, *infinitely* costly grace. When I know that I am the recipient of this kind of costly grace, when I know Jesus Christ went to hell's heart for me and was loving and obedient for me . . . There. *That's* what changes me. *That's* tears. *That's* amazement. *That's* exhilaration. *That's* galvanizing. It changes me because at the very same time, on the one hand, it humbles me out of my pride and self-centeredness and it affirms me out of my inferiority and self-pity. It makes me hate my sins because it led to his death. But it forbids me to hate myself because he did it for me, to make me free.

There is nothing that changes you like this. There are no inferiority complexes—because I'm so loved. There are no superiority complexes—because I'm a sinner saved only by grace. Understanding the cry of Jesus on the cross is the key to personal transformation—and it is the great key to the work of human forgiveness and reconciliation.

CHAPTER 9

RECEIVING GOD'S FORGIVENESS

Long my imprisoned spirit lay
Fast bound in sin and nature's night;
Thine eye diffused a quick'ning ray—
I woke. The dungeon flamed with light;
My chains fell off, my heart was free,
I rose, went forth, and followed thee.

—CHARLES WESLEY[1]

M acbeth knew that his wife, famously plagued with a guilty conscience, could be delivered only by some "sweet . . . antidote" that would wipe away the "perilous stuff that weighs upon her heart." That antidote is the forgiveness of God. You will never be able to fully forgive others for their sins against you unless you first experience God's forgiveness of your sins against him. Our guilt must be dealt with if we are to deal rightly with others' guilt.

The Problem of Self-Forgiveness

It is common for counselors to hear people say, "Yes, I asked for God's forgiveness. But the problem is . . . I can't forgive myself."

There is a large industry of self-help books and many kinds of therapy that attempt to help people with self-forgiveness. The vertical dimension—the relationship to God—is left out completely, and guilt is seen as strictly to be dealt with on the internal and horizontal levels.

The main ideas of self-forgiveness therapy include: (a) asking for forgiveness from anyone you've wronged, (b) taking responsibility for what you have done wrong, but then (c) learning lessons from the event, (d) being as compassionate to yourself as you would be to others, and finally (e) then moving on with life, accepting yourself.

While individual steps mentioned can be helpful, the overall approach falls short. We struggle to know if what we did really *was* wrong, and secular approaches have no way to help anyone judge between true guilt and false guilt feelings. Also, many have asked forgiveness of other human beings—they have done all required of them—but still can't rid themselves of guilt and shame.[2]

How do we respond to someone who says, "I cannot forgive myself"? Modernity has declared that we are our own highest authorities. Gail Sheehy's bestseller *Passages* spells this out as a foundational rule of life. You "find yourself" only as you free yourself from all other institutional claims and from all other people's agendas and approval. Relationships should be tentative and engaged only as long as they support your chosen identity and interests. We alone can validate ourselves or judge whether something is good or bad. No one else has the right to tell us who we are or judge us by their standards.[3]

But what happens then when the self is weighed down in guilt nonetheless? No outside agent has the power to overturn the sanctions that the self inflicts upon itself. Who has the right to tell the modern self, "Your evaluation of yourself is all wrong"? The Bible reveals the core of this problem: "If our hearts condemn us, we know that God is greater than our hearts" (1 John 3:20).

Here is the essence of what Christianity gives us. Only God is the final judge of who we are and what we have done. If—and only if—he is, then God can overrule our heart's guilt and self-condemnation. If he says we are forgiven, then we are, and we can tell our hearts to quiet themselves. The secular framework, however, has nothing to give the wounded conscience to heal it. It has nothing to say to the self who feels it is unworthy of love and forgiveness. Anyone who has seen the depths of their sin and what they are capable of will never be mollified by the bromide of "Be nice to yourself—you deserve it."

In his book, *Radical Self-Forgiveness*, Colin Tipping sees the limits of a wholly secular approach and so incorporates Eastern mysticism. Tipping advises us to look at our life in a framework of reincarnation and karma. We are souls that exist in the present life to experience many things that will educate us for better practice in future lives. In this worldview, all things that happen to us and all things we do to others, even wrongdoing, are lessons we learn in order to grow through many lifetimes into perfection and bliss. To achieve self-forgiveness, we tell ourselves: "While I remain accountable for what I do in the human world, in purely spiritual terms nothing wrong ever happens."[4]

Tipping deals with sin not by absolving it but by minimizing it. This is deeply unsatisfying because we know intuitively that the evils committed here are indeed *evils*. Christianity does not minimize the wrongness of sin yet still provides a powerful antidote for guilt.

The "sweet antidote" that Macbeth yearned for does exist. It is divine forgiveness. But to experience divine forgiveness requires making a crucial distinction—between true and false guilt. After doing this, it requires turning to God.

True and False Guilt

There are two kinds of guilty people. Some people *should* feel guilty for their deeds because some things are objectively evil and the perpetrators are guilty regardless of their beliefs and feelings about the deed. But we recognize another group of people who have inordinate guilt feelings that seem too great in proportion to the deed.

There are true guilt feelings and false guilt feelings, and a person who "cannot forgive themselves" must start by determining whether their guilt is warranted or not.

At this point Christianity is of enormous help. The only way to discern true from false guilt is if you have a standard by which to do so. In one of Jesus's many critiques of the religious leaders of the day, he says, "You experts in the law, woe to you, because you load people down with burdens they can hardly carry, and you yourselves will not lift one finger to help them" (Luke 11:46; cf. Mark 7:11–13). Jesus is referring to "the heavy weight of religious duties added to the law which burden the people . . . [and make them] devastated because of their failure to . . . please God."[5] Jesus here shows that, while people should feel guilty if they violate the law of God—murdering, stealing, committing adultery—they should not feel guilty for failures to keep all the numerous, legalistic, man-made religious rules added to that.

Jesus's distinction and warning can also apply to those who are part of legalistic religious bodies. They too can be racked with false guilt, because their culture or community or family or their own selves put unrealistic burdens on them. So the first step in helping someone with guilt is to ask if it is truly a violation of the will and Word of God.[6]

Nevertheless, making this distinction is not always simple. There are situations in which true and false guilt are intertwined in complex ways.

Many of us are wracked with guilt because we have said yes to so many people and then we find we don't have time in the day or the week to do it all. On the one hand, you should keep your promises and be true to your word (Matthew 5:37; Proverbs 11:3, 20:25). But it is not God who has given you more than you can do—it is you yourself who have done that. You must not feel guilty for not being able to do all people request for you to do. You are only duty-bound to do what God asks you to do in his Word.

What about the driver whose laughter at a joke on the radio causes a momentary lapse in attention, leading to an accident that seriously injures people? The driver's guilt will be overwhelming. Yet there was no great moral lapse or violation of a law or rule. "It could have happened to anyone," say the driver's friends, rightly, but it doesn't help him. There is certainly some warrant for regret that he was not driving more carefully and slowly, but his guilt, by using God's Word as a standard, is disproportionate. A counselor will have to help him see that if he is emotionally debilitated by this for years, or, worse, he will be only compounding the tragedy. Instead, he should secure God's forgiveness for his lack of circumspection and then rely on the loving support of others who reinforce God's acceptance of him.

Another example under this heading is "survivor's guilt." Many soldiers who lost comrades-in-arms in war survived and came home alive. But instead of feeling relief and peace, they find themselves filled with guilt. Why were they spared? This guilt, I think, comes because they know they were not more brave or skillful or virtuous than their deceased friends and yet somehow they feel they *ought* to have been. Again, the only way to deal with this understandable but persistent guilt is to look to the Word of God. It is God who determines why, in his plan, some people get sick and die in their twenties, or die in battle, and others continue to live on. There should be no guilt in that.

The distinction between true guilt and false guilt feelings is a crucial one to make. Why? Because *time will not heal true guilt.* There are absolute moral norms embedded in the universe, and your soul, made in the image of God, senses them (Romans 1:18–20, 2:14–16). The only way to deal with true guilt is to take it to the grace and mercy of God. On the other hand *moral effort and prayer will not heal false guilt.* The only way to deal with false guilt is to take it to the will of God and understand it in light of his Word.

Taking Your Guilt to God

What, then, do you do with real guilt? There is no better place to look for an answer than Psalm 51, perhaps the most famous prayer of confession in the entire Bible.

> Have mercy on me, O God, according to your unfailing love;
> according to your great compassion blot out my transgressions.
> Wash away all my iniquity and cleanse me from my sin. (Psalm 51:1–2)

The occasion for this prayer of David is described in the heading. He had an extramarital affair with Bathsheba, had her husband killed, and then took her as his wife. God exposed David's sin to the world through the prophet Nathan. Then he began to pray.

What if I told you that, no matter how much you had blown up your life, there was a way to get through it? That way is what the Bible calls repentance, and repentance is a process. What does Psalm 51 teach us about it?

It teaches us that there are three things we must stop doing, two things we must start doing, and finally one thing to receive.

The Counterfeits of Repentance— Blame Shifting

> For I know my transgressions, and my sin is always before me.
> Against you, you only, have I sinned and done what is evil in your
> sight; so you are right in your verdict and justified when you judge.
> Surely I was sinful at birth, sinful from the time my mother con-
> ceived me. (Psalm 51:3–5)

There is a true repentance that is "unto life" (Acts 11:18, KJV), that
brings strength, freedom, and peace, but according to the Bible there is also
false repentance, a sorrow or remorse that may masquerade as repentance
but "brings death" (2 Corinthians 7:10)—brings frustration, continuing
guilt, and despair. There are things that look like life-giving, guilt-removing
repentance but are not.

One counterfeit is *blame shifting*. "I'm sorry, but you know it really
wasn't my fault." But real repentance takes full responsibility for your sin.

One way to shift blame is to justify our sin. The seventeenth-century
writer Thomas Brooks called it "painting sin with virtue's colors."[7] We
look at ourselves and say, "I'm not greedy, I'm just thrifty"; "I'm not proud,
just assertive"; "I don't drink too much, I'm just the life of the party"; "I'm
not abrasive, I just 'tell it like it is.'"

Another way is to shift responsibility. "I wouldn't have had an affair if
you had been a better spouse." "I shouldn't have said that, but she provoked me. Anyone would have done the same." "I've suffered a lot; I think
I deserved this."

A third form of blame shifting is insisting that the accuser is exaggerating. "Okay, that was wrong, but you are being far too sensitive." "Sure, I
probably shouldn't have done that—but remember back when you did this
other thing? That was terrible. Now stop pointing to me."

The Bible's opening scene shows the deadliness of blame shifting—Eve blaming the serpent, Adam blaming Eve and even God ("the woman *you* gave me") for what they did. We can only begin to deal with our guilt when blame shifting ends. David prays, "You are right in your verdict, and justified when you judge" (Psalm 51:4). There isn't the slightest effort to diminish responsibility. There are no excuses. True repentance looks its own responsibility full in the face and says to God, "In all that has happened to us, you have remained righteous . . . while we acted wickedly" (Nehemiah 9:33). There is no note of blaming God for being too harsh. There is no hint of blaming circumstances or anyone else for the sin. Only when there is no longer pretense or evasion can the conscience be cleared.

In light of what he has done, David adds a remarkable insight about his own heart: "Surely I was sinful at birth, sinful from the time my mother conceived me" (Psalm 51:5). Is David merely speaking about the classic doctrine of "original sin"—namely, that all human beings are sinful in their inward nature? Probably, but David's concern here is not to teach theology. He is being much more personal.

David sees a family resemblance between the common sins of his youth and murder. He sees that they were not two radically different things. In the right circumstances, the capacity for cruelty that comes from self-assertion and self-centeredness in every person's heart can, if nourished properly, become murder. It comes from the same seed.

In the popular BBC series *Broadchurch*, the mystery is who in this lovely little seaside town could have murdered a boy. The local detective, Ellie Miller, is dubious that anyone from the town could have done it. This is a tight-knit community of good people. "We don't have these problems," she says. In response, Detective Inspector Alec Hardy argues with her.

Hardy: "Anybody's capable of murder, given the right circumstances."

Miller: "Most people have moral compasses."

Hardy: "Compasses break."[8]

The fictional detective inspector is telling us exactly what the Bible says at this point. You must not be in denial about your capacity for evil. You will do some really bad things in your life that will utterly shock you unless you get hold of this particular truth from the Bible. Blame shifting is therefore one of the most dangerous things you can do.

Here is the language of a repentant heart: "Yes, Lord, I have been mistreated, and I've had troubles, but I did not react to these conditions as I should have. It is my own sin that is the reason I am miserable today. I take full responsibility!" Repentance begins where blame shifting ends.

The Counterfeits of Repentance—Self-Pity

Another counterfeit is *self-pity*. "I really made a mess of my life!" But real repentance involves grief over *sin itself* and the offense and grief it is to *God*.

False repentance is sorrow over the *consequences* of the sin and the trouble it has caused you. David has just wronged Bathsheba by using his kingly power to have an affair with her, a married woman, and has wronged Uriah, her husband, by having him killed. He also betrayed his people's trust in him as king by abusing his power. Yet David says to God, "Against you, you only, have I sinned and done what is evil in your sight" (Psalm 51:4). How can he say that?

David's statement is not primarily a piece of theological teaching—it is literally a cri de coeur. The doubling of a word in Hebrew indicates intensity of emotion—passion, longing, and love. His heart is breaking as he realizes what he has done he has done to the God who anointed him as king, saved him over and over again from the hands of a jealous King Saul, and installed him as the king of Israel.

David certainly is not saying that he did *not* sin against Uriah and Bathsheba, but rather that his sin against God—the God to whom he owes literally everything—was foundational to it all. David recognized that his sin against God was the cause of his sin against all the others. Martin Luther, in his *Large Catechism*, argues that you never harm others (commandments five through ten) without breaking the first commandment—"Have no other gods before me." So if you lie in order to make money, then you have made money more important than God, a greater love, at that moment. If you lie in order to protect your reputation, you have done the same thing.

David grasps this. This concentration on our sin against God is the opposite of self-pity. Wallowing in self-pity may appear to be repentance, but it is not. When our wrongdoing brings down real-world problems on our head, we cry, "I wish I hadn't done that!" But our sorrow isn't over how we wronged God or others but over the trouble it has brought to us. We are not truly troubled by the sin, and if the consequences go away, we slide back toward the wrongful behavior. That proves that the seeming repentance was just self-pity.

Some years ago I was doing pastoral counseling with a married couple. The man continually lapsed into harsh, angry, insulting language to his wife that deeply grieved and hurt her. Over a three-year period he agreed to see me for counseling, but it became clear this happened only when she threatened to leave him. Then he came in and was willing to make changes to his behavior. But those changes faded away as soon as the threat of separation and divorce receded. In other words, he was not primarily sorry for how he was wronging his wife, how he was dishonoring his God. He was not sorry for the *sin* but for himself. And self-pity never leads to change. To be sorry for the sin itself takes love. If he had really been loving his wife—and loving his God—he would have hated the sin itself, and it would then have begun to lose its attractive power over him. Self-pity led to superficial changes that never really affected his heart and therefore made no lasting change to his behavior.

Self-pity looks like repentance, but it is self-absorption, and that is the essence of sin. Only if you see that you haven't just broken God's law but you have broken his heart, that you have dishonored and grieved him, do you begin to change.

Just as real repentance starts where blame shifting ends, it also starts where self-pity ends. The British pastor Richard Sibbes wrote in his classic *The Bruised Reed* (1630) that self-pity ends only when you stop thinking about the consequences. Repentance is "not a little bowing down our heads . . . but a working our hearts . . . [until] sin is more odious unto us than punishment."[9]

A near contemporary, Stephen Charnock, who wrote *A Discourse of Conviction of Sin*, makes a vivid distinction between what he called legalistic repentance—marked by self-pity—and truly "evangelical" or gospel-based repentance. Legalistic repentance arises chiefly from a fear of punishment, while true repentance arises from a consideration of God's goodness and therefore a sense of one's own ingratitude and lack of love. So false repentance "cries out, 'I have exasperated a power that is as the roaring of a lion. . . . I have provoked one that is the sovereign Lord of heaven and earth, whose word can tear up the foundation of the world." But an evangelically convicted person cries, "I have incensed a goodness that is like the dropping of the dew; I have offended a God that had the deportment of a friend. . . . Oh my . . . hard heart . . . to run from so sweet a fountain to rake in puddles!"[10]

Here is the language of a repentant heart: "Yes, Lord, I am in sorrow because of the consequences of my sin. But they have only awakened me to the wrongness of what I have done—how it has wronged others and especially you, my Creator, Provider, and Redeemer." Repentance begins where self-pity ends.

The Counterfeits of Repentance— Self-Flagellation

Finally, there is a kind of false repentance that is excessive. The person is filled with loud and intense self-loathing, cries, and tears. Listeners feel compelled to tell them they aren't that bad, they aren't that guilty. And that is the very point of such self-flagellation—it tries to pressure others and even God not to accuse but to excuse and pardon. The inner logic goes something like this: "If I beat myself up enough, surely this will atone for my sin and no one will ask me for anything else."

The use of self-hating contrition as a way to atone for one's sin rejects God's forgiveness as much as its opposite—a proud denial that you have done anything wrong. They are both forms of self-righteousness. The eighteenth-century Anglican minister John Newton wrote to a young man who was constantly depressed, with a sense of being sinful and unworthy. Newton was not put off. He wrote that it shows great spiritual pride and self-righteousness to shamelessly excuse oneself *or* indulge in morbid self-hatred. He wrote:

> Your [understanding] of the gospel is sound, but there is a legal[istic] something in your experience which perplexes you. . . . You cannot be too [aware] of the inward and inbred evils you complain of, but you may be—indeed you are—improperly affected by them. . . . You express not only a low opinion of yourself, which is right, but too low an opinion of the person, work, and promises of the Redeemer, which is certainly wrong. . . .
>
> Satan . . . sometimes offers to teach us humility, but though I wish to be humble, I desire not to learn in his school. His premises [about our sinfulness] are perhaps true . . . but he then draws abominable conclusions from them, and would teach us, that

therefore we ought to question either the power, or the willingness, or the faithfulness of Christ.

Indeed, though our [self-recriminations] are good so far as
they show dislike of sin, yet when we come to examine them
closely, there is often so much self-will, self-righteousness, unbe-
lief, pride, and impatience mingled with them, that they are little
better than the worst evils we complain of.[11]

The reception of God's forgiveness is simple—repent and ask for mercy!
Yet many or perhaps most people never experience this grace because they
don't repent. True repentance begins where whitewashing ("Nothing really
happened") and blame shifting ("It wasn't really my fault") and self-pity
("I'm sorry because of what it has cost *me*") and self-flagellation ("I will feel
so terrible no one will be able to criticize me") end.

Turning to God

If blame shifting, self-pity, and self-flagellation are the counterfeits, what
is the true repentance that connects us to God? There are two things to
look for. For these we turn to a remarkable but often overlooked verse in
the book of Proverbs.

In Proverbs 28:13 (ESV) we read: "Whoever conceals his transgressions will not prosper, but he who confesses and forsakes them will obtain
mercy."[12] First, we must "confess"—a word that is helpfully contrasted in
the proverb with the word *conceal*. To confess is to *make a full, clean admission of what you have done wrong*, without qualification or excuse, without
minimizing or relativizing. It is to take full responsibility. The Hebrew
word *ydh*, translated here as "confess," always has the sense of praising and
thanking God. So confessing a sin is not merely telling the truth, nor is it
an abstract "I deserve punishment of some kind." Rather, it is admitting

that you have been failing to love and honor God, and at this moment you begin to glorify him by admitting how you have wronged him and others.

One man recounts his experience of this. He had lived for years with a defensiveness and inner discomfort that darkened his life.

> In my search for inner peace I pursued various religions and studied psychology but never received more than partial answers. . . . The pivotal experience came inexplicably and unexpectedly: I was suddenly aware what an enormous avalanche of wrongs I had [done and] left behind me. Before, this reality had been masked by pride and my wanting to look good in front of others. . . . I had no excuses for myself—youth, circumstances, or bad peers. I was responsible for what I had done. On one page after another I poured it all out in clear detail. I felt as though an angel of repentance was slashing at my heart with his sword, such was the pain. I wrote dozens of letters to people and organizations I had cheated, stolen from, and lied to. Finally I felt truly free.[13]

However, Proverbs 28:13 moves on and says it is not enough to confess or admit a sin—you must also forsake it. To forsake is to *make a full renunciation of the sinful behavior, both in your heart attitude and in practical action.* When John the Baptist led people to the brink of repentance, they asked, "What then shall we do?" He answered, "Bear fruits in keeping with repentance" (Luke 3:8, ESV), and by that he meant practical action that reversed their wrong behavior.

> Tax collectors also came to be baptized and said to him, "Teacher, what shall we do?" And he said to them, "Collect no more than you are authorized to do." Soldiers also asked him, "And we, what shall we do?" And he said to them, "Do not extort money from

anyone by threats or by false accusation, and be content with your wages." (Luke 3:12–14, ESV)

So repentance means not only an admission of wrong but also a heart that finds the sin repugnant and therefore plans to change. Concrete steps are offered: "From now on I'll never go to . . ." "From now on I will not do . . ." Bridges are burned; accountability structures are put into place.

Of course, many such plans fail or fail in part. Christian growth is a process. But without sincere renunciation and concrete designs for change, true repentance is not at work. False repentance is sentiment only. True repentance offers a change in behavior.

A man named Leonard offered this account. He was a middle-aged businessman who was highly successful and well off. He wrote:

> I was, from a human point of view, a good person, keeping the laws and being responsible to the community. I was also religious, attending church faithfully, giving my money to good causes, and even trying to "witness for Christ."

However, one Sunday he heard a sermon on being "poor in spirit." It was a biblical call to be a humble person who cared nothing for one's own status but who served others. He was deeply convicted. The sermon "made me fear that I was not so good as I thought." He experienced a "new restlessness" and began to examine the ground motives of his life. To his shock, he came to see that he was driven by envy and a desire to prove himself better than others through acquiring wealth. He saw that the love of money was the driving force in his life but he had hidden that powerful drive from himself and others. "Now I was certain I was far from God. . . . [I] had a great need for his forgiveness and I wanted Christ to take away this terrible spirit of envy in my mind."

He turned to Christ intent on changing his behavior. He determined to be less ruthless in business, more generous to customers, employees, and stakeholders, and more generous with his wealth in general. He was ready to forsake his sin, but he knew he would not be forgiven for only good intentions. "I asked him to forgive me and trusted that His death took away my sins." This was the turning point in his life.[14]

Receiving God's Forgiveness

Finally, there is one thing to receive. After repenting must come rejoicing—rejoicing in the free mercy of God. Repentance without rejoicing leads to despair.

Proverbs 28:13 tells us that repentance entails a third action, namely, *the willing reception and acceptance of God's free mercy.* The Hebrew word for obtaining "mercy" (Hebrew *rhm*) is the word for womb. Old Testament scholars tell us the word came to have its meaning from the feelings of parents toward their newborn infants. "The verb is always used in connection with the emotion of mercy from . . . parents to children."[15] The love of a mother for the child of her womb is not something "merited" by the child—it comes simply because the heart of the mother powerfully moves her. In other words, the mercy God offers to the repentant person is completely free, undeserved, unstinting, and deeply personal, and this is an important part of repentance that is often missed. Real repentance involves an acceptance of God's free mercy.

False repentance, however, demands that forgiveness be earned. And this is why it is common to find people who do the first and second actions of repentance—confessing and forsaking—but insist that they don't "feel forgiven" or even that they "can't forgive themselves." Many despair over their sin because they never believed their standing with God was by sheer mercy to begin with. Though they gave lip service to the idea of

God's grace, they based their justification on their sanctification—their performance. That is, they believe God loved and accepted them on the basis of their moral performance and their relative freedom from sin and wrongdoing. When a person falls into sin who is still functionally operating on the belief that they are saved by their moral life, their very foundations are shaken.

Such a person wants to "work off" her sin, to atone for the sin, to earn forgiveness. She cannot take it to God and leave it there. She carries the guilt around as a way of paying for the sin herself, hoping that God and others will eventually declare that she has suffered enough and can be forgiven. But instead she should let the greater recognition of her sinfulness lead her to see the magnitude of God's mercy and to greater amazement at his grace.

In summary, repentance begins when blame shifting, self-pity, and self-righteous despair end. It begins when confession, renunciation, and the acceptance of free grace take place. Then the clouds of guilt and shame can lift—and we can sing:

> Sometimes a light surprises the Christian as he sings;
> It is the Lord who rises, with healing in his wings.[16]

Keeping God's Mercy "New"

The default mode of the human heart is to maintain control of one's life by earning one's own salvation. The idea of free grace, unmerited, is both insulting and unnatural to the self-absorbed human heart. Jean Valjean is famously overthrown by the bishop's forgiveness in *Les Misérables*. He realizes that it robs him of the self-pity and self-righteousness that made him rationalize an angry and selfish life.

So even if we initially accept the fact of God's forgiveness and acceptance, we need to spend the rest of our lives deepening our understanding of it and refreshing our experience of it.

One way to do this is to look up, study, and meditate regularly on the biblical texts that directly teach about God's forgiveness. (See appendix B.)

A second way to grow in your experience of God's forgiveness is to continually go deeper in the study of the various doctrines that are the basis for it. They include the doctrine of substitution (that Jesus paid the penalty for your sin fully and in your place) and the doctrine of justification (that when we put our faith in Christ, we have his righteousness, his perfect record, legally "imputed" to us).

Perhaps the single most comprehensive biblical theme that encompasses all these blessings is the idea that when we believe in him we are united with him, both legally and vitally, in his life and death (Romans 6:1–4) and his ascension (Ephesians 2:6). What can it mean that we died with him or that we are seated in the heavenly places *now* with him? As the hymn says, "I scarce can take it in."[17]

We are so united in Christ in the Father's eyes that when he sees us, he sees Jesus. Christians are so one with Christ that we are as forgiven as if *we* had already died for our sins, as if we had already been raised. We are so one with Christ that when the Father sees us, he treats us as if we deserve all the glory and honor that Jesus deserves. Over 160 times in the New Testament, Paul speaks of our being "in Christ" or "in him." He calls himself "a man in Christ" (2 Corinthians 12:2). It utterly dominated Paul's self-understanding and it must dominate ours.

One of the many wonderful dimensions of this great truth is found in 1 John 2:1, where the apostle writes that if we sin, we should remember that "we have an advocate with the Father—Jesus Christ, the Righteous One."

Some years ago I read the outline of a chapel sermon delivered by

Charles Hodge to the students of Princeton Theological Seminary in 1861. In the sermon Hodge explores the idea of an "advocate" before a court of justice for a person accused of a crime. Imagine the charges are against you, but you have a defense attorney. What is that relationship like? Hodge writes that the relationship of an advocate to a client should be one of great intimacy and power. If your defense attorney is brilliant in court, your case is brilliant. If she is eloquent in court, your case is eloquent. Whatever your attorney does is imputed to you. "The former [the advocate] *personates* the latter [the client], puts himself in the client's place. It is while it lasts, the most intimate relation. The client . . . is not heard . . . not regarded. He is lost in his advocate. This is the relation in which Christ as our advocate stands to us. He appears before God for us. We are lost in him. He, not we, is seen, heard and regarded . . . Christ thus assumes our position."[18]

Is Jesus radiant? Beautiful? Spotless? Is he "the fairest among ten thousand"? Then that's how you appear to the universe's bar of justice. You are lost in your advocate.

When I first read this sermon, it struck me in a powerful way. I began to realize that my overwork was a way of seeking to be my own advocate. It was as if I had the most brilliant defense attorney in the world and I kept getting up and saying, "Let *me* speak. Let *me* question the witness. Let *me* make the case to the jury." But only Jesus Christ has an infallible case. He can say of me, "Father, I have fulfilled every demand of yours on his behalf, in his place. Now accept my friend, my brother, my son, because of what I've done."

When our hearts condemn us, Jesus is infinitely greater than our hearts, and we can feel that greatness the more we know the teaching of the Word about God's free grace and forgiveness.

In Luke 7 Jesus was eating in the courtyard of the home of Simon the Pharisee when "a woman of the city" approached him. The term was a euphemism for a sex worker. She knelt at Jesus's feet weeping and anointing them in an act of devotion. Simon recognized her as a "sinner" and was amazed that Jesus accepted her public expressions of love rather than recoiling from her. Jesus responded with a parable of two debtors—one who owed ten times more than the other—who were both forgiven their debts by their lender. "Which of them will love him more?" Jesus asked Simon (Luke 7:40–42). He got the obvious answer—the one who was forgiven more.

Jesus proceeded to point out that Simon himself, who clearly did not see himself as a sinner in need of forgiveness, had given Jesus a fairly stiff and formal greeting, but the woman's great love and warmth proceeded from the joy of the great forgiveness she experienced. The lesson is not in any way that it's better to live a life of big, scandalous, notorious sins. As the entire New Testament teaches, Simon was as much in need of forgiveness, if not more, for his pride as the woman was for her immorality. If we turn to Christ for forgiveness, we will know love and joy through the power of the Holy Spirit.

The prophet Micah says God will "tread our sins underfoot" and "hurl all our iniquities into the depths of the sea" (Micah 7:19). The famous Dutch writer Corrie ten Boom would often say that when God throws our sins into the deepest sea, he puts up a sign: "No fishing!" God has dealt with your sins. Don't go back to them to feel guilty about them all over. Go forward in love.[19]

The Blood of Christ

Let's return to Psalm 51. David knows he has sinned and "done what is evil in your sight" (verse 4). He knows he is guilty of "bloodguiltiness" (verse 14, ESV). And yet he has confidence that God will forgive him because of his *chesedh*—"steadfast love"—his unconditional covenantal love. David senses his complete *unworthiness*, and yet he has *confidence* that he is still accepted. If you feel only unworthy and not confident, then repentance will not work. You will beat yourself up, hoping God will have mercy. If you have confidence but not a sense of deep unworthiness, you will feel self-pity and will not change. David is absolutely humble and sees he is unworthy, and yet is completely confident.[20]

We have no excuses, then, because on this side of the cross and the resurrection we see clearly what David could only know "through a glass, darkly" (1 Corinthians 13:12, KJV). David prayed, "Cast me not away from thy presence" (Psalm 51:11, KJV), and God did not. But that was because on the cross Jesus *was* cast away from the divine presence—he got what David deserved. Jesus cried, "My God, my God, why have you forsaken me?" (Matthew 27:46) so David didn't have to.

This is the secret to really changing. It is not enough to say, "God is a loving God and I have broken his heart." That is too abstract. Jesus was on the cross, looking at all of us, and saw us denying and betraying him, and yet, in the greatest act of love in the history of the world, Jesus Christ stayed. He saw what we are like and he stayed on the cross. When you see Jesus dying for you like that, and you know the reason he died is because of the sins you do every day, you will want nothing to do with your sins.

> All have sinned and fall short of the glory of God, and all are justified freely by his grace through the redemption that came by Christ Jesus. God presented Christ as a sacrifice of atonement, through the shedding of his blood—to be received by faith. (Romans 3:23–25)

In 1955 Billy Graham was invited to speak at Cambridge University to the students in Great St Mary's Hall for a week of evening meetings. When it came out to the public that he was going to be doing that, letters appeared in *The Times* of London very upset that this fundamentalist Baptist American preacher was going to come and speak to Britain's best and brightest about a primitive kind of religion based on blood and atonement and hell.

Graham admits that this got to him. He smarted under the characterization of being an uneducated provincial. So the first three nights he was there, he quoted intellectuals and scholars and sought to speak in more of an academic mode—but he could sense that his message was falling flat. And so he got down on his knees, prayed, and determined to throw out his prepared notes and simply preach about the blood of Christ and the cross.[21]

Dick Lucas, who for many years was rector of St Helen's Bishopsgate Anglican church in London, recalled in a taped sermon what he saw that last night.

> I'll never forget that night. I was in a totally packed chancel, sitting on the floor at Great St Mary's [Church] with the Regius Professor of Divinity sitting on one side of me and the chaplain of the college (who was a future bishop) on the other side of me. Both of these were good men, but completely against the idea that we needed salvation from sin by the blood of Christ. Dear Billy Graham got up that night and began at Genesis and went right through the whole Bible and talked about *every single sacrifice* in it.
>
> The blood was flowing all over the great hall, everywhere, for three quarters of an hour. Both my neighbors were horribly embarrassed by this crude proclamation of the blood of Christ and also must have been sure that no bright, sophisticated, young British person was going to believe any of this stuff. But at the end of the sermon, to everyone's shock, four hundred young men and women stayed to commit their lives to Christ. [There were only eight thousand students in the student body then.]
>
> I remembered meeting a young pastor some years later, a Cambridge graduate, at Birmingham Cathedral. Over a cup of tea I said, "Where did Christian things begin for you?"

"Oh, at Cambridge in fifty-five," he said.

"When?"

"Billy Graham."

"What night?"

"It was Wednesday night."

"How did that happen?"

"Well," he said, "all I remember is that I walked out of Great St Mary's for the first time in my life thinking 'Christ really died for me.'" [22]

The forgiveness of God finally became real to him, and he was never the same again.

What was unbelievable to the dons was that a man like that, preaching a sermon like that—so simple, about the blood of Christ forgiving sin—could have totally changed the life of a young person like that. But so it did. And it can for you.

CHAPTER 10

GRANTING OUR FORGIVENESS

> No happy reconciliation was to be had with him—no cheering
> smile or generous word. . . . When I asked him if he forgave me,
> he answered that he was not in the habit of cherishing the re-
> membrance of vexation; that he had nothing to forgive; not hav-
> ing been offended.
>
> And with that answer, he left me. I would much rather he had
> knocked me down.
>
> —CHARLOTTE BRONTË, *JANE EYRE*[1]

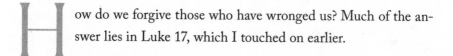ow do we forgive those who have wronged us? Much of the an-
swer lies in Luke 17, which I touched on earlier.

So watch yourselves. "If your brother or sister sins against you,
rebuke them; and if they repent, forgive them. Even if they sin
against you seven times in a day and seven times come back to you
saying 'I repent,' you must forgive them." (verses 3–5)

In these verses Jesus explains that to be his disciple is to live a life of perpetual forgiveness. It's an astonishing call, and the disciples immediately
cry, "We don't have the faith for this!" But a closer look at this biblical

text, and others, will show us that Christians do indeed have the resources for such a life.

Why Do We Need to Live a Life of Forgiveness?

Let's not overlook Jesus's very first sentence. He says, "So watch *yourselves*," and then he goes on to talk about forgiveness when someone wrongs you. That's counterintuitive. When someone wrongs us, we pay great attention to the wrongdoer. Jesus says, however, "When someone does something wrong to you, that's when you need to be looking especially closely at yourself."

The premise behind this warning is that it is extremely easy to develop an unforgiving spirit and to not see it in yourself. Hebrews 12:15 (ESV) says, "See to it that . . . no 'root of bitterness' springs up and causes trouble, and by it many become defiled." The image is telling. You go to a corner of a field that belongs to you, and you say, "I don't want this tree here anymore," you cut down the tree and you pull out the stump and you say, "That's that." But that's *not* that, because some time later you come back to that corner of the field and, to your surprise, you find there's a young tree that has sprung up again. Why? Because there were roots left under the surface, hidden from your sight, that grew.

The Bible means it is hard to admit how angry you are at the people who have wronged you. Our first response is always to say, "Oh, I'm fine. No, I'm not angry—maybe a little upset." To maintain our image of ourselves as good people, we deny how embittered we are. "I've forgiven," you say (meaning you aren't actively seeking revenge), "but I can't forget" (meaning that you are rooting for the person's downfall and that you are still filled with resentment).

When Jesus says to those wronged, "Watch yourselves," and the Hebrew writer says, "See to it" (a term that means to pay close attention to something), it means we should assume that we are more resentful and less forgiving and more controlled by what people have done to us than we think we are. Hidden roots work in hidden ways; unless you dig around to find them, you may never see them until they have sprouted and you have done or said something cruel that shocks you.

Unless you forgive deliberately, thoroughly, and with all the help Christ offers, your anger will "defile" you, as Hebrews says. Our English word *wrath* comes from the same Anglo-Saxon root as our word *wreath*. *Wrath* means to be twisted out of your normal shape by your anger.

And the same Anglo-Saxon word also gives us the now somewhat archaic word *wraith*. We don't use it much anymore (unless you read *The Lord of the Rings*), but it's an old word for a ghost, a spirit that can't rest. Ghosts, according to legend, stay in the place where something was done to them, and they can't get over it or stop reliving it. If you don't deal with your wrath through forgiveness, wrath can make you a wraith, turning you slowly but surely into a restless spirit, into someone who's controlled by the past, someone who's haunted.

For example, if somebody has done something wrong to you and you haven't been able to forgive, at the very least you get a low-level spiritual fever called self-pity. That gives you a sense of entitlement—you feel that for what you have gone through, you deserve a break, some good treatment. If that good treatment is not forthcoming, you may slide into joyless cynicism about people and life. Or say you can't forgive the person who broke up with you. That may affect your whole attitude toward romantic relationships.

If you cannot forgive your parents for the things they've done, it will distort your relationship with authority figures. If you have your own children, you may overcompensate and do either *more* than or *the opposite* of what your parents did to you. You might end up parenting your children not according to their needs but according to your own.

Watch yourselves. We live in a world where canceling, ghosting, and insults are the norm. You will experience snubs on a regular basis, and in some cases will experience real injustice. How are you going to keep it all from turning you into a wraith controlled by the past? You must forgive and forgive well.

The Parts of Internal Forgiveness

Heart forgiveness includes *identifying with the wrongdoer, inwardly paying the debt,* and then *willing good for the wrongdoer.* This is hard but necessary to keep you from becoming someone whom—if you could see into the future—you would never want to be.

First, forgiveness means *identifying with the wrongdoer.* In Luke 17 Jesus says, "If your brother or sister sins against you . . . and if they repent, forgive them."

Some believe this text teaches that you don't have to forgive those who have wronged you unless they repent. But Mark 11:25 says if you are praying and realize you hold *anything* against *anyone*, you must forgive them at that moment. (See chapter 7 above.) There is no need to pit these verses against each other. Real forgiveness always hopes for a full restoration of the offender and the relationship. But if, as is so often the case in our fallen world, that reconciliation does not happen, Mark 11:25 tells us we still need (and are required) to forgive in our hearts.

See Jesus's implication—the brother or sister who sins against you is still a brother or sister like you whom you are to love (1 John 3:14). The neighbor is still a neighbor you must love as much as you love yourself (Luke 10:25–37). The crucial truth is *you are the same.* But when you are wronged, it is extraordinarily easy to lose sight of this.

If a cartoonist wants to make someone look ludicrous, she can create a caricature. She can take something about a person's face that's unusual or a bit unattractive and exaggerate it, making it prominent so that the person looks foolish. That's exactly what your heart does when someone wrongs you. You think of them one-dimensionally, in terms of that one thing they've done to you.

If somebody has lied to you, you tell yourself, "She lied because she is just a liar!" But if you ever are caught in a lie, and someone asks why *you* lied, you say, "Well, yes, but it's complicated. I didn't mean . . ." Yes, you did lie, but you are basically a good person. So while you continue to think of yourself as a three-dimensional, complex human being, you start to think of the person who lied to you as a one-dimensional villain.

The person you are angry at for lying has been reduced in your mind to the lie. It's a self-justification engine that takes hold of the wrong and says, "*I* would never do something like that." This impulse to compare yourself and feel superior to the person is an instinctive way the heart tries to push back against the perpetrator. To look down on the wrongdoer feels like a small victory against them—but it leads to self-righteousness, and self-righteousness in the heart is always deadly. Lewis Smedes writes:

> Resentment is bittersweet. If we did not cherish it, we would let it go. What sort of rewards do we get from our resentment? Why do we keep score? First, it makes us feel superior to the person we resent. . . . [Also, we] enjoy the feeling of hurt that the memory kindles. . . . We feel noble and worthy as the decent person who was wrongly hurt. Resentments serve a double purpose: they give us treasured pain, and they give us a chance to justify ourselves. . . . [Yet] it depresses us, robs us of gratitude, sneaks into other relationships.[2]

Resentment always makes us feel morally superior to the wrongdoer, which in turn makes it harder to shed the resentment. If you don't see that you too are a sinner needing grace, your resentment will twist and defile you. Miroslav Volf has a classic statement about this:

> Forgiveness flounders because I exclude the enemy from the community of humans even as I exclude myself from the community of sinners. But no one can be in the presence of the God of the crucified Messiah for long without overcoming this double exclusion. . . . When one knows that the torturer will not eternally triumph over the victim, one is free to rediscover that person's humanity and imitate God's love for him. And when one knows that God's love is greater than all sin, one is free to see oneself . . . and so rediscover one's own sinfulness.[3]

If you are going to forgive, you must identify with the wrongdoers—as Volf says, you must realize you are co-sinner and they are co-humans. That's the first thing.

Absorbing the Debt

The second element of forgiveness is to *inwardly pay the debt of the wrongdoer yourself rather than make him pay it*. The very word *forgive* used here—*aphiemi*—means to cancel or to "remit" a debt.[4] To remit something is to refuse to make the person who owes you pay—and therefore to pay or assume the cost yourself. Here we come to the heart of the Christian meaning of forgiveness.

When you are wronged, the perpetrator owes you a debt. It may be literal. What if a guest at a party in your home carelessly breaks an expensive lamp. He apologizes profusely but you say, "Don't bother about it"—in other words, you forgive him. However, now you must either pay to replace the lamp or go without light in that part of the room. In any case your forgiveness means now you bear the cost of what the man has done, rather than him bearing it. There is always a cost to wrongdoing and it must fall on someone. Either the wrongdoer bears it or someone else must. This is true even if the wrong is not something that can be measured financially. The cost may be in reputation or relationship or health or something else. To forgive is to deny oneself revenge (Romans 12:17–21), to absorb the cost, to *not* exact repayment by inflicting on them the things they did to you in order to "even the score." Therefore forgiveness is always expensive to the forgiver, but the benefits—at the very least within your heart, and at best in the restoration of relationship and a witness to the power of the gospel—outweigh the cost.

Forgiveness is inwardly giving up the desire to get even. To forgive is to give the perpetrator a gift they do not in any way deserve. In love you are absorbing the debt that they owe you. Here you are truly walking in Christ's footsteps. Forgiveness is always a form of voluntary suffering that brings about a greater good.

As we will see in the next chapter, it is possible to seek justice without seeking revenge. Nevertheless, when you see a perpetrator receive justice, it can be very satisfying to you, the victim. However, Jesus's words in Mark 11:25 mean we are to forgive the wrongdoer before *we know how he or she will respond, or whether you will ever see justice done in this life.* Jesus is clear: "When you stand praying, . . . forgive." The reasoning here is both theological and practical. As we saw in the Matthew 18 parable, we owe it to God to forgive others as graciously as he has forgiven us. But practically, unless you do at least some of the work toward forgiving the perpetrator, when you go to him or her, you will not be seeking justice but revenge, and the wrongdoer will sense it and will merely go into combat mode. So forgiveness is not the opposite of seeking true justice. It is, among many other things, its precondition.

In a small classic essay on forgiveness, Dan Hamilton describes how he and his fiancée forgave each other over time after a painful breakup.[5] He insightfully describes how, while forgiveness can be granted to someone in a moment, it is still an inward process for the forgiver that can take time. "Forgiveness can be like buying an expensive gift for someone on credit. The gift is received in one moment [when you say to the person, 'I forgive you'] and enjoyed from there on, but the giver will continue to pay unseen until the full debt is satisfied."[6] He provides himself as a case study:

> Once upon a time, I was engaged to a young woman who changed her mind. I forgave her . . . but [only] in small sums over a year. . . . [They were made] whenever I spoke to her and refrained from rehashing the past. Done whenever I saw her with another man. Done when I had to renounce jealousy and self-pity, when I prayed for her as she moved into other relationships. Done when I praised her and spoke of her value, though I wanted to slice away at her reputation. Those were the payments—but she never saw them. And her own payments were unseen by me. . . . But I do know that she forgave me. . . . [Forgiveness] is more than a matter of refusing to hate someone. It is also a matter of choosing to demonstrate love and acceptance to the offender. . . .
>
> [Forgiveness] is to deal with our emotions . . . by denying ourselves the dark pleasures of venting them or fondling them in our minds. . . . Pain is the consequence of sin; there is no easy way to deal with it. Wood, nails and pain are the currency of forgiveness, the love that heals.[7]

Common Misunderstandings of Forgiveness

Jesus's teaching means that many common understandings of forgiveness today are wrong.

It is typical for requests for forgiveness to be met with shrugs and "Think nothing of it" or "No problem" or "Just forget it and move on." When in the novel Jane Eyre turns down the proposal of marriage from St. John, she asks his forgiveness, and he gives a cold answer: "When I asked him if he forgave me, he answered that he was not in the habit of cherishing the remembrance of vexation; that he had nothing to forgive; not having been offended. And with that answer, he left me. I would much rather he had knocked me down."⁸ Jane Eyre means, by this last sentence, that she would have felt better if he had actually punished her or actually forgiven her. But he did neither. He would not acknowledge any wrong. He minimized and excused rather than forgiving. So let's learn what forgiveness is *not*:

Excusing. An excuse eliminates the need for forgiveness. And sometimes if perpetrators are confronted and give a good explanation of the reasons for their actions, we may accept it and excuse them. But that is not forgiveness—it is determining there was no real debt to begin with.

Denying or whitewashing. Forgiveness is not pretending a sin is not a sin. It is not denial or pretense that it did not happen. In fact, forgiveness starts by taking the full measure of the debt and the cost. The price cannot be paid unless it is reckoned.

Only refraining from active revenge. Many say, "I forgive but I cannot forget." That often means: "I won't actively seek to harm you now, but I will treat you with coldness and root for you to fail, because you still owe me." In short, you refuse to make the inward payments and instead you wait for bad things to happen to the person until you feel they have paid.

Suspending judgment. It is possible to say, "I'll forgive you this time, but next time I won't be so nice." That means: "I am counting this against you, but it is not enough for full revenge yet. But I am keeping it in your account! You are on probation."

Weaponizing condescending mercy. There is a way to say "I forgive you" that is really saying, "Look how much better I am than you—I am overlooking this!" It is also a way of implying, "Since I have forgiven you, I expect a whole lot out of you." You are actually saying, "You owe me a lot of bowing and scraping, since I did not go after revenge." That *is* a form of revenge.

Abandoning justice. Justice is calling the wrongdoer to admit the sin to God and to the wronged and to bear whatever penalty either God's law or human law requires.[9] Justice is pursued for God's sake, for other potential victims' sake, and even for the perpetrator's sake. (It is never loving to allow someone to go on sinning in a grievous way—Galatians 6:1.) People tend to either seek personal revenge in the belief that that *is* justice or not seek any justice at all. One is vindictiveness and the other cowardice.

Immediate trust. Sometimes people think that forgiveness means we have to immediately resume the relationship with the wrongdoer at the level it was before. But until a person shows evidence of true change, we should not trust the person. To immediately re-trust a person with sinful habits could actually be enabling him or her to sin. Infamously, many churches have fully restored molesters to places of trust and authority because, they say, this is what forgiveness entails. But Jesus did not automatically restore Peter without a well-known and thorough process (John 21). Trust must be restored, but the speed at which this occurs depends on the response of the offender to correction.

Willing Their Good

The third part of forgiveness is *willing the good of the wrongdoer.* On the cross Jesus said, "Father, forgive them, for they do not know what they are doing" (Luke 23:34). By turning to the Father and praying for them,

Jesus showed us an important aspect of forgiveness. He acknowledged that they were sinning (otherwise they would not need forgiveness), but he also sympathetically observes their inability to fully understand what they are doing. As Stephen does later (Acts 7:60), he asks for mercy for his killers.

"Willing the offender's good" is a kind of test. If you have both identified with the wrongdoer *and* begun the process of inwardly paying down the debt, you will be freed to will their good.

A secret to overcoming evil is to see it as something distinct from the evildoer. Our true enemy is the evil in the person, and we want it defeated in him or her and in us. When we do that, the spread of evil is checked toward us. Its hatred and pride do not infect us. The perpetrator does not draw us into a cycle of anger and payback. But in addition, the spread of evil may be checked in the evildoer. He or she may be softened and helped by our love. We can't know that for certain, but if it is to happen, that is the only way. So we determine to wish them good and will their growth and healing. We determine to pray for them.

Vengeance is all about you—not about the honor of God or the good of the victims or the offender. But on the other hand, complete withdrawal is about you as well. Many people, when they're wronged, say, "I don't want to deal with that person. I just don't want to talk to them. I don't want to have anything to do with them." But when someone wrongs you, if you resent them on the inside but stay courteously mute on the outside, you are the opposite of a disciple of Christ. He calls you to utterly forgive them on the inside (Mark 11:25) so you can speak the truth to them in love on the outside (Matthew 18:15–20; Ephesians 4:15).

How can this be done? The best way to start is to pray for the wrongdoer. Jesus tells us to both love and pray for our enemies (Matthew 5:44) as he himself did on the cross. It also means to refrain internally from recounting what they did to you (see below). It also means going beyond mere courtesy to being genuinely affirming of the person's assets and strengths.

In *Team of Rivals: The Political Genius of Abraham Lincoln*, we learn that Lincoln appointed Salmon Chase as chief justice of the Supreme Court. Chase was extremely qualified and competent, but as secretary of the Treasury he had undermined Lincoln. When someone pointed this out to the president, he responded: "I should despise myself if I allowed personal differences to affect my judgment of his fitness for the office." Later his personal secretary would reminisce that he had never met a man who had "the degree of magnanimity to forgive and exalt a rival."[10] We are called to the same magnanimity by the one who said,

> But I tell you, love your enemies and pray for those who persecute you, that you may be children of your Father in heaven. He causes his sun to rise on the evil and the good, and sends rain on the righteous and the unrighteous. If you love those who love you, what reward will you get? Are not even the tax collectors doing that? And if you greet only your own people, what are you doing more than others? Do not even pagans do that? Be perfect, therefore, as your heavenly Father is perfect. (Matthew 5:44–48)

The Practices of Forgiveness

When the disciples were told they had to forgive wrongdoers "seventy times seven" (i.e., indefinitely, always), they cried, "Increase our faith!" (Luke 17:5). And many readers will be feeling the same way, thinking, "I could never do this." But you can. Christianity gives you both *practices* and *resources* for forgiveness.

Forgiveness in Christianity is a set of practices—including practices of prayer (Mark 11:25; Matthew 6:12,14–15) and of community (Matthew

5:21–24, 18:15–17). It is not primarily and originally an emotion. Forgiveness is granted (often a good while) before it is felt—not felt before it is granted. It is a promise to *not* exact the price of sin from the person who hurt you. Forgiveness is a promise we make to keep despite our feelings. It is likely you have always thought, "Well, I have to feel it before I grant it. I have to start feeling less angry before I start to not hold them liable." If you wait to feel it before you grant it, you'll never grant it; you'll be in an anger prison.

When Jesus says in Mark 11:25, that if you are standing and praying and "you hold anything against anyone" you must "forgive," he is obviously talking about an act of the will. Forgiveness is a practice before it is a feeling. It is something you can begin to do daily, and if you do, eventually your heart will soften instead of harden and you'll escape the prison.

What, then, are these daily disciplines?

First, take an inventory of all the ways you can exact payment from the offender. Each time you refrain from doing so, you are absorbing the cost and paying down the debt. In the list below are the ways in which we tend to exact payments:

✦ In our dealings with the offender:

- We can make cutting remarks and drag out the past.

- We can be far more demanding and controlling with the person than we are with others, because "they owe us."

- We can punish with self-righteous "mercy," which makes them feel small.

- We can avoid them or be cold to them in overt or subtle ways.

- We can actively scheme to harm them, taking from them something they value.

✦ In our dealings with others:

- We can run them down to others under the guise of "warning" people about them.

- We can run them down to others under the guise of seeking sympathy and sharing our hurt.

✦ In our dealings with ourselves:

- We can replay the "recordings"—vividly recalling the details in our memory—of what they did to us, to feed our anger and hostility.

- We can cheer for their failure or pain.

Forgiveness is a promise not to keep bringing the matter up to the person, to others, or even to ourselves. At each point when we are tempted to exact payment, we should refuse and do something positive. Take steps such as these.

✦ When speaking with the person: In your dealings with the person, you should be as courteous and warm as possible. If the person is repentant, you should restore the relationship as much as possible. Why say "as much as possible"? If the person has done grievous wrong, it may mean the trust can be restored only by degrees. If the person is continuing in a hostile manner, you must not make it easy for them to sin against you. And there are other circumstances. If the person is a former love interest, then to re-create the same relationship may be inappropriate. The speed and degree of this restoration entails the re-creation of trust, and that takes time, depending on the nature and severity of the offenses involved. Part of real repentance usually means the wrongdoer asking, "What could I do that would make you trust me?" Part of real forgiveness means being open to the possibility of change in the offender and being truly unbiased and willing to offer more trust little by little.

✦ When speaking with others: When you speak to others about the wrongdoer, you must not airbrush their flaws. If the perpetrator has done something egregiously wrong and illegal (such as sexual abuse), then seek justice through the best channels—but even in this situation, express your desire for the person's repentance and forgiveness. If the sin against you was private, and the person stays in a hostile and unrepentant mode, it may be necessary to warn someone about him or her, but you should watch your motives. Are you truly warning others or setting up a situation in which the person may get confronted in a redemptive way, or are you eagerly trying to destroy his or her reputation?

✦ When speaking with ourselves: What does it mean to "not bring it up to yourself"? It means not to dwell on it in the heart, and not to replay the videos of the wrong in your imagination, in order to keep the sense of loss and hurt fresh and real to you. It means you should pray for the person and yourself, remind yourself of the cross (see below) and turn your mind to other things.

The Resources

Forgiveness requires two inner resources that the experience of divine forgiveness provides for us. They can be called "inner poverty" or humility about our sin and "inner wealth" or assurance of God's love.

Spiritual humility. The Bible is explicit in telling us to forgive "as God in Christ forgave you" (Ephesians 4:32, ESV). There is no better way to get the humility necessary for forgiveness than to accept what the gospel says about us. It tells us that we were made by God and owe him everything—we owe it to him to put him first in our lives. None of us love him with all our heart, soul, strength, and mind (Mark 12:30; Luke 10:27). We have seen how Jesus helps us get spiritual humility in the Matthew 18 parable. He asks us to compare the debt we owe God with the debt anyone owes us. We are to say, "Lord, you did not exact payment for my debts from me, but Jesus paid for them with his life. Now, what right do I have to exact payments for their debts to me?"

Paul in Romans 12 shows us another way to think of forgiveness. He says, "Leave room for the wrath of God; for it is written, 'Vengeance is mine . . . says the Lord'" (verse 19, NRS). He reminds us that those pursuing vengeance put themselves in God's judgment seat. Humility reminds us that only God is qualified to be judge (we are imperfect and deserve judgment ourselves), that only God knows enough to be judge (we don't know all about the offender, what he or she has faced and deserves), and that Jesus took the judgment of God for us.

Spiritual wealth. People who are rich in their experience of God's love in Christ can be generous to others. They have the ultimate good reputation—their names are written in heaven (Luke 10:20) and over the heart of our great high priest, Christ, as he stands before the heavenly throne (Exodus 28:12,29; Hebrews 4:14–10:18). They have the applause and praise of God (Romans 2:29). They also have the ultimate riches (2 Corinthians 8:9)—they are heirs of God and joint heirs with Christ (Romans 8:17). So what if someone here on earth hurts your reputation? So what if you are swindled out of some money? For God's sake and the perpetrator's sake, you should confront and seek justice. But you should be emotionally and spiritually wealthy enough to bear these losses.

If you are a poor person who is not sure where your next meal will come from, and someone steals a five-dollar bill from your pocket—that is deeply traumatic, maybe the last straw. But if you are worth fifty billion dollars and you lose a five-dollar bill, it is no big deal. Spiritually and emotionally, Christians are like the wealthy, not the poor, if we only grasp what the gospel tells us about who we are and will be in Christ. You can look at an offender and say, "You cannot ruin me. You can't ultimately rob me of my real wealth and goods."

The Possibilities

These practices and resources have great power. Ordinarily they work slowly, like an acorn grows eventually into a mighty oak. But God can work swiftly as well.

Corrie ten Boom was a Dutch Christian whose family hid Jews and helped them escape during the Nazi occupation of the Netherlands in World War II. (The story is told in the 1972 book *The Hiding Place*.)[11] She and her sister Betsie were caught and sent to Ravensbrück concentration camp, where Betsie died but Corrie survived. In 1947 Corrie went to Germany on a speaking tour where she was telling people about the gospel. At one of these meetings, she said to the audience that through Jesus Christ, God has thrown our sins into the bottom of the sea.

At the end of the meeting, while people were leaving, she saw a man walking toward her whom she recognized.

> This man had been a guard at Ravensbrück concentration camp where we were sent. . . . It came back with a rush: the huge room with its harsh overhead lights, the pathetic pile of dresses and shoes in the center of the floor, the shame of walking naked past this man. I could see my sister's frail form ahead of me, ribs sharp beneath the parchment skin. Betsie, how thin you were! . . . I remembered the leather crop swinging from his belt. Now he was in front of me, hand thrust out: "A fine message, *fräulein*! How good it is to know that, as you say, all our sins are at the bottom of the sea!"[12]

Though he did not recognize Corrie as having been one of his prisoners, he was asking a Dutch woman for confirmation that the sins of a concentration camp guard could be forgiven. It was the first time she had met any of her former captors, and so, she said, the woman who had just given a speech about God's forgiveness kept her hand in her pocket.

He then told her that he had been a guard at Ravensbrück and that he had turned to Christ and had sought forgiveness "for all the cruel things I did there." That did not help Corrie. "I stood there—I whose sins had every day to be forgiven—and could not. Betsie had died in that place—could he erase her slow terrible death simply for the asking?" She stood there—his hand thrust out, her hand unmoving.

But Corrie remembered what she knew about Christian forgiveness. She knew she had to do it. She had seen many people post–World War II who could not and who had through their "bitterness remained invalids." She also knew that "forgiveness is not an emotion. . . . [It] is an act of the will." Silently she prayed, "Jesus help me. . . . I can lift my hand, I can do that much."

> And so woodenly, mechanically, I thrust my hand into the one stretched out to me. And as I did, an incredible thing took place. The current started in my shoulder, raced down my arm, sprang into our joined hands. And then this healing warmth seemed to flood my whole being, bringing tears to my eyes.
>
> "I forgive you, brother!" I cried. "With all my heart!" . . . I had never known God's love so intensely as I did then.

There are some real dangers in this story. Dan Hamilton's metaphor of making slow, steady payments over time is a far more normal experience than this dramatic story by Corrie ten Boom. Yet notice that Corrie cites all the fundamentals of Christian forgiveness—it is not optional, it is an act of the will, and it requires divine help. The actual experience was a gift of God to her—perhaps there would have been no other way forward for her. God will give us whatever we need as well. The other reason I include this story is that Corrie insisted forgiveness is indeed hard.

I wish I could say that merciful and charitable thoughts just naturally flowed from me from then on. But they didn't. If there's one thing I've learned at 80 years of age, it's that I can't store up good feelings and behavior—but only draw them fresh from God each day.[13]

Why We Can Live Such a Life

"Even if they sin against you seven times in a day and seven times come back to you saying 'I repent,' you must forgive them."

The apostles said to the Lord, "Increase our faith!"

He replied, "If you have faith as small as a mustard seed, you can say to this mulberry tree, 'Be uprooted and planted in the sea,' and it will obey you." (Luke 17:4–6)

We began this chapter looking at Jesus's teaching on forgiveness and the disciples' incredulity. This chapter should be read as an answer to those who complain: "This idea of forgiveness is beyond me. It's impossible. We don't have enough faith." Jesus says, "If you had the faith the size of a mustard seed, you could do what I'm asking." That is, if you understand the gospel at all, if you understand what Jesus Christ has done for you at all, you have what you need to forgive.[14]

Nevertheless, forgiveness still seems to us to be such a high wall to scale. How is it possible? Jesus speaks to this with a miracle.

Now on his way to Jerusalem, Jesus traveled along the border between Samaria and Galilee. As he was going into a village, ten men who had leprosy met him. They stood at a distance and called out in a loud voice, "Jesus, Master, have pity on us!" When he saw them, he said, "Go, show yourselves to the priests." And as they went, they were cleansed.

One of them, when he saw he was healed, came back, praising God in a loud voice. He threw himself at Jesus' feet and thanked him—and he was a Samaritan. Jesus asked, "Were not all ten cleansed? Where are the other nine? Has no one returned to give praise to God except this foreigner?" Then he said to him, "Rise and go; your faith has made you well." (Luke 17:11–19)

Jesus meets ten lepers who ask for healing. Jesus's directive to them makes sense only if we realize they needed two kinds of healing. First, of course, their bodies needed to be physically healed. But second, because they had been legally excluded from social interaction, the lepers needed to be socially healed. They needed to be officially reinstated into society. That's the reason Jesus tells them to go to the priests. He means, "Go to the priests, and when they see you are physically whole, they'll let you back into the worshipping community." The lepers needed to be reconciled with the community from which they had been excluded. Only the priest could do that.

But as we see by the one returning leper, these men were not all Jews. The question it raises, as biblical scholar Joel Green puts it, is to *"which priests"* was Jesus sending them?[15] The Jews had their priests in Jerusalem, and the Samaritans had their priests and temple on Mount Gerizim.

As the lepers went, they found they were physically healed by God's power, but only the Samaritan turned back and threw himself at Jesus's feet, an action of deep reverence and absolute submission. Jesus had told him to go to the temple and the priests for full reconciliation. Why did he turn back before he got to his priests? Was he being disobedient to Jesus? No. Many commentators point out that by returning to Jesus, and receiving Christ's approval for doing so, he had figured out who the True Priest really was.

Jesus is the ultimate priest. Jesus is the final temple. Jesus is the sacrifice to end all other atoning sacrifices. Jesus, then, is the place you get your reconciliation—to God, to others, and eventually to all things in creation (Ephesians 1:10).

> For God was pleased to have all his fullness dwell in him, and through him to reconcile to himself all things, whether things on earth or things in heaven, by making peace through his blood, shed on the cross. (Colossians 1:19–20)

Don't let yourself be twisted. Take in what Jesus Christ has done, put your little story about what people have done to you into the big story of what he did for you, and you'll have all the power you need to grant forgiveness.

CHAPTER 11

EXTENDING FORGIVENESS

REBECCA: Ted, I lied to you. I hired you because I wanted this team to lose. I wanted you to fail. And I sabotaged you every chance I've had. . . . Ted, I'm so sorry.

TED LASSO: I forgive you.

REBECCA: You—What?! Why?!

TED LASSO: Divorce is hard. . . . It makes folks do crazy things. . . . You and me . . . we're okay.

—*TED LASSO*[1]

To forgive is first to release the wrongdoer from liability by absorbing the debt oneself. To forgive is then to aim for reconciliation and restoration of the relationship that was broken by the wrongdoing. This is what we have called the third dimension of forgiveness—the horizontal.

In this chapter we will look at what Jesus and later what Paul tell us practically about how to extend forgiveness and reconcile a broken relationship.

The Principle: Jesus on Anger

"You have heard that it was said to the people long ago, 'You shall not murder, and anyone who murders will be subject to judgment.' But I tell you that anyone who is angry with a brother or sister will be subject to judgment. Again, anyone who says to a brother or sister, 'Raca,' is answerable to the court. And anyone who says, 'You fool!' will be in danger of the fire of hell. Therefore, if you are offering your gift at the altar and there remember that your brother or sister has something against you, leave your gift there in front of the altar. First go and be reconciled to them; then come and offer your gift. Settle matters quickly with your adversary who is taking you to court. Do it while you are still together on the way, or your adversary may hand you over to the judge, and the judge may hand you over to the officer, and you may be thrown into prison." (Matthew 5:21–25)

In the first verses Jesus gives his well-known exposition of the sixth commandment, "Thou shalt not kill." He extends its meaning to the inner states that lead to murder, namely anger, contempt, and indifference. Any failure to love others is linked to murder and forbidden.

Many have argued that Jesus is prohibiting all anger, but that is not what he is doing. First of all, God himself, who is holy and perfect, gets angry. Anger is not intrinsically sinful. It can be energy released to remove an object that is harming something we love. The biblical text explicitly states in Mark 3:5 and John 11:33 that Jesus got angry. He got angry when defending the honor of his Father's house (Matthew 21:12–13; John 2:13–16) and when defending Lazarus from death. In fact we are told that at the tomb of Lazarus he was filled with rage (John 11:33,38).[2]

Jesus, then, is talking about sinful anger, not anger per se. But what is the difference?

The two examples he gives help us understand it. If your anger leads you to call someone "raca"—an Aramaic word that means to be inconsequential—or "you fool," it is sinful. To do so even in one's heart is to dismiss, disdain, and belittle. To do so out loud is to punish and hurt.

So when we get angry, we should ask: "What am I defending?" If we do that, we will see how often we are defending our ego, pride, agendas, and image. God's anger is always righteous because he is perfect love. So his anger is always in defense of the good, true, and beautiful, and his anger is always released to destroy evil, sin, and death.

Before Jesus gives us practical instruction on reconciliation in the Christian community, he warns us in the strongest terms about sinful anger as a violation of the commandment against murder. Just as an acorn contains the entire tree—and millions of other acorns—all within its small cup, so murder begins with the seed of inward, sinful anger. When you indulge in it, you step onto a path that could end in murder. We are grateful that the vast majority of people who set foot on the road never go to its destination, but along that road are bitterness, grudges, hate, and a host of other griefs and injustices.

The Practical: Jesus on Reconciliation

It is possible to inwardly forgive without being able to reconcile with the offending party. Yet anyone who truly forgives from the heart will be open to and willing to reconcile. Immediately after Jesus warns about anger, he gives us case studies on reconciliation:

> Therefore, if you are offering your gift at the altar and there re-
> member that your brother or sister has something against you,

leave your gift there in front of the altar. First go and be reconciled to them; then come and offer your gift. Settle matters quickly
with your adversary who is taking you to court. (verses 23–25)

The first concerns a fellow believer and the second an adversary, an
enemy—the "brother" and the "adversary" both have something against
you. Jesus's directions are surprising.

The first surprise is that Jesus does *not* give his listeners an example of
when *they* get angry. He has just warned his disciples against anger, but he
does not then turn and say, "This is what you must do if someone has
made you angry," but rather, "This is what you must do if you have made
someone else angry." Jesus's disciples are to be so concerned to stop the
spread of sinful anger and hate that they should be "no less concerned
when [they] engender them in others" as when they experience them
themselves.[3]

The second surprise is the urgency of Jesus. He asks listeners to imagine worshipping in the temple and recalling that a fellow believer has
something against them. He urges them to drop everything, even leaving
the gift at the altar, and go to make things right. This reflects the same
principle in Paul's teaching: "Do not let the sun go down on your anger"
(Ephesians 4:26, ESV). In both cases, Jesus and Paul are not so much laying down literal rules for timing as they are denouncing the procrastination and avoidance that characterize almost all of us when we know there
has been a breach in a relationship.

In Jesus's most famous statement on reconciliation, he says:

"If your brother or sister sins, go and point out their fault, just
between the two of you. If they listen to you, you have won them
over. But if they will not listen, take one or two others along, so
that 'every matter may be established by the testimony of two or
three witnesses.' If they still refuse to listen, tell it to the church;

and if they refuse to listen even to the church, treat them as you
would a pagan or a tax collector." (Matthew 18:15–17)

Here it is the believer who has been sinned against—the relationship
has been broken from the other side. Most significantly, Jesus says that the
relationship breach between two Christians is not the concern only of the
two parties. It is the concern of the entire church, and it may be necessary
to use the resources and involvement of the community in order to repair
the relationship.

In this situation, Jesus says, first *go privately*. At first, then, do *not* involve others. "Go and point out their fault, just between the two of you." I
think it would be good to take Jesus literally here, despite the differences
between our time and his. I think that ordinarily you should not phone or
write or email. Both studies and anecdotal evidence tell us that young
"digital natives" are extremely intimidated by the challenge to *go*. It is far
easier to simply refuse to answer texts and emails—to ghost. However,
confronting a person *and* seeking a repair of the relationship is a highly
complicated, delicate operation. Everything must be mustered—body language, tone, facial expression, words, feelings—in order to convey a balance
between truth and love, justice and mercy.

If it is possible, go and talk to him or her face to face. And do this before talking to others, so that you can honestly tell the person you have not
been spreading around complaints about them. Go to them in such a way
as not to embarrass them.

Second, Jesus says *go positively*. Yes, the phrase "point out their fault"
translates the Greek *elencho*, meaning a sharp, painful admonition. Nevertheless, the goal of the criticism is all important. Why are you confronting
them? Jesus's answer—it must be *to win the person, not the argument* (verse
15). The aim is to persuade the person and to restore or maintain the relationship. One commentator points out that "the concern [should not be]
mainly the safety and/or reputation of the whole community but the spir-

itual welfare of the individual[s]."[4] That is an important insight in light of the many accounts of a church silencing sexual abuse victims in order to protect the reputation of the church and its leaders.

How is it possible, if you have been wronged, to be so positive in your aim and motivation? Here we must remember the multidimensional nature of forgiveness. Jesus taught (Mark 11:25) that we must forgive inwardly— or at least start the internal forgiveness process—before we go ask the wrongdoer to repent. If you go to the perpetrator before you forgive them, you are likely to go not to regain your brother or sister. You will most likely be going not to persuade and reclaim them but just to tell them off and so to pay them back. They will sense the ill will immediately and will become defensive and angry and will not admit where they have been wrong. And so they will be far less likely to ever repent in response to your confrontation.

Some read this text as saying that you are to speak to the wrongdoer only one time, but the text doesn't say to "go *once* privately" but simply to go privately. It is normal and wise for this stage of relationship mending to take more than one encounter. So, thirdly, *go repeatedly* if necessary. Often the person being challenged will be surprised and defensive and may need time to process it all. If you have been wronged but your goal is love and restoration, you will be patient and perhaps meet several times to work through the various issues surrounding your relationship.

Fourth, Jesus says that if the first stage stalls or is rejected, *involve the community*. What if the person will not hear you or respond to your appeals for reconciliation? Jesus says that if there is no progress, it is warranted and wise to involve others from the Christian community. We see that he first says to take "one or two others" (Matthew 18:16, ESV). This means that it is still necessary to keep things as private as possible at every stage.

Despite the words *testimony* and *witnesses*, we are not talking about formal legal proceedings; "one or two" shows that Jesus is giving general guidance rather than a strict procedure. He is also being realistic. It may be that you are not being persuasive because the perpetrator thinks you are not being objective. And that may be the case. "It behooves the person taking the initiative to make sure that the 'sin' is not simply a matter of personal preference; the eventual involvement of the 'one or two' and then of the church should minimize that danger."[5]

The one or two others have a dual function. On the one hand, they can help you refine your understanding of what happened and speak more persuasively. They can call you out if you are speaking excessively or unhelpfully. On the other hand, they can confirm to the perpetrator that he or she is truly in the wrong and that repentance is required. Two or three is more persuasive than one. To involve one or two others is in some ways a strategy for holding both parties accountable.

Fifth and finally, if this stage does not work, you should "*tell it to the church*" (verse 17). This phrase means to finally, as a last resort, speak to the local church as a whole. The way this process looks will depend on matters like church polity and government. For example, in a church governed by elders, "telling it to the church" could simply mean taking it to them. This is clearly not to be done precipitously—the procedure Jesus outlines avoids this if at all possible. Yet notice that the purpose even of such a meeting is not to humiliate, shame, or punish but to appeal and persuade. The idea is that the offender might "listen even to the church." "The offender, faced by the disapproval of the whole local disciple community, ought [hopefully] to recognize that this was not just a personal grievance on the part of the initiator."[6]

Michael Green, for many years the rector of St Aldate's Church in the midst of Oxford University, recalls an incident in which a Christian who was a staff member of a local business and a member of his church was judged to be guilty of financial malfeasance. Green recounts: "He was seen alone. He strenuously denied it. So I as the Rector and three others saw him. He confessed what he had done when faced by incriminating evidence in the presence of witnesses."[7] But over the years, Green saw that "sometimes even that does not suffice. It is necessary to tell the church.

That is a painful last resort. I have once or twice had to take it, [when] it will simply not do to conduct things behind closed doors."[8]

If the person will not "listen to the church," Jesus says the man or woman cannot continue in the church's fellowship as if nothing has happened. To treat them "as a pagan or a tax collector" does not, of course, mean anything like shunning, since Jesus was famous for speaking to tax collectors and sinners.[9] The context of the whole passage indicates that even this measure of church discipline is designed for the purpose of reclaiming and restoring the wrongdoer.[10]

Matthew 5 and 18 in Tandem

What do we learn from reading both of these short case studies together?

First, from the two passages emerges a single principle. If a relationship has broken down, *it is always your move* to initiate relationship repair. Matthew 5 says, "If your brother has something against you, go to him," while Matthew 18 says, "If you have something against your brother, go to him," so it doesn't matter who started it. A Christian is responsible to begin the process of reconciliation, regardless of how the alienation began. If you say, "Well, she started it—let her approach *me*," nothing will ever happen, since she may be out there saying the same thing in her heart about you.

Second, while sometimes the perpetrator's wrongdoing is egregious and unprovoked (as in the case of sexual assault), in many cases of relationship breakdown *there are usually some things for which both sides can confess and both sides forgive.* Seldom does just one party bear all the blame for a tattered relationship. Almost always reconciliation is best done by *both* repenting *and* forgiving—by both admitting your own wrong and pointing out the wrong of the other. Of course, it may be the case that one party is far more in the wrong, but if the other party is willing to confess anything at all, it may make it far easier for the perpetrator to "come clean."

Only the gospel prepares you for both sides of the Christian reconciliation model. It humbles you enough to make you able to be a forgiver and, at the same time, affirms and fills you with such a sense of worth and love that it makes you able to be a repenter. It is only great humility and great joy that will help us as a church, a community, to keep relationships in repair.

Paul on Reconciliation

Bless those who persecute you; bless and do not curse. Rejoice with those who rejoice; mourn with those who mourn. Live in harmony with one another. Do not be proud, but be willing to associate with people of low position. Do not be conceited. Do not repay anyone evil for evil. Be careful to do what is right in the eyes of everyone. If it is possible, as far as it depends on you, live at peace with everyone. Do not take revenge, my dear friends, but leave room for God's wrath, for it is written: "It is mine to avenge; I will repay," says the Lord. On the contrary: "If your enemy is hungry, feed him; if he is thirsty, give him something to drink. In doing this, you will heap burning coals on his head." Do not be overcome by evil, but overcome evil with good. (Romans 12:14–21)

Paul lays out a principle, and gives us five practical ways to realize that principle. *The principle: "Do not be overcome by evil, but overcome evil with good"* (verse 21). *Overcome* is a military word that means "to defeat, conquer." There are only two possibilities: either you will be defeated by evil, *or* you will conquer and defeat evil by responding to it with good. If, when someone hurts you, you hurt the person back or even want in your heart to see them hurt, then you are being defeated by evil because you are being influenced by it.

Evil wins when it distorts your relationships with others. When someone harms you and you continue wanting to hurt them, or even nourish a low-level anger, it ruins relationships.

Evil wins when it distorts your view of yourself. When you replay the video in your imagination of what the other person did to you, you think about what is wrong with them and how noble you are by contrast. You feel self-pity and self-righteousness. There is nothing that makes you more open to being cruel than feeling: "Nobody knows how much I have suffered." It makes you open to temptation, and when you have an opportunity to do something dishonest, you will do it, because deep in your heart you will think you are giving yourself reparations. You are more open to evil. Evil has won.

Evil wins when, through you, it helps the perpetrator in his or her self-justification. If you maintain your anger, coldness, and ill will toward the wrongdoers, that can make *them* feel more justified. They tell themselves what a cruel person you are and how you deserved it. If we don't defeat evil through forgiveness, evil wins—in the world, in the perpetrator, in you.

You must defeat, and can only defeat, evil if you respond not by hurting the person back or wanting the person to be hurt but with good. Here are five ways to overcome evil with good:

1. **Pray for them.** "*Bless* those who persecute you." To "bless" may mean many things, but above all it means to pray for them—to pray for God to bless them. It is hard to stay angry at someone if you are praying for them. It is also hard to stay angry unless you feel superior, and it is hard to feel superior if you are praying for them, since in prayer you approach God as a forgiven sinner. Praying for them knocks down the superiority, and it turns your heart so you are starting to will them good.

2. **Forgive them.** "Do not repay anyone evil for evil. . . . Do not take revenge . . . but overcome evil with good." Here we see that the essence of forgiveness is a turning away from the pursuit of revenge. We tell the wrongdoer they have done wrong—that's telling the truth. But we do so not to pay back and hurt them as they hurt us, but in order to seek the "good." We confront for their sake, for other victims' sake, for God's sake—not for revenge. To confront without revenge *is* forgiveness. It means you've canceled the personal debt between the two of you. You may confront or even go to the law if that is necessary, but not in revenge.

3. **Don't avoid them.** Verse 18 reads: "If it is possible, as far as it depends on you, live at peace with everyone." Some say, "I have forgiven the person, but I want nothing to do with them," but that is actually a form of retaliation. Even if the other person remains hostile so you can't restore the relationship, you don't contribute to the hostility. You act as kindly, as helpfully, as respectfully as you can—you are always seeking a relationship.

4. **Give them what they need, to whatever degree they allow.** "If your enemy is hungry, feed him; if he is thirsty, give him something to drink." This means if there is an opportunity to do something for a wrongdoer in order to meet his or her needs, do it. This takes much discernment, however. As we have been saying, it may be that what they need is a confrontation, since it is never loving to make it easy for someone to go on sinning. If you are afraid to confront, you may be failing to love them. If you confront with too much relish and anger, you may be failing to love them. If you give them help in such a way that it enables them to abuse you, you are failing to love them enough to want them to change.

5. **Do it humbly.**[11] Verse 16 says all this must be done without pride or conceit. Some "forgiveness" is done to take the high moral ground, to show one's superiority. As the scare quotes in the previous sentence show, that isn't real forgiveness at all. Forgiveness is a gift given by a sinner saved by sheer grace to another. If you confront not for their sake, not for truth's sake, not for the world's sake, but for *your* sake, you will make the perpetrator worse. But if you have

the humility and love and have forgiven them, they may not like what you are saying, but they will see that you care for them, and you may actually be able to help them.

The Power for It All

What are the implications of "Leave room for God's wrath . . . 'I will repay,' says the Lord"?

It means that Christians, of all people, should not need to see full justice done in this life. We should pursue what we can, but we rest in the knowledge that, in the end, God will square every account, and absolutely everything will be made right. So the Christian does not desire vengeance. Our job is to get as full a justice as we can and leave the rest to God.

However, this metaphor about God's wrath points to something else. Before looking at it, one more story of forgiveness.

Australians Graham and Gladys Staines were Christian medical missionaries working at clinics and at a home for lepers in one of the poorest parts of India. On January 22, 1999, Graham and their two sons, Philip (age ten) and Timothy (age six), were burned alive by an anti-Christian mob. The next morning, as Gladys received official confirmation of the deaths, her friends were around her but unprepared for what she did and said:

> Mrs. Staines shook with grief and, for a time, moved very slowly as if struggling to part her way through the air. She seemed to be impaled in the middle of a thought, which finally, with a quavering voice, she shared. "Whoever did this, we will forgive them," she said. . . . "That's the good news . . . that there is forgiveness for every sin through the vessel of Jesus Christ."[12]

The rest of her life demonstrated that she did this. Rather than leave India, Gladys and her daughter stayed and continued to minister in the same place to the same people. She built the leper home into a full hospital. In 2005 she was awarded the Padma Shri, an award given by the government of India to civilians who have made distinguished contributions to the nation.

How can anyone have the strength and love to forgive like this and live such a life?

"Leave room for God's wrath" has often been interpreted like this: "Yes—leave it to God. God will let them have it! And in a way that you cannot!" British pastor Dr. Martyn Lloyd-Jones had heard this idea and responds, "The moment you say that, you have denied the entire spirit of this injunction."[13] Lloyd-Jones goes on to cite the incident in 1 Samuel 25 where Abigail narrowly prevents David from taking angry personal revenge on Nabal. Everything in the Bible tells the Christian that "We must never desire the harm of the person who has offended us—never!"[14]

What, then, *does* it mean to leave room for God's wrath? Lloyd-Jones says it does not mean "a kind of flabby passivity,"[15] as all the surrounding admonitions show. It takes strength of will and heart to refuse to avoid someone who has wronged us but also to forgive and be kind and serve them wherever possible, all in a context of truth telling.

This call is not for the faint of heart. Who has ever been strong and loving enough to follow this pattern? Of course, it is Jesus himself. When he died on the cross, he responded to mocking with respect, to cruelty with love, to cursing with blessing, to evil with forgiveness and good—and in that very act he overcame the evil.

If we don't tell God what to do with his wrath but allow him to send it when and where he wills, what does he do with it? In Jesus Christ God comes and takes the penalty of justice himself. The old King James Version of the Bible translates verse 19 as "Vengeance is mine," and that reminds us that the wrath that should have come to us came to him. The vengeance due to us literally became his.

Do you want a heart for forgiveness? Do you want a heart that overcomes evil with good? Do you want a heart that doesn't feel superior, that doesn't need to justify itself? Look at Jesus taking the vengeance that was your due. Vengeance is his! He received it.

The enduring lesson of the parable of the Unforgiving Servant is this: it is only when we see a King acting as a servant voluntarily for our sake that we servants will stop acting like little kings and judges.

No one learns to love by trying. Before love is something you give, it is someone you receive. You learn to love by first *experiencing* love and passing it on. You will be patient only if you see someone saving you through the costliest patience and forgiving you even as he dies: "Father, forgive them. They don't know what they are doing." That is what can change you. And that is what will change you.

EPILOGUE

The movie *Places in the Heart* (1984) is a tearjerker. It has a conventional story line about hardworking, common people who remain steadfast in the face of terrible circumstances and disappointments. Sally Field won an Oscar for playing the role of Edna Spalding, who suddenly becomes a young widow when her husband, Royce, the local sheriff, is shot to death accidentally by a drunk Black teenager. The story takes place in a small, segregated Texas town during the Great Depression. Racist members of the community find Wylie, the African American shooter, and tie him to the back of a truck and drag him to death.

Without her husband's salary Edna cannot afford to make the loan payments on the farm. The rest of the movie shows Edna doing all she can to save her farm, aided by a blind man who rents a room, Mr. Will (John Malkovich), and a Black farmhand, Moze (Danny Glover). Together they save the farm by winning a hundred-dollar prize for the season's earliest bale of cotton. Yet the happy ending is stolen away, because the local Ku Klux Klan beats Moze to within an inch of his life. He is saved from death only by Mr. Will, who recognizes the robed and hidden Klansmen's voices and names them. Although Moze survives, he decides to leave the farm for Edna's sake and his own.

Up to this point the movie is a typical Hollywood tribute to American humanistic values. Terrible circumstances can be overcome through individual effort. Black and white people can work together. Good white people respect Blacks even though there are bad white people who do not. Innumerable other movies have given the same message to audiences. Be like the good people in the story, not like the bad. Even though there will be setbacks, we can make the world a better place.

However, *Places in the Heart* is rightly famous for its final scene, which takes the movie into a category of its own.

The final scene shows us a scattering of townspeople sitting in a service at the local church on a Sunday morning. The minister reads from 1 Corinthians 13 on love, and then the choir sings "In the Garden" as the communion trays are passed. The camera allows us to see only one or two persons at a time, and we are more and more surprised when we see nearly every character to whom we have been introduced throughout the movie, taking communion and passing the trays along. Then we are amazed to see Moze there, sitting in the pew and taking a cup. It is an integrated church service, something that did not exist in Texas at that time. We begin to realize that we have left the realm of this-world reality.

Finally the communion tray comes to Edna, who hands it to her husband, Royce Spalding, who in turn hands it to Wylie, the Black youth who shot him. They are alive again, and they quietly say to one another, as they commune, "Peace of God." The audience is strangely and deeply moved as the camera fades.

The shocking ending gives us a far richer and more complex analysis of the human situation than we were expecting.

The movie shows it understands the evils of racism and poverty are more entrenched and endemic to our fallen human nature than we want to believe. They can't be overcome with the pieties of American liberalism, with better education, and simply all trying harder to be good people. While we must indeed fight these things; it is going to take something more than we can muster to defeat them. It is going to take something supernatural, something not of this world, to change it.

And yet at the same time, the movie shows us that there is hope for everyone and anyone, that you can be granted love regardless of what you have done. This final scene, then, in which killed and killer greet each other with God's peace, is a picture of the future kingdom of God, in which divine forgiveness heals all wounds and wipes away every tear.

The screenplay writer and director Robert Benton was asked about this ending. He responded, "I had the ending before I ever finished the screenplay, although I knew audiences would be confused by it." So then why did he include it? "There are certain things images can explain that words cannot. There is something in the image of the man who has been killed handing the communion plate to the boy who killed him that seems very moving to me in ways I cannot explain."[1]

Indeed. The Bible tells us this future is possible because the thing that moved Robert Benton has actually happened. There is one who, though he was being killed on the cross, called for forgiveness and offered his peace to those who were killing him. To all of us, then, no matter what we have done, he offers the "peace of God." This gift came at an infinite cost to him, but he offers it to us gladly. Let us receive it and pass it along to others in the same way.

ACKNOWLEDGMENTS

As always, I am indebted to Brian Tart of Viking Books and David McCormick of McCormick Literary for their counsel, support, and friendship. They have decades of rich experience in the literary and publishing worlds, and I am the beneficiary of all that wealth.

COVID and cancer treatments have changed my life in many ways, yet, as always, God works things for good. My wife, Kathy, and I have spent far more time together these last two years than we would have otherwise, and we have seen the importance of the daily exercise of asking for and granting forgiveness. Although Kathy did not cowrite this book with me, we have colearned the meaning and practice of forgiveness together over the decades.

FORGIVENESS PRINCIPLES

1. *The difficulty of forgiveness lies in that it is unnatural—it is not the nature of things.* It is counterintuitive to our basic human instincts and nature. A holy God's forgiveness was a mystery (before the coming of Christ), as God himself proclaimed in Exodus 34:7. Forgiveness is therefore always a wonder and surprise, and it needs to be accounted for rather than ever taken for granted.

2. *The dynamic of forgiveness is the atoning death of Christ,* which provides satisfaction for sin through the self-substitution of God. This is what makes forgiveness possible (from both God and humans) despite its difficulty and unnaturalness. Our forgiveness of others is based on and empowered by (theologically, motivationally, and practically) God's forgiveness of us through the cross.

3. *The fading of forgiveness comes because of the inadequacy of contemporary forgiveness models, which lack the vertical dimension.* Christian forgiveness (a) differs from the therapeutic model because it seeks justice and reconciliation; (b) differs from the merited or transactional forgiveness model because it offers internal forgiveness; (c) differs from the modern antipathy toward any forgiveness because it shows us the need for it, the costliness of it, and the power of it.

4. *The history of forgiveness is rooted in the Bible.* While all cultures have some idea of forgiveness, the dominant ideas about it in the world today derive from the Old and New Testaments. The loss of orientation to for-

giveness today has to do with both the decline of Christian faith and the distortion of the concept within the churches.

5. *The definition of forgiveness is to renounce revenge and be open to reconciliation.* Revenge is being satisfied by another person's unhappiness, especially that inflicted by you. To forgive is to (a) name the wrong truthfully as indeed wrong and punishable (rather than merely excusing it) but also to (b) identify with the perpetrator as a fellow sinner, to (c) release the wrongdoer from liability from personal payback by absorbing the debt oneself (rather than merely pardoning), and finally to (d) aim for reconciliation and the restoration of the relationship that was broken by the wrong.

6. *The dependencies of forgiveness.* (a) Internal or attitudinal forgiveness is *not* dependent on the response of the perpetrator. It can be done in any circumstances. (b) The work of actual reconciliation *is* dependent on the wronged person doing internal forgiveness and the repentance of the perpetrator.

7. *The resources for forgiveness are twofold:* (a) poverty of spirit—and the humility that comes from knowing our salvation is by sheer grace, not merit, and (b) wealth of spirit—and the assurance of love that comes from knowing our salvation is by sheer grace, not merit.

8. *The dimensions of forgiveness are threefold:*

   a. *The vertical or upward dimension.* The character and reception of God's forgiveness: (1) God's salvation is more than past forgiveness but the basis for future forgiveness: justification and adoption. (2) The instrument(s) that receive this divine forgiveness and salvation are repentance and faith.

   b. *The internal or inward dimension.* The character and granting of human forgiveness: (1) It is granted before felt because it is a promise and a practice. (2) It entails costly suffering, as it absorbs the debt rather than seeking revenge.

   c. *The horizontal or outward dimension.* The character and extension of human forgiveness: (1) It pursues both mercy and justice together and interdependently, since both are forms of love. (2) It holds out the offer of a reconciled relationship and, eventually, a restoration of trust.

BIBLICAL TEXTS ON GOD'S FORGIVENESS

1 John 1:9. If we confess our sins, he is faithful and just to forgive us our sins and to cleanse us from all unrighteousness.

Ephesians 1:7. In him we have redemption through his blood, the forgiveness of our trespasses, according to the riches of his grace.

Isaiah 1:18. Come now, let us reason together, says the Lord: though your sins are like scarlet, they shall be as white as snow; though they are red like crimson, they shall become like wool.

Isaiah 55:7. Let the wicked forsake his way, and the unrighteous man his thoughts; let him return to the Lord, that he may have compassion on him, and to our God, for he will abundantly pardon.

Acts 2:38. And Peter said to them, "Repent and be baptized every one of you in the name of Jesus Christ for the forgiveness of your sins, and you will receive the gift of the Holy Spirit."

Acts 3:19. Repent therefore, and turn back, that your sins may be blotted out.

COLOSSIANS 1:13–14. He has delivered us from the domain of darkness and transferred us to the kingdom of his beloved Son, in whom we have redemption, the forgiveness of sins.

MATTHEW 26:28. For this is my blood of the covenant, which is poured out for many for the forgiveness of sins.

PSALM 103:10–14. He does not deal with us according to our sins, nor repay us according to our iniquities. For as high as the heavens are above the earth, so great is his steadfast love toward those who fear him; as far as the east is from the west, so far does he remove our transgressions from us. As a father shows compassion to his children, so the Lord shows compassion to those who fear him. For he knows our frame; he remembers that we are dust.

HEBREWS 10:17. Then he adds, "I will remember their sins and their lawless deeds no more."

PSALM 86:5. For you, O Lord, are good and forgiving, abounding in steadfast love to all who call upon you.

PSALM 32:5. I acknowledged my sin to you, and I did not cover my iniquity; I said, "I will confess my transgressions to the Lord," and you forgave the iniquity of my sin. Selah

2 CHRONICLES 7:14. If my people who are called by my name humble themselves, and pray and seek my face and turn from their wicked ways, then I will hear from heaven and will forgive their sin and heal their land.

ACTS 10:43. To him all the prophets bear witness that everyone who believes in him receives forgiveness of sins through his name.

HEBREWS 8:12. For I will be merciful toward their iniquities, and I will remember their sins no more.

MICAH 7:18–19. Who is a God like you, pardoning iniquity and passing over transgression for the remnant of his inheritance? He does not retain his anger forever, because he delights in steadfast love. He will again have compassion on us; he will tread our iniquities underfoot. You will cast all our sins into the depths of the sea.

ISAIAH 43:25. I, I am he who blots out your transgressions for my own sake, and I will not remember your sins.

PROVERBS 28:13. Whoever conceals his transgressions will not prosper, but he who confesses and forsakes them will obtain mercy.

EPHESIANS 2:8–9. For by grace you have been saved through faith. And this is not your own doing; it is the gift of God, not a result of works, so that no one may boast.

PSALM 130:4. But with you there is forgiveness, that you may be feared.

1 JOHN 2:1. My little children, I am writing these things to you so that you may not sin. But if anyone does sin, we have an advocate with the Father, Jesus Christ the righteous.

ROMANS 8:1. There is therefore now no condemnation for those who are in Christ Jesus.

JEREMIAH 31:34. And no longer shall each one teach his neighbor and each his brother, saying, "Know the Lord," for they shall all know me, from the least of them to the greatest, declares the Lord. For I will forgive their iniquity, and I will remember their sin no more.

ISAIAH 53:5. But he was pierced for our transgressions; he was crushed for our iniquities; upon him was the chastisement that brought us peace, and with his wounds we are healed.

ZEPHANIAH 3:15,17. The Lord has taken away the judgments against you. . . . The Lord your God is in your midst, a mighty one who will save; he will rejoice over you with gladness; he will quiet you by his love; he will exult over you with loud singing.[1]

APPENDIX C

FORGIVENESS PRACTICES

1. WHAT FORGIVENESS IS

When speaking of forgiveness, Jesus uses the image of "debts" to describe the nature of sins (Matthew 18:21–35, 6:12).

When someone seriously wrongs you, there is an unavoidable sense that the wrongdoer *owes* you. The wrong has incurred an obligation, a liability, a debt. Anyone who is wronged feels a compulsion to make the other person pay down that debt. We do that by hurting them, yelling at them, making them feel bad in some way, or even just waiting and watching and hoping that something bad happens to them.

Only after we see them suffer in some commensurate way do we sense that the debt has been paid and the feeling of obligation is gone. This sense of debt/liability and obligation is impossible to escape. Anyone who denies it exists has simply not been wronged or sinned against in any serious way.

What, then, is forgiveness? Forgiveness means giving up the right to revenge, the right to seek repayment from the one who harmed you. It must be recognized that forgiveness is a form of voluntary suffering. What do we mean?

Think about how monetary debts work. If a friend breaks my lamp, and if the lamp costs fifty dollars to replace, then the act of lamp breaking incurs a debt of fifty dollars. If I let him pay for and replace the lamp, I get fifty dollars. But if I forgive him for what he did, the debt does not somehow vanish into thin air. When I forgive him, I absorb the cost and payment for the lamp. (Either I will pay the fifty dollars to replace it or I will lose the lighting in that room.) To forgive is to cancel the debt by paying it or absorbing it yourself. Someone *always* pays every debt.

This is the case in all situations of wrongdoing, even nonmonetary situations. When you are sinned against, you lose *something*—whether it is happiness, reputation, peace of mind, a relationship, an opportunity, or something else. There are two things to do about a sin. Imagine, for example, that someone has hurt your reputation. You can try to restore it by paying the other person back, by vilifying them and ruining *their* reputation. Or you can forgive them, refuse to pay them back, and therefore absorb the damage to your reputation. (You will have to restore it over time.)

But in all situations, when wrong is done, there is always a debt, and there is no way to deal with it without suffering—either you make the perpetrator suffer for it or you forgive and suffer for it yourself. Either you make the debtor pay by hurting them until you feel things are even or you pay by forgiving and absorbing the pain within yourself.

Forgiveness is always costly. It is emotionally very expensive—it takes much blood, sweat, and tears. So in forgiveness you pay the debt yourself in several ways:

✦ First, by refusing to hurt the person directly. You refuse vengeance, payback, or the infliction of pain in order to try to relieve the sense of debt you feel. Instead, you are as cordial as possible. Beware of subtle ways that we can try to exact payment in our relationship.

· Don't make cutting remarks and drag out the past over and over.

· Don't be far more demanding and controlling with the person than you are with others, all because you feel deep down that they still owe you.

- Don't punish them with self-righteous "mercy" that is really a way to make them feel small and to justify yourself.

- Don't avoid them and be cold to them in overt or more subtle ways.

✦ Second, by refusing to cut the person down to others. You refuse to diminish them in the eyes of others by innuendo or "spin" or hint or gossip or direct slander.

- Don't run them down to others under the guise of "warning" people about them.

- Don't run them down to others under the guise of seeking sympathy and support and sharing your hurt.

✦ Third, by refusing to indulge in ill will in your heart.

- Don't continually replay the "videotapes" of the wrong in your imagination, in order to keep the sense of loss and hurt fresh and real to you so you can stay actively hostile to the person and feel virtuous yourself.

- Don't vilify or demonize the offender in your imagination. Rather, recognize the common sinful humanity you share with them.

- Don't indulge in "rooting for them to fail," hoping for their pain. Instead, pray positively for their growth.

Forgiveness, then, is granted before it is felt. It is a promise to refrain from the three things above and pray for the perpetrator as you remind yourself of God's grace to you. Though it is extremely difficult and painful (you are bearing the cost of the sin yourself!), forgiveness will deepen your character, free you to talk to and help the person, and lead to love and peace rather than bitterness.

And by bearing the cost of the sin, you are walking in the path of your master (Colossians 3:13; Matthew 18:21–35). It is typical for non-Christians today to say that the cross "makes no sense." "Why did Jesus have to die? Why couldn't God just forgive us?" But *no* one who has been deeply wronged "*just* forgives"! If someone wrongs you, there are only two options: (a) you make them suffer, or (b) you refuse revenge and forgive them, and then you suffer. And if *we* can't forgive without suffering, how much more must God suffer in order to forgive us? For if *we* sense the obligation and debt and injustice of sin unavoidably in our soul, how much more does God know it? On the cross we see God forgiving us, and that is possible only if God suffers. On the cross God's love satisfied his own justice by suffering, bearing the penalty for sin. There is never forgiveness without suffering, nails, thorns, sweat, blood. Never.

2. WHAT WE NEED IN ORDER TO FORGIVE

The experience of the gospel gives us the two prerequisites for a life of forgiveness:

Spiritual poverty or humility. You can stay bitter toward someone only if you feel superior, if you feel that you "would never do anything like that!" Those who won't forgive show they have not accepted the fact of their own sinfulness. When Paul says he is the "chief of sinners," he is not exaggerating. He is saying that he is as capable of sin as the worst criminals are. To remain unforgiving means you remain unaware of your own need for forgiveness.

Spiritual wealth or assurance. You can't be gracious to someone if you are too needy and insecure. If you know God's love and forgiveness, then there is a limit to how deeply another person can hurt you. He or she can't touch your *real* identity, wealth, and significance. The more we rejoice in our own forgiveness, the quicker we will be to forgive others.

Jesus says: "If you do not forgive others their sins, your Father will not forgive your sins" (Matthew 6:15). This does not mean we can earn God's forgiveness through our own forgiving but that we can disqualify ourselves from it. No heart that is truly repenting toward God could be unforgiving toward others. A lack of forgiveness toward others is the direct result of a lack of repentance toward God. And as we know, you must repent in order to be saved (Acts 2:38).

3. GOD'S FORGIVENESS AND OURS

When God reveals his glory to Moses, he says he is a God who "[*forgives*] *wickedness*" yet "*does not leave the guilty unpunished*" (Exodus 34:6–7). Not until Jesus do we see how God can be both completely just and yet forgiving; it is through his atonement (1 John 1:7–9). In the cross God satisfies *both* justice *and* love. God was so just and desirous to judge sin that Jesus *had* to die, but he was so loving and desirous of our salvation that Jesus *was glad* to die.

We, too, are commanded to forgive, "Bear with each other and forgive one another if any of you has a grievance against someone," (Colossians 3:13) on the basis of Jesus's atonement for our sins: "Be kind and compassionate to one another, forgiving each other, just as in Christ God forgave you" (Ephesians 4:32).

But we are also required to forgive in a way that honors justice, just as God's forgiveness does. "If your brother sins, rebuke him, and if he repents, forgive him" (Luke 17:3, ESV). Since God forgives us yet in a way that honors justice, so *we* should also forgive in a way that honors justice. Christians "are called to abandon bitterness, to be forbearing, to have a forgiving stance even where the repentance of the offending party is conspicuous by its absence; on the other hand, their God-centered passion for justice, their concern for God's glory, ensure that the awful odium of sin is not glossed over."1

4. PURSUING TRUTH, LOVE, AND RELATIONSHIP

The gospel calls us, then, to keep an equal concern (a) to speak the truth and honor what is right, yet (b) to be endlessly forgiving as we do so, and (c) to never give up on the goal of a reconciled, warm relationship.

First, God requires forgiveness whether or not the offender has repented and has asked for forgiveness. Mark 11:25: "And when you stand praying, if you hold anything against anyone, forgive them." This does not say "Forgive him *if* he repents" but rather "Forgive him right there—as you are praying."

Second, God requires speaking the truth. That is why Jesus tells his disciples in Luke 17:3–4 to "rebuke" the wrongdoer and "if they repent, forgive them." Many readers think that Jesus is saying that we can hold a grudge if the person doesn't repent, but we can't read Luke 17 to contradict Mark 11. Jesus is calling us here *both* to inner forgiveness *and* to rebuke and correct. We must completely surrender the right to pay back or get even, yet at the same time we must never overlook injustice and must see serious wrongdoings redressed.

+ This is almost the very opposite of how we ordinarily operate. Ordinarily we do not seek justice on the outside (we don't confront or call people to change and make restoration), but meanwhile we stay hateful and bitter on the inside. The Bible calls us to do the exact opposite. We deeply forgive on the inside so as to have no desire for vengeance, but then we are to speak openly about what has happened with a desire to help the person see what was done wrong.

+ And in reality, inner forgiveness and outward correction work well together. Only if you have forgiven inside can you correct unabusively—without trying to make the person feel terrible. Only if you have forgiven already can your motive be to correct the person for God's sake, for justice's sake, for the community's sake, and for the person's sake. And only if you forgive on the inside will your speech have any hope of changing the perpetrator's heart. Otherwise it will be so filled with disdain and hostility that he or she will not listen to you.

+ Ultimately, to forgive on the inside *and* to rebuke/correct on the outside are not incompatible because they are *both* acts of love. It is never loving to let a person just get away with sin. It is not loving (a) to the perpetrator, who continues in the grip of the habit, (b) nor to the others who will be wronged in the future, (c) nor to God, who is grieved. This is difficult, for the line is very thin between moral outrage for God's sake and self-righteous outrage because of hurt pride. To refuse to confront is not loving, then, but just selfish on your part.

Third, we are to speak the truth in love (Ephesians 4:15); we are to pursue justice gently and humbly in order to redress wrongs and yet maintain or restore the relationship (Galatians 6:1ff.).

There is a great deal of tension among these three things! Almost always, one is much more easily attained if you simply drop any concern for another (or the other two).

For example, it is easy to "speak the truth" if you've given up on any desire to maintain a warm relationship. But if you want both, you will have to be extremely careful in how you speak the truth!

Another example: It is possible to convince yourself you have forgiven someone, but if afterward you still want almost nothing to do with them (you don't pursue a continuing relationship), then that is a sign that you spoke the truth without truly forgiving.

Of course, it is possible that *you* may keep these three things together in your heart and mind but the other person simply cannot. There is no culture or personality type that holds these together. Virtually everyone will believe that "if you are confronting me, you don't forgive/love me" or "if you really loved me, you wouldn't be rebuking me." God recognizes that many people simply won't let you pursue all these things together, and so says: "As far as it depends on you, live at peace with everyone" (Romans 12:18). That is, "Do your part and have as good and peaceful a relationship with people as they will let you have."

RECONCILIATION PRACTICES

1. WHEN DO WE NEED TO CONFRONT/RECONCILE?

Jesus tells us that if we have been sinned against, we may need to go and speak to the offender. "If your brother sins, rebuke him, and if he repents, forgive him" (Luke 17:3, ESV). But *when* do we "rebuke"? Every time anyone wrongs us? 1 Peter 4:8 (ESV) says famously that "love covers a multitude of sins," and Proverbs 10:12 backs this up. This means we are not to be thin-skinned, and it would be wrong to bring up every matter every time we have been treated unfairly or insensitively. But passages like Matthew 18 and Luke 17 say there are some times when we should make an appeal and complaint. When do we do so?

This is where Galatians 6 gives us guidance. "If someone is caught in a sin, you who live by the Spirit should restore that person gently. But watch yourselves, or you also may be tempted" (verse 1). We should give correction under two conditions:

+ First, we should correct when the sin is serious enough to cool off or rupture the relationship. Matthew 18:15 indicates that the purpose of such a rebuke is to "win" your brother—i.e., rescue the relationship. That is implied in Galatians 6:2 (ESV) when it tells us that correcting someone is a way to "bear one another's burdens"—it is an expression of an interdependent relationship.

✦ Second, we should correct when the sin against us is evidently part of a pattern of behavior that the other person is seriously "stuck" in. Galatians 6:1 ("If . . . caught in any transgression, you who are spiritual should restore"). The image is of someone trapped in a pattern of behavior that will be harmful to the person and to others. In love it should be pointed out. So we do it for the person's sake—to "restore" him. Our concern is his growth.

✦ And *how* do we do it? "If someone is caught in a sin, you who live by the Spirit should restore that person gently" (Galatians 6:1). This could not be more important. If the motive of the correction is the growth of the person, then we will be loving and gentle. Verses 2 and 3 indicate that we should do this very humbly. We are making ourselves servants by doing the correction. Ultimately, any love that is afraid to confront the beloved is really not love but a selfish desire to *be* loved. Cowardice is always selfish, putting your own needs ahead of the needs of the other. A love that says, "I'll do *anything* to keep him or her loving and approving of me!" is not real love at all. It is not loving the person—it is loving the love you get from the person. True love is willing to confront, even to "lose" the beloved in the short run if there is a chance to help him or her.

Nevertheless, it is clear that there are plenty of times when we should *not* correct and *not* "seek an apology" even when we are owed one. The stronger a Christian you are, the less sensitive and easily hurt you will be. Thus, when people "zing" you or snub you or ignore you or let you down in some way, it should not immediately cool you off to them. A mature Christian immediately remembers (a) times when you did the same thing to others or (b) times when people who did this to you before were later revealed to have a lot on their mind and heart. If you find that any wrongdoing immediately cools you off to people and makes you need apologies, you should inquire as to the level of your own emotional humility and emotional wealth in Christ. Love should cover a multitude of sins (that is, most of them!). You should be able to treat warmly people who by rights owe you an apology but whom you haven't corrected because the slights were rather minor or the time wasn't right to speak about it or you didn't know them well enough to be sure it is a major pattern in their lives.

How do you know if you have a relationship that needs reconciliation? Here are seven signs (or levels), each more serious than the one before, by which this dynamic begins to work on the heart and cool your relationships.

+ *You roll your eyes inside and think: "You idiot. What a mess you are."*

   When you do this and there is no sadness or sympathy but instead disdain and sneering, that is the beginning of a relationship going bad, the beginning of your heart getting haughty and hard. You are calling them "raca" or "fool" in your heart.

+ *You hear about the person having a problem, and it is very satisfying.*

   You realize you have tied your happiness to their unhappiness, and that is a terrible sign.

+ *You start to find most things they do irritating.*

   You realize that something *that* person did is irritating or infuriating, but you would overlook it if someone else did it.

+ *You start to feel awkwardness in the relationship.*

   The awkwardness might come from just one side or both sides. Awkwardness is a sense of unease when around each other.

+ *You start avoiding the person.*

   This can mean avoiding places you know they will be or, when in the same place, taking pains to not have to meet or talk.

+ *You get a chance to pass along negative information about the person and enjoy it.*

+ *You are hardly speaking to each other, and there is a lot of very obvious friction that others can see.*

Know the difference between a reconciled and an unreconciled relationship.

+ An unreconciled relationship is one in which you see (a) avoidance, (b) coldness, or (c) irritability (i.e., the same action performed by another person does not disturb you as much as it does when *this* person does it!) If you find yourself avoiding or being cold to or very irritated with the other person (or if you can tell the other person is cold or irritable or avoiding you), then you probably have an unreconciled relationship.

+ On the other hand, "I forgive you" does *not* mean "I trust you." Some people think they haven't reconciled until they can completely retrust the person who did the wrong. That is not the case. Forgiveness means a willingness to try to reestablish trust, but that reestablishment is always a process. The speed and degree of this restoration entails the re-creation of trust, and that takes time, depending on the nature and severity of the offenses involved. Until a person shows evidence of true change, we *should not* trust the person. To immediately retrust a person with sinful habits could actually be enabling him to sin. Trust must be restored, and the speed at which this occurs depends on the behavior. Just because you don't (and shouldn't) trust a person who wronged you as you did before doesn't mean you don't have a reconciled relationship with him or her.

+ Note: This also applies to the people who owe you an apology but whose sins have been "covered" (see above). A person who has let you down but whom you don't correct is someone who has damaged your trust in minor ways. If he or she comes to apologize, it would restore the trust and respect level you had before, but until that happens, you can still have a civil relationship with him or her.

2. HOW DO WE RECONCILE?

We can look at Matthew 5 and Matthew 18 as two different approaches— Matthew 5 is what you do when you believe you have (or may have) wronged someone else, while Matthew 18 is what you do when you believe someone has wronged you. But it is also possible to look at these passages as giving us two stages of the normal reconciliation process, because seldom does just one party bear all the blame for a tattered relationship. Almost always reconciliation is best done by *both* repenting *and* forgiving—by both admitting your own wrong and pointing out the wrong of the other. If we put these two approaches together, we can create a practical outline like the one that follows.

✦ Stage 1 (Matthew 5 phase): Begin by confessing anything you may have done wrong.

- Begin with yourself. Even if you believe that your own behavior is no more than 5 percent of the problem, start with your 5 percent! Look for what you have done wrong, and collect the criticism.

- Start by listing whatever you think you have done wrong and by asking the other person to add to the list (of what he or she thinks you have done wrong or contributed to the breakdown in the relationship).

  - Example: "I'm here because I don't like what has happened to our relationship (or—if the term applies—"our friendship"). It appears to me that there is a problem between us; am I wrong?" Or "Here is what I believe I have contributed to the problem— where I've wronged you and contributed to the relationship problem. But where *else* have I wronged you or contributed to the relationship problem in your estimation?"

  - If you are almost totally "in the dark" about what went wrong, you may have to simply offer to listen. Example: "It appears to me that there is trouble between us and I have offended you. Am I right? Please tell me specific ways I have wronged you. I am really ready to listen. Honest."

- Then listen well to the criticism you've invited. Seek to distill the criticism of you into something clear and specific. Eventually (to do so too quickly may seem defensive), ask for as many specific examples as possible. If they say, "You are bullying," you need to discover what actual words or actions or tones of voice strike the other person as "bullying."

A Practical Checklist for Reconciliation:

+ Pray silently, asking God to give you wisdom and to sense his love for you.

+ Assume that he is speaking to you through this whole thing and is showing you ways you should be more careful or change.

+ Assume he is speaking to you even through a flawed person.

+ Beware of being defensive. Don't explain yourself too quickly, even if you have a good answer or can show the person he or she was mistaken. Be sure that you don't interrupt or keep the person from expressing frustration. Show sympathy even if you were misunderstood.

+ Always ask, "Is there anything else? I really want to know!" In stressful situations it is easy for someone to hold back some of their complaints or concerns. Get them all out on the table or you will be doing this again!

+ Make it *safe* to criticize you—support individual criticisms with "That must have been hard; I see why you were concerned."

+ Look beneath the criticism for needs in the critic that may be there and with which you can be concerned.

+ Now respond to the criticism by repenting.

  • *Please, forgive me for* _____. (This is your repentance, confession of sin.)

- Admit it without excuses and without blaming any other circumstances. Even if there are exaggerations, extract the real fault and confess it. Even if only 10 percent of the problem is you, admit it. Provide plans for changing your behavior.

- Don't just "apologize" but ask for forgiveness.

- If you can think of something, say, "And here is what I am going to do to change so I will not do such a thing again in the future." Ask him or her if there is anything you can do to restore trust. (If you really cannot see any validity in any of the criticism, ask if you can get back to the person later after checking with others about the criticism.)

+ Avoid:

  - Overexpressions of just "how terrible I feel over what I've done!" Some confessions are designed to be painful catharsis that is a way to (a) relieve one of guilt feelings (the confession is a kind of atonement/punishment) or (b) get people to provide sympathy.

  - On the other hand, avoid being deadpan, lighthearted, or even flip. Confession can be done in such a way as to preserve pride, to technically fulfill the requirement, to force the other person to let you off the hook without your showing any real contrition or emotional regret at all.

  - Most of all, do not make a confession that is really an attack. "If I upset you, I am sorry" is in this category. It means, "If you were a normal person, you would not have been upset by what I did." Do not repent to the person of something that you are not going to repent to God for nor take concrete steps to change.

  - "Please, accept my explanation for _____."
    - "Here's how I see it. Can you see that my motive or meaning was very different from what you inferred?"

- "Can you understand my point of view? Can you accept that I could have perceived this very differently and had the motives I am describing?"

- "Is there some way, since we see this issue so differently, that we can avoid hurting each other like this again?"

- Real repentance has three aspects:

  - confession to God

  - confession to the person wronged

  - the offering of a concrete plan for change that avoids the sin in the future (cf. Luke 3:7–14)

✦ Stage 2 (Matthew 18 phase): Now (if necessary) address any ways that the other person has wronged you.

- If you have done all of the above, very often you will find that this approach elicits a confession from the other person without your having to ask for it or extract it! This is far and away the best way to get reconciliation!

- If the other person is not forthcoming, begin: "From my point of view, it looks to me like . . .

  - you did this _____,

  - and it affected me this way: _____.

  - I think it would be far better for all concerned if instead you did this: _____.

  - I am coming to ask you if my understanding is accurate or distorted. Correct me if I am wrong. Could you explain what happened?" Be sure your list of things he or she has done is specific, not vague.

- If the other person offers an apology, grant forgiveness—but avoid using the term unless it is asked for! Say: "Well, I won't hold this against you" or "Let's put that in the past now" or "Think no more of it." To say "I forgive you" may sound humiliating.

- General guidelines for this part of the process:

  - Have a loving and humble tone. Tone of voice is extremely important. Overly controlled and nice and calm may sound patronizing and be as infuriating as fury. Don't resort to flattery and fawning syrupiness or fall into abusive or angry tones.

  - Attack the problem, not the person (e.g., not "You are so thoughtless" but "You have forgotten this after making repeated promises that you would not").

  - Suggest substitutes and solutions for alternative courses of action or behavior. Make sure all criticism is specific and constructive. Never say, "Don't do this" without saying "Instead, do this."

  - In the heart of the discussion you may discover some underlying goal or need that the other person is trying to meet that could be met in more constructive ways.

  - Keep in mind differences in culture. Another culture may consider your approach incredibly disrespectful and demeaning when you think you are being respectful.

Know what to do if the other person won't be reconciled to you.

+ *If it is a person who does not share your Christian beliefs:*

- Christians are commanded to seek peace and reconciliation with "everyone" (Hebrews 12:14; Romans 12:18), not just Christians. However, non-Christians may not feel the same responsibility to live in reconciled relationships.

- If that occurs, you must "take what you are given." Romans 12:18ff. gives you a lot of good ideas about how to stay gracious, kind, open, and cordial to persons who still are being standoffish to you.

✦ *If it is a Christian from your church:*

Matthew 18 indicates that if a person will not reconcile after repeated skillful efforts on your part, you should go to stage B—getting some other Christian friends (preferably who are respected by the other person) to go along with you to reconcile the relationship. If that does not work, at stage C you "tell it to the church" and ask the elders to speak to the person. There is much that can be said here, and we have done so elsewhere.

✦ *If it is a Christian from some other church:*

If the person you are seeking reconciliation with is a Christian but from another region or another church, you should use the Matthew 18:15ff process as far as you can. However, if you are not both members of the same church, it may not be possible to go to the final step of "telling it to the church." Again, you may have to "take what you are given" and live as cordially and as graciously as possible with someone who is not reconciled to you.

✦ *General advice:*

- Learn to accept the apologies/repentances you get without demanding that people admit more than they honestly believe. If they repent pretty much as extensively as you feel they should, then the relationship can be almost what it was before. If they go only halfway, then you are better off, though the relationship is weakened because you still don't fully trust their wisdom and self-knowledge.

- It is usually harder to forgive someone who will not admit any wrong and who stays haughty. Internal forgiveness may be a longer process. Use all the spiritual resources we have in our faith:

  - Look at God's commands to forgive. This is our obligation.

  - Remember God's forgiveness of us. We have no right to be bitter.

- Remember that God's omniscience is necessary to be a just judge. We have insufficient knowledge to know what others deserve.

- Remember that we are being defeated by evil when we allow the evil to keep us in bondage through bitterness! (Romans 12 tells us to "overcome" or defeat evil with forgiveness.)

- Remember that we undermine the glory of the gospel in the world's eyes when we fail to forgive.

3. WATCHING FROM THE SIDELINES

When two people are having a conflict with each other within the church, it can wreak a lot of havoc in the hearts and lives of the Christians around them who are not immediately involved in the dispute.

The worst thing (but the common thing!) that happens is that rather than suspending judgment and praying and encouraging the parties toward reconciliation, we take sides in the dispute in a very world-typical way.

It is hard not to sympathize with the party you know best. It is also hard for that person not to "share" his or her hurt with you in a way that vilifies the other party in the conflict.

As a result, you can have second- and third-order unreconciled relationships. That is, you feel alienated from people who are friends of the person your friend is alienated from! The problem with this is obvious—there is no direct way to heal breaches like this. If someone is avoiding you because your friend is mad at his or her friend, there is no wrong that you can confess or repent for. It is a spiritually poisonous situation.

The problem here is not that you have sinned or have been sinned against but that you have heard a bad report about another Christian and you let it pass into your own heart and take root as distrust and hostility.

What should we do? First, see what James says about *passing along* bad reports:

✦ James 4:10–11. "Humble yourselves before the Lord. . . . Brothers and sisters, do not slander one another." The verb translated as "slander" (*kata-lalein*) simply means to "speak against." It is not necessarily a false report, just an "against-report"—one that undermines the listener's respect and love for the person being spoken about. ("Like a north wind that brings unexpected rain is a sly tongue—which provokes a horrified look," Proverbs 25:23.) The link of slander to pride (James 4:10) shows that slander is not the humble evaluation of error or fault, which we must constantly be doing. Rather, in slander the speaker speaks as if he never would do the same thing himself. Nonslanderous evaluation is gentle, is guarded, and always shows that speakers sense how much they share the frailty, humanity, and sinful nature of the one being criticized. It always shows a profound awareness of your own sin. It is never "against-speaking."

✦ James 5:9. "Don't grumble [literally, don't groan and roll your eyes] against one another." This refers to the kind of against-speaking that is not as specific as a focused slander or attack. It is hinting with not words but body language. It means shaking heads, rolling eyes, and reinforcing the erosion of love and respect for someone else (e.g. "You know how they do things around here!") It accomplishes the same thing as slander. It brings angry looks, and it undermines love and respect.

Second, see what the book of Proverbs says about *receiving* bad reports:

• Proverbs 17:9. "Whoever would foster love covers over an offense, but whoever repeats the matter separates close friends." The first thing to do when hearing or seeing something negative is to seek to cover the offense rather than speak about it to others. That is, rather than letting it "pass in," you should seek to keep from letting the matter destroy your love and regard for a person. How?

  • First, by remembering your own sinfulness. "All a person's ways seem pure to them, but motives are weighed by the Lord"

(Proverbs 16:2). You realize you may not be seeing things well. Your motives are never as pure as you think they are.

- Second, by remembering there is always another side. "In a lawsuit the first to speak seems right, until someone comes forward and cross-examines" (Proverbs 18:17). You never have all the facts. You are never in a position to have the whole picture, and therefore when you hear the first report, you should assume you have far too little information to draw a conclusion.

- Summary: If you hear a negative report about another, you must either keep it from passing in *or* go to the person, so as not to permanently lose respect for them.

What happens if you think the injustice is too great or grievous for you to ignore? In Derek Kidner's commentary on Proverbs 25:7–10 he writes that when we think someone has done wrong, we should remember, "One seldom knows the full facts (v. 8) and one's motives in spreading a story are seldom as pure as one pretends (v. 10). To run to the law or to the neighbors is usually to run away from the duty of personal relationship—see Christ's clinching comment in Matthew 18:15b."[1] In short, if you feel the problem is too great and you can't keep it from destroying your regard for the person, you must go to them personally before you go to anyone else.

- When? Galatians 6:1–2 says we are to go to someone if they are *caught in a trespass*. That means there should be some kind of pattern. Don't go the first time you see or hear of someone doing wrong. As we said above, there's always another side and our motives are never totally pure when we get indignant. Galatians 6 says we should go if they seem to us "caught"—that is, in a pattern of behavior.

- How? Galatians 6 says we are to *restore gently* and in humility. Jesus in Matthew 18 says we should also do it persistently. If the person won't listen to us, take another with you whom they might listen to. Matthew 5:23ff., 18:15ff.: *reestablish broken relationships with one another.*

In summary, from the Old Testament to the New Testament, the principle is this: If you hear a bad report about another Christian, you must *either*

cover it with love or go to them personally before speaking of it to any others.
The first thing to do is to simply suspend judgment. The second thing to
do is cover it in love. The last thing to do is go and speak to them personally. What you should never do is (a) withdraw from them or (b) pass the
negative report on to others.

SUMMARY

Receiving God's forgiveness

+ For the first time:

  • See your need for it and the cost of it.

  • Offer authentic repentance.

  • Understand/experience forgiveness as part of salvation.

+ Ongoing forgiveness:

  • Engage in self-examination of both sins and gifts.

  • Make a confession/repent: (1) for sin, (2) for sins under sins, and
    (3) for danger and guilt.

  • Reexperience forgiveness as part of salvation: (1) Jesus as sacri-
    fice, (2) Jesus as advocate, and (3) Jesus as desire of the nations.

Giving and receiving human forgiveness

+ It is always your move.

+ Internal forgiveness:

  • Tap resources from divine forgiveness: spiritual poverty (identi-
    fying with sinner) and spiritual wealth (identity in Christ).

- Forgiveness is granted before it is felt. It is a promise: to not keep bringing it up to the person (apart from reconciliation offer—see below), to not keep bringing it up to others, and to not keep bringing it up to oneself.

+ External reconciliation:

  - Tell the truth—name the wrong and do all justice.

  - Offer any repentance you can that is warranted; offer forgiveness, declaring the put-aside of getting even.

  - Overcome evil with good—more than just forgiving.

  - Be open to rebuilding a trust relationship.

NOTES

THE PARABLE OF THE UNFORGIVING SERVANT

1. Author's note: All biblical quotes in this book will be from the New International Version (NIV) unless otherwise noted.

INTRODUCTION: "NO FUTURE WITHOUT FORGIVENESS"

1. "A Life in Quotes: bell hooks," *The Guardian*, December 15, 2021, www.theguardian.com/books/2021/dec/15/bell-hooks-best-quotes-feminism-race.
2. Desmond Tutu, *No Future without Forgiveness* (New York: Doubleday, 1999). This approach is sometimes called "restorative justice." Despite a lot of admirable things being done under this heading, the definitions and practices of restorative justice differ. To paraphrase Alasdair MacIntyre, the question is "Which restorative justice?" My volume is here to explore all the dimensions of forgiveness and to do so biblically. I will not try to adjudicate the complex legal, political, and philosophical issues surrounding restorative justice or lay out my own version of it.
3. Timothy Keller (@timkellernyc), "Many argue 'forgiveness culture' helps abusers escape accountability. Desmond Tutu argued that without forgiveness abusers hold us in thrall," Twitter, December 28, 2021, 11:39 p.m., https://mobile.twitter.com/timkellernyc/status/1476095414310998016.
4. Michael Eric Dyson, "Where Is the Forgiveness and Grace in Cancel Culture?," *The New York Times,* December 28, 2021, www.nytimes.com/2021/12/28/opinion/desmond-tutu-america-justice.html?referringSource=articleShare.
5. Elizabeth Bruenig (@ebruenig), "There's just something unsustainable about an environment that demands constant atonement, but actively disdains the very idea of forgiveness," Twitter, June 18, 2020, time unknown (tweet since deleted).

6. Mark Tooley, "Elizabeth Bruenig on Atonement and Forgiveness," *Juicy Ecumenism* (blog), July 13, 2020, https://juicyecumenism.com/2020/07/13/elizabeth-bruenig -interview.

7. Oscar Blayton, "Ain't Your Grandparents' Civil Rights Movement," *The Philadelphia Tribune*, October 22, 2014, https://www.phillytrib.com/commentary/ain-t -your-grandparents-civil-rights-movement/article_35df1b39-99f1-53bd-905d -472be169a61d.html.

8. Nathan Hersh, "Whoopi Goldberg Apologized. Punishing Her Further Is Un-Jewish," *The New York Times*, February 9, 2022, https://www.nytimes.com/2022/02 /09/opinion/whoopi-goldberg-the-view-apology.html.

9. Stacey Patton, "Black America Should Stop Forgiving White Racists," *The Washington Post*, June 22, 2015.

10. Kevin Powell, "The Insanity of White Justice and Black Forgiveness: Reducing Another Tragic Loss of Black Life to a Hallmark Card Is Not Justice," *Progressive Magazine*, October 4, 2019, https://progressive.org/latest/insanity-of-white-justice -black-forgiveness-powell-191004.

11. Preston Mitchum (@PrestonMitchum), "Black people are historically forced to show empathy to colonizers and made to feel bad when we don't," Twitter, October 2, 2019, 7:58 p.m., https://twitter.com/PrestonMitchum/status/11795914921570 34497.

12. Barbara Reynolds, "I Was a Civil Rights Activist in the 60s, but It Is Hard for Me to Get behind Black Lives Matter," *The Washington Post*, August 24, 2015.

13. Sabine Birdsong, "To Hell with Forgiveness Culture," *Medium* (blog), June 5, 2018, https://medium.com/@vvitchplease/to-hell-with-forgiveness-culture-bf805 648b43a.

14. Sabine Birdsong, "On Forgiveness, Repentance, and Necessary Mercy," *Medium* (blog), September 24, 2018, https://medium.com/@vvitchplease/on-forgiveness -repentance-and-necessary-mercy-4ec6bf1826ff.

15. Johann Christoph Arnold, *Why Forgive?* (Walden, NY: Plough, 2010), 178–80. For a book-length treatment of this revival, see Friedrich Zuendel, *The Awakening: One Man's Battle with Darkness* (Walden, NY: Plough, 2000).

CHAPTER 1: A STORY OF FORGIVENESS

1. This portion of the Talmud can be found at www.sefaria.org/Yoma.86b?lang=bi.

2. R. T. France, *The Gospel of Matthew* (Grand Rapids, MI: Wm. B. Eerdmans, 2007), 705.

3. Craig L. Blomberg, *Matthew* (Nashville: Broadman Press, 1992), 283.

4. John R. W. Stott, "The Problem of Forgiveness," in *The Cross of Christ* (Downers Grove, IL: InterVarsity Press, 1986), 87–110.

5. Despite the basic biblical teaching that we should have mercy on and forgive others as God had mercy on and forgave us, nevertheless, there will be differences. For

example, the way we have pity on other human beings is not how God has pity on us. Part of our pity is recognizing the same weakness and sinfulness we see in the wrongdoer in ourselves. God, obviously, does not have pity on us like that.

6. See Ashraf H. A. Rushdy, *After Injury: A Historical Anatomy of Forgiveness, Resentment, and Apology* (Oxford: Oxford University Press, 2018), 31–32.

7. William Cowper, "Love Constraining to Obedience," in *The New Oxford Book of Christian Verse*, ed. Davie Donald (Oxford: Oxford University Press, 1981), 195–96.

8. C. S. Lewis, *Mere Christianity* (New York: Macmillan, 1952), 167.

9. In the Matthew 18 story line, the king gives the servant forgiveness and then withdraws it. When Jesus concludes, "So also my heavenly Father will do to . . . you, if you do not forgive" (ESV), he could be read as saying that it is possible to be saved and forgiven by God and then to have it withdrawn if you fail to forgive. But in light of the rest of Jesus's and scriptural teaching, that seeks to make the parable metaphor "walk on all fours." As biblical scholar R. T. France writes about these verses: "Is refusal to forgive therefore an unforgivable sin? [But in] 12:31–32 we have been told that there is only one unforgivable sin and that is not simply a refusal to forgive, so that to set the present passage against the wider spread of Jesus' teaching may suggest some qualification of its absolute language. . . . But such considerations, appropriate as they may be to the compilation of a systematic theology, must not be allowed to weaken the impact of this sobering parable and of the solemn words in 6:14–15 which it illustrates. Those who will not forgive must not expect to be forgiven." R. T. France, *The Gospel of Matthew* (Grand Rapids, MI: Eerdmans, 2007), 708. Craig Blomberg argues similarly: "The subordinate details of the parable should not be pressed. Verse 34 does not promulgate any doctrine of purgatory. Even when one allegorizes the prison, torturers, and repayment, one winds up with a picture of hell, not purgatory, since this man could almost certainly never repay his debt or escape. Nor is it obvious that the retraction of [the king's] forgiveness has a clear spiritual analogue [with God]. Jesus may be teaching that no true disciple could ever act as this servant did; those who do so show that they have not really received forgiveness. Alternately, he may be indicating that God makes forgiveness available for everyone, but only those who appropriate it by a life of forgiving others show that they have genuinely accepted his pardon. Similar teaching occurs in the Sermon on the Mount (6:14–15), in which Jesus makes clear that those who are lost were never previously saved (7:21–23). Frighteningly, many in Christian circles today seem in danger of this judgment because they refuse to forgive fellow believers, speak kindly to them, cooperate with them, or accept their apologies." Craig Blomberg, *Matthew*, The New American Commentary, vol. 22 (Nashville: Broadman & Holman, 1992), 285.

10. Hashim Garrett's story can be found at The Forgiveness Project, www.theforgivenessproject.com/stories-library/hashim-garrett. It is also recounted in Johann Christoph Arnold, *Why Forgive?* (Walden, NY: Plough, 2010), 24–29. The quotes by Hashim are from the book *Why Forgive?*

CHAPTER 2: THE FADING OF FORGIVENESS

1. Delia Owens, *Where the Crawdads Sing* (New York: Putnam, 2018), 198.
2. Salma Hayek, "Harvey Weinstein Is My Monster Too," *The New York Times*, December 12, 2017, www.nytimes.com/interactive/2017/12/13/opinion/contributors/salma-hayek-harvey-weinstein.html.
3. Danielle Berrin, "Should We Forgive the Men Who Assaulted Us?," *The New York Times*, December 22, 2017.
4. Earthling (Pacific Northwest), comment on Berrin, "Should We Forgive?," https://nyti.ms/3wvJqLu#permid=25318811.
5. See "Dianna Ortiz, Nun Previously Abducted by Guatemalan Military, Dies at 62," Robert F. Kennedy Human Rights, February 19, 2021, https://rfkhumanrights.org/in-the-news/dianna-ortiz-nun-previously-abducted-by-guatemalan-military-dies-at-62.
6. Dianna Ortiz, "Theology, International Law, and Torture: A Survivor's View," *Theology Today* 63, no. 3 (2006): 346, cited in Jacob and Rachael Denhollander, "Justice: The Foundation of a Christian Approach to Abuse," *Fathom*, November 19, 2018, www.fathommag.com/stories/justice-the-foundation-of-a-christian-approach-to-abuse.
7. Susan Waters, The Forgiveness Project, undated, www.theforgivenessproject.com/stories/susan-waters.
8. Helen Blake and Nicola Lock, "Forgiveness and Reconciliation for Survivors of Sexual Abuse" (paper presented at 8th Biennial Safe as Churches? Conference, Melbourne, Australia, May 16–17, 2017), www.ncca.org.au/images/SafeChurch/Updated_Forgiveness_and_Reconciliation_for_Survivors_of_Sexual_Abuse_Updated_11.5.17FINAL.pdf.
9. Blake and Lock, "Forgiveness and Reconciliation."
10. Jennifer Wright, "Should We Forgive Men Accused of Sexual Assault?," *Harper's Bazaar*, March 8, 2018, www.harpersbazaar.com/culture/politics/a19156505/forgiving-men-accused-of-sexual-assault.
11. Anne Theriault, "What Women Want from Jian Ghomeshi," *Flare*, September 14, 2018, https://www.flare.com/news/ghomeshi-essay.
12. Scrimshaw Jen (@ScrimshawsFire), "Forgiveness is completely overrated and just serves to create power imbalances. 'I forgive you' = 'I am morally superior to you' however you look at it," Twitter, May 29, 2021, 10:40 a.m., https://twitter.com/ScrimshawsFire/status/1398695723567353856.
13. Jesse Dizard (@Tr4shdr4g0n), "It is a function of what Nietzsche called the slave morality of modern bourgeois society," Twitter, May 31, 2021, 7:45 p.m., https://twitter.com/Tr4shdr4g0n/status/1399512374911004672.
14. This is Nussbaum's summary of Nietzsche's position. See Martha C. Nussbaum, *Anger and Forgiveness: Resentment, Generosity, Justice* (Oxford: Oxford University Press, 2016), 73–74.
15. Nussbaum, *Anger and Forgiveness*, 10.

16. Nussbaum, *Anger and Forgiveness*, 11. Italics are mine.

17. Nussbaum, *Anger and Forgiveness*, 10. See Nussbaum's chapter 3 ("Forgiveness: A Genealogy") for a full critique of transactional forgiveness, which she mistakes for Christian forgiveness.

18. Malcolm Gladwell, *David and Goliath: Underdogs, Misfits, and the Art of Battling Giants* (New York: Little, Brown, 2013), 248–50.

19. Wilma Derksen, The Forgiveness Project, undated, www.theforgivenessproject .com/stories/wilma-derksen.

20. Derksen, The Forgiveness Project.

21. This account is given in Robert Enright, "Two Weaknesses of Forgiving: It Victimizes and Stops Justice," *Psychology Today*, August 10, 2017, www.psychology today.com/us/blog/the-forgiving-life/201708/two-weaknesses-forgiving-it-victi mizes-and-stops-justice.

22. Amanda Borschel-Dan, "Holocaust Survivor Preaches Forgiveness of Nazis as 'Ultimate Revenge,'" *Times of Israel*, December 8, 2016, www.timesofisrael.com /holocaust-survivor-preaches-forgiveness-of-nazis-as-ultimate-revenge.

23. "María Gabriela De Faría on Growth, Empowerment, and Positive Change," *Global Heroes*, February 11, 2021, www.globalheroes.com/maria-gabriela-de-faria -empowerment.

24. Rebecca Manley Pippert, *Hope Has Its Reasons: From the Search for Self to the Surprise of Faith* (New York: Harper & Row, 1989), 113–14.

25. L. Gregory Jones, *Embodying Forgiveness: A Theological Analysis* (Grand Rapids, MI: Eerdmans, 1995), 37.

26. Jones, *Embodying Forgiveness*, 64.

27. Jones, *Embodying Forgiveness*, 65.

28. Bradley Campbell and Jason Manning, "Microaggression and Moral Cultures," *Comparative Sociology* 13 (2014): 692–726; Bradley Campbell and Jason Manning, *The Rise of Victimhood Culture: Microaggressions, Safe Spaces, and the New Culture Wars* (Cham, Switzerland: Palgrave MacMillan, 2018).

29. The intellectual and social roots of this new shame-and-honor/cancel culture are many. Good arguments can be made that social media inherently moves us toward it. But more interestingly, many contend that Herbert Marcuse and other twentieth-century neo-Marxist thinkers wedded the therapeutic insights of Freud with the Marxist reduction of culture to the exercise of power.

30. Andrew Sullivan, "Is Intersectionality a Religion?," *New York*, March 10, 2017; John McWhorter, "Antiracism, Our Flawed New Religion," *Daily Beast*, July 27, 2015; Michael Lind, "The Revenge of the Yankees: How Social Gospel Became Social Justice," *Tablet*, November 14, 2020; Joshua Mitchell, *American Awakening: Identity Politics and Other Afflictions of Our Time* (New York: Encounter Books, 2020); Eric Kaufmann, "Liberal Fundamentalism: A Sociology of Wokeness," *American Affairs* 4, no. 4 (Winter 2020): 188–208; Antonia Senior, "Identity Politics Is Christianity without Redemption," *UnHerd*, January 20, 2020; Jonathan

Haidt, "Why Universities Must Choose One Telos: Truth or Social Justice" (lecture, Duke University, Durham, NC, October 6, 2016), available at https://hetero doxacademy.org/blog/one-telos-truth-or-social-justice-2.

31. Sullivan, "Is Intersectionality a Religion?"

32. See Émile Durkheim, *The Division of Labor in Society* (New York: Free Press, 2014).

33. See Émile Durkheim, *Selected Writings*, ed. Anthony Giddens (Cambridge, UK: Cambridge University Press, 1972); Christian Smith, *Religion: What It Is, How It Works, and Why It Matters* (Princeton, NJ: Princeton, 2017); Émile Durkheim, *The Elementary Forms of Religion* (Oxford, UK: Oxford University Press, 2008); Steven Lukes, *Moral Relativism* (New York: Picador, 2008); Jonathan Haidt, *The Righteous Mind: Why Good People Are Divided by Religion and Politics* (New York: Pantheon, 2012). Durkheim did believe that the transition to a secular grounding for moral values would be possible though difficult. Alan Jacobs thinks if Durkheim were alive today, he would be concerned that maybe the transition was going to be harder than he thought. See Alan Jacobs, "The Paradoxical Relevance of Durkheim to Our Time," *Hedgehog Review*, December 15, 2020, https://hedgehogre view.com/blog/thr/posts/the-paradoxical-relevance-of-durkheim-to-our-time.

34. Tom Holland, *Dominion: How the Christian Revolution Remade the World* (New York: Basic Books, 2019).

35. Ayjay (Alan Jacobs), "Vengeance," *Snakes and Ladders* (blog), June 26, 2017, https:// blog.ayjay.org/vengeance.

36. "Pennsylvania: The Revolt of Leo Held," *Time*, November 3, 1967, http://content .time.com/time/subscriber/article/0,33009,837437,00.html.

37. D. A. Carson, *Love in Hard Places* (Wheaton, IL: Crossway Books, 2002), 72.

38. Seamus Martin, "Atrocities by Former 'Good Guys' Seen as 'Understandable' Desire for Revenge," *Irish Times*, August 7, 1999, www.irishtimes.com/news/atrocities -by-former-good-guys-seen-as-understandable-desire-for-revenge-1.214374.

39. William Makepeace Thackeray, *Vanity Fair: A Novel without a Hero* (London: Bradbury and Evans, 1853), 8.

40. Hannah Arendt, *The Human Condition* (Chicago: University of Chicago Press, 1958), 237.

41. Martin Luther King Jr., *A Gift of Love: Sermons from "Strength to Love" and Other Preachings* (Boston: Beacon Press, 1963), 45–46.

42. Donald B. Kraybill, Steven M. Nolt, and David L. Weaver-Zercher, *Amish Grace: How Forgiveness Transcended Tragedy* (San Francisco: Jossey-Bass, 2010).

43. Kraybill, Nolt, and Weaver-Zercher, *Amish Grace*, 176–77.

44. Kraybill, Nolt, and Weaver-Zercher, *Amish Grace*, 181.

45. See article XIV of the Dordrecht Confession at https://gameo.org/index.php?title =Dordrecht_Confession_of_Faith_(Mennonite,_1632).

46. Readers will detect here—or already know, of course—that the Anabaptists were pacifists. Critics of the position can question whether taking up arms to defend

one's country against invaders and enslavement is a form of revenge and retaliation. But all Christians will agree with the substance of this admirable paragraph.

CHAPTER 3: THE HISTORY OF FORGIVENESS

1. Carrie Fisher, *The Best Awful: A Novel* (New York: Simon & Schuster, 2005), 30. While it does appear in Fisher's novel, there's no consensus on who was the original author of the quote.
2. Hannah Arendt, *The Human Condition* (Chicago: University of Chicago Press, 1958), 238.
3. David Konstan, *Before Forgiveness: The Origin of a Moral Idea* (Cambridge: Cambridge University Press, 2012), ix. While Konstan agrees that ancient cultures had little concept of (or appreciation for) forgiveness, he argues that our current understanding of forgiveness owes more to Kant than to the Bible or Christianity. I find this thesis quite unconvincing. Not only do I find his analysis of the biblical material spotty, showing little close reading of passages such as Matthew 18, but he overlooks how much Christianity informed Kant's views.
4. Charles L. Griswold, *Forgiveness: A Philosophical Exploration* (Cambridge: Cambridge University Press, 2007), 2. Griswold says that the "conceptual framework" his book assumes is "secular."
5. Herman Bavinck, *Reformed Dogmatics*, vol. 4, *Holy Spirit, Church, and New Creation*, ed. John Bolt, trans. John Vriend (Grand Rapids, MI: Baker, 2008), 179.
6. Homer, *The Iliad*, trans R. Lattimore (Chicago: University of Chicago Press, 1961), 399.
7. Another example: in Euripides's *Iphigenia in Tauris*, Electra asks the goddess Artemis for *sungnome* by reminding her of her own love for her brother Apollo, but again, this is a request not for acquittal but for leniency. Griswold, *Forgiveness*, 4.
8. Aristotle, *Nicomachean Ethics* 1110a24–26, cited in Griswold, *Forgiveness*, 4.
9. Griswold, *Forgiveness*, 4n5.
10. Griswold, *Forgiveness*, 8.
11. Griswold, *Forgiveness*, 14.
12. Griswold, *Forgiveness*, 9. See also Nicholas Wolterstorff, *Justice in Love* (Grand Rapids, MI: Eerdmans, 2015), 184.
13. Kenneth J. Dover, quoted in David J. Leigh, "Forgiveness, Pity, and Ultimacy in Ancient Greek Culture," *Ultimate Reality and Meaning* 27, no. 2 (June 2004): 152–61, https://utpjournals.press/doi/pdf/10.3138/uram.27.2.152.
14. Griswold, *Forgiveness*, 10–14.
15. Griswold, *Forgiveness*, 15.
16. See Larry W. Hurtado, *Why on Earth Did Anyone Become a Christian in the First Three Centuries?* (Milwaukee: Marquette University Press, 2016).
17. Kenneth Scott Latourette, *A History of the Expansion of Christianity*, vol. 1 (San Francisco: HarperOne, 1975), 167.

18. Cited and discussed in Alan Kreider, *The Patient Ferment of the Early Church: The Improbable Rise of Christianity in the Roman Empire* (Grand Rapids, MI: Eerdmans, 2016), 28.
19. Kreider, *Patient Ferment*, 29.
20. Kreider, *Patient Ferment*, 29.
21. C. John Sommerville, *The Decline of the Secular University* (Oxford: Oxford University, 2006), 69.
22. Sommerville, *Decline of the Secular University*, 69.
23. Sommerville, *Decline of the Secular University*, 69.
24. Sommerville, *Decline of the Secular University*, 70.
25. Sommerville, *Decline of the Secular University*, 70.
26. See Kwame Anthony Appiah, *The Honor Code: How Moral Revolutions Happen* (New York: W. W. Norton, 2010).
27. Arendt, *Human Condition*, 214–15.
28. Wolterstorff, *Justice in Love*, 185.
29. Derek Kidner, *The Message of Ecclesiastes: A Time to Mourn, a Time to Dance* (Downers Grove, IL: InterVarsity Press, 1991), 39.
30. Ian Power, "Why Does This Mozart Piece Make Me Cry Even Though It's Stupid and Probably Evil?," *Medium* (blog), January 11, 2019, https://medium.com/@ian poweromg/why-does-this-mozart-piece-make-me-cry-even-though-its-stupid-and -probably-evil-80c63c60fc7f.
31. *Amadeus* (1984), directed by Miloš Forman, adapted from a play by Peter Shaffer.
32. Phillip Gorski, "Where Do Morals Come From?," *Public Books*, February 15, 2016, www.publicbooks.org/where-do-morals-come-from.
33. Leonard Bernstein, *The Joy of Music* (Pompton Plains, NJ: Amadeus Press, 2004), 29.

    L.B. (Leonard Bernstein)—Beethoven broke all the rules, and turned out pieces of breath-taking rightness. Rightness—that's the word! When you get the feeling that whatever note succeeds the last is the only possible note that can rightly happen at that instant, in that context, then chances are you're listening to Beethoven. Melodies, fugues, rhythms—leave them to the Tchaikovskys and Hindemiths and Ravels. Our boy has the real goods, the stuff from Heaven, the power to make you feel at the finish: Something is right in the world. There is something that checks throughout, that follows its own law consistently: something we can trust, that will never let us down.

    L.P. (Lyric Poet)—(Quietly) But that is almost a definition of God.

    L.B.—I meant it to be.

CHAPTER 4: THE BOOK OF FORGIVENESS

1. Ashraf H. A. Rushdy, *After Injury: A Historical Anatomy of Forgiveness, Resentment, and Apology* (Oxford: Oxford University Press, 2018), 31.
2. Cited in Rushdy, *After Injury*, 31.

3. Augustine, *The City of God* 13.12, cited in Derek Kidner, *Genesis: An Introduction and Commentary* (Downers Grove, IL: Inter-Varsity Press, 1972), 69.
4. Kidner, *Genesis*, 76.
5. Kidner, *Genesis*, 76.
6. Kidner, *Genesis*, 86.
7. Derek Kidner, *Psalms 73–150* (London: InterVarsity Press, 1973), 446.
8. Kidner, *Psalms 73–150*, 446.
9. Possidius, *Life of Augustine* 31.2, trans. H. T. Weiskotten, M. M. Muller, and R. Deferrari, in Early Christian Biographies (Washington, D.C.: Catholic University of America Press, 1952), 67–124.
10. Rudolf Bultmann, "Ἀφίημι, Ἄφεσις, Παρίημι, Πάρεσις," in *Theological Dictionary of the New Testament*, ed. Gerhard Kittel, Geoffrey W. Bromiley, and Gerhard Friedrich (Grand Rapids, MI: Eerdmans, 1964), 509.
11. Two other words are *apolyo*, "to release," used in Luke 6:37, and *paresis*, "to pass over," used in Romans 3:25.
12. We do not have time to discuss two aspects of the gospels' teaching on forgiveness that are often seen as problems. Leon Morris briefly addresses them: "Two difficulties must be mentioned. One is that of the sin against the Holy Spirit which can never be forgiven (Mt. 12:31f.; Mk. 3:28f.; Lk. 12:10; cf. 1 Jn. 5:16). This sin is never defined. But in the light of NT teaching generally it is impossible to think of it as any specific act of sin. The reference is rather to the continuing blasphemy against the Spirit of God by one who consistently rejects God's gracious call. This is blasphemy indeed." In other words, the sin against the Holy Spirit is the rejection of Jesus Christ as Savior. Since it is faith in Christ alone that brings forgiveness for all sin, rejecting Christ is the one and only sin that cuts you off from all forgiveness, including for the sin of rejecting Christ. "The [second difficulty] is Jn. 20:23, 'If you forgive the sins of any, they are forgiven.' It is more than difficult to think of Christ as leaving in men's hands the determination of whether the sins of other men are to be forgiven or not. The important points are the plural ('any' is plural in the Gk.; it points to categories, not individuals), and the perfect tense rendered 'are forgiven' (it means 'have been forgiven', not 'will be forgiven'). The meaning of the passage then seems to be that as they are inspired by the Holy Spirit (v. 22) the followers of Jesus will be able to say with accuracy which categories of men have sins forgiven, and which not." In other words, when Jesus gives disciples the ability to forgive sins, it means he gives them the gospel, which explains to people how they can receive forgiveness. That means they can declare who has received forgiveness (those who have rested in Christ's salvation through sincere faith) and who has not. These quotes are from L. L. Morris, "Forgiveness," in *New Bible Dictionary*, ed. D.R.W. Wood et al. (Leicester, UK, and Downers Grove, IL: InterVarsity Press, 1996), 382.
13. See note 4 of chapter 5 for a discussion of the "simplicity" of God—the doctrine that there cannot be a true tension or contradiction between any of the attributes of God.

14. C. S. Lewis, "On Forgiveness," in *The Weight of Glory and Other Addresses* (New York: Touchstone, 1980), 133.
15. Lewis, "On Forgiveness," 134–35.
16. Lewis, "On Forgiveness," 135–36. The italics are mine.

CHAPTER 5: THE GOD OF LOVE AND FURY

1. Herman Bavinck, *Reformed Dogmatics*, vol. 2, *God and Creation*, ed. John Bolt, trans. John Vriend (Grand Rapids, MI: Baker, 2004), 219.
2. Herman Bavinck, *Reformed Dogmatics*, vol. 4, *Holy Spirit, Church, and New Creation*, ed. John Bolt, trans. John Vriend (Grand Rapids, MI: Baker, 2008), 179–80.
3. L. L. Morris, "Forgiveness," *New Bible Dictionary*, ed. D.R.W. Wood et al. (Leicester, UK, and Downers Grove, IL: InterVarsity Press, 1996), 381.
4. This is part of the doctrine of the "simplicity" of God. The simplicity of God means that all his attributes are identical with his one essence. God's love and justice cannot ever be ultimately opposed to each other because they are merely different facets of his essential being. The righteous wrath of God upon the sin destroying us is an expression of his love, and his love is an expression of his righteousness. The cross, then, is not something that "resolves a contradiction" between God's love and justice. Rather it is an expression in real time of how God's love and justice cohere. For more on the simplicity of God, see Herman Bavinck's *Reformed Dogmatics*, volume 2. "The oneness of God does not only consist in a unity of singularity, however, but also in a unity of simplicity. The fact of the matter is that Scripture, to denote the fullness of the life of God, uses not only adjectives but also substantives: it tells us not only that God is truthful, righteous, living, illuminating, loving, and wise, but also that he is the truth, righteousness, life, light, love, and wisdom (Jer. 10:10; 23:6; John 1:4–5, 9; 14:6; 1 Cor. 1:30; 1 John 1:5; 4:8). Hence, on account of its absolute perfection, every attribute of God is identical with his essence. Theology later taught this doctrine of Scripture under the term 'the simplicity of God.'" Bavinck, *Reformed Dogmatics*, vol. 2, 173–77.
5. C. S. Lewis, *The Abolition of Man* (New York: HarperOne, 2015), 27.
6. Bavinck, *Reformed Dogmatics*, vol. 4, 179–80.
7. Bavinck, *Reformed Dogmatics*, vol. 4, 179–80.
8. Annie Dillard, *Pilgrim at Tinker Creek* (New York: HarperCollins, 1974).
9. Rebecca Manley Pippert, *Hope Has Its Reasons*, rev. ed. (Downers Grove, IL: IVP Books, 2001), 101. See chapter 4, "What Kind of God Gets Angry?"
10. This phrase is my own translation.
11. See the brief but helpful biographical essay on Bonar by Sinclair Ferguson at www.desiringgod.org/articles/his-hymns-make-souls-feel-whole.
12. Horatius Bonar, *The Everlasting Righteousness* (1874; repr. Edinburgh: Banner of Truth Trust, 1993), 3–4.

13. John R. W. Stott, *The Cross of Christ* (Downers Grove, IL: InterVarsity Press, 1986), 160.
14. Bonar, *Everlasting Righteousness*, 4.
15. Quoted by J. I. Packer, "Sacrifice and Satisfaction" in *Our Savior God: Studies on Man, Christ, and the Atonement*, ed. James M. Boice (Grand Rapids, MI: Baker, 1980), 137.
16. Bonar, *Everlasting Righteousness*, 12.
17. William Cowper, "Love Constraining to Obedience," in *The New Oxford Book of Christian Verse*, ed. Davie Donald (Oxford: Oxford University Press, 1981), 195–96.

CHAPTER 6: JUSTICE AND LOVE, HONOR AND ABUSE

1. William Shakespeare, *The Merchant of Venice*, act 4, scene 1.
2. Robert Yarborough, "Forgiveness and Reconciliation," in *New Dictionary of Biblical Theology*, ed. T. Desmond et al. (Downers Grove, IL: InterVarsity Press, 2000), 500.
3. R. K. Harrison, *Leviticus: An Introduction and Commentary*, vol. 3, Tyndale Old Testament Commentaries (Downers Grove, IL: InterVarsity Press, 1980), 202. "This so-called 'golden rule' was quoted by Christ (Matt. 19:19; 22:39; Mark 12:31; Luke 10:27, etc.) as an ideal of altruistic behavior in society. The sentiment underlying this aphorism was unique in the ancient world, and represents one of the Old Testament's most outstanding moral precepts."
4. See especially Jay Sklar, *Leviticus: An Introduction and Commentary*, ed. David G. Firth, vol. 3, Tyndale Old Testament Commentaries (Nottingham, UK: Inter-Varsity Press, 2013), 246–47.
5. For the Old Testament teaching on how to receive a rebuke properly, see Psalm 141:5 and Proverbs 9:7–8 and 15:12.
6. Henri Nouwen, *The Road to Daybreak* (New York: Doubleday, 1990), 68.
7. Rachael Denhollander, *What Is a Girl Worth?* (Carol Stream, IL: Tyndale, 2019), 140.
8. Denhollander, *What Is a Girl Worth?*, 140–41.
9. Makonagasawa, "Atonement in Scripture: Why Penal Substitution is a Gateway Drug to Right-Wing Extremism," Anástasis Center for Christian Education & Ministry, February 22, 2016, https://newhumanityinstitute.wordpress.com/2016/02/22/atonement-in-scripture-why-penal-substitution-is-a-gateway-drug-to-right-wing-extremism/#_ftnref10.
10. Steve Chalke and Alan Mann, *The Lost Message of Jesus* (Grand Rapids, MI: Zondervan, 2004), 182–83.
11. The website for the podcast is www.christianitytoday.com/ct/podcasts/rise-and-fall-of-mars-hill.
12. Rick Pidcock, "I Lived in the Culture of 'The Rise and Fall of Mars Hill' and There's One Part of the Story That's Wrong," *Baptist News Global*, August 24, 2021,

https://baptistnews.com/article/i-lived-in-the-culture-of-the-rise-and-fall-of
-mars-hill-and-theres-one-part-of-the-story-thats-wrong/#.YdDAcxPMJhF.

13. Denhollander, *What Is a Girl Worth?*, 99.
14. Denhollander, *What Is a Girl Worth?*, 100–101.
15. Denhollander, *What Is a Girl Worth?*, 103.
16. Jacob and Rachael Denhollander, "Justice: The Foundation of a Christian Approach to Abuse" (paper presented at the 70th Annual Meeting of the Evangelical Theological Society, Denver, CO, November 13, 2018), www.fathommag.com/stories/justice-the-foundation-of-a-christian-approach-to-abuse. This important paper is addressed to the evangelical Protestant community, but it is just as relevant to other branches of the Christian church, notably the Roman Catholic, where there have also been decades of sexual abuse and cover-up.
17. Fleming Rutledge, *The Crucifixion: Understanding the Death of Jesus Christ* (Grand Rapids, MI: Eerdmans, 2017), 129.
18. Denhollander, "Justice."
19. Miroslav Volf, *Free of Charge: Giving and Forgiving in a Culture Stripped of Grace* (Grand Rapids, MI: Zondervan, 2005), 145.
20. John R. W. Stott, *The Cross of Christ* (Downers Grove, IL: InterVarsity Press, 1986), 133.
21. Denhollander, "Justice." Italics are mine.
22. Denhollander, "Justice."
23. The subject of abuse is an enormously important and contested one. See appendix B.
24. Denhollander, "Justice."
25. Denhollander, "Justice."
26. Denhollander, "Justice."
27. Denhollander, *What Is a Girl Worth?*, 310.
28. Mez McConnell, *The Creaking on the Stairs: Finding Faith in God through Childhood Abuse* (Fearn, Ross-shire, UK: Christian Focus Publications, 2019).
29. Mez McConnell, "The Rock-Solid Hope of Penal Substitutionary Atonement (Part 3)," 20 Schemes Equip, October 8, 2020, https://20schemesequip.com/rock-solid-hope-penal-substitutionary-atonement.

CHAPTER 7: THE BASICS OF FORGIVENESS

1. Fyodor Dostoyevsky, *The Brothers Karamazov*, trans. Constance Garnett (Theophania Press, 2011), 270.
2. Robert H. Gundry, *Mark: A Commentary on His Apology for the Cross*, vol. 2 (Grand Rapids, MI: Eerdmans, 1993), 649.
3. Craig A. Evans, *Mark 8:27–16:20*, vol. 34B, Word Biblical Commentary (Dallas: Word, 2001), 193. "One misses the nature of the reciprocity in all these passages if God's forgiveness is somehow seen as caused or earned by one's forgiving of others. As the parable of the Unforgiving Servant in Matt 18:21–35 illustrates, one's own

forgiving of others must grow out of one's being forgiven. Therefore, to be forgiven and not forgiving, to have obtained mercy and not be merciful, is in reality to have failed to experience God's gracious acceptance and makes a mockery out of prayer as understood in vv 22–24 as an expression of one's relationship to God."

4. James R. Edwards, *The Gospel According to Luke*, The Pillar New Testament Commentary, ed. D. A. Carson (Grand Rapids, MI, Cambridge, and Nottingham, UK: Wm. B. Eerdmans and Apollos, 2015), 478.

5. Church of England, Articles of Religion, www.churchofengland.org/prayer-and-worship/worship-texts-and-resources/book-common-prayer/articles-religion#XX.

6. D. A. Carson, *Love in Hard Places* (Wheaton, IL: Crossway Books, 2002), 81.

7. I am here borrowing terms from two writers who make the same formulation of two aspects of forgiveness, David Powlison, *Good and Angry: Redeeming Anger, Irritation, Complaining, and Bitterness* (Greensboro, NC: New Growth Press, 2016), 84–87, and Carson, *Love in Hard Places*, 82.

8. Carson, *Love in Hard Places*, 85.

9. Johann Christoph Arnold, *Why Forgive?* (Walden, NY: Plough, 2010), 183–84.

10. Arnold, *Why Forgive?*, 185.

11. Powlison, *Good and Angry*, 86.

12. D. A. Carson, "Matthew," in *The Expositor's Bible Commentary*, vol. 8, ed. Frank E. Gaebelein (Grand Rapids, MI: Zondervan, 1995), 155–57.

13. John R. W. Stott, *Christian Counter-culture: The Message of the Sermon on the Mount* (Leicester, UK, and Downers Grove, IL: InterVarsity Press, 1978), 105.

14. R. T. France, *The Gospel of Matthew*, The New International Commentary on the New Testament (Grand Rapids, MI: Wm. B. Eerdmans, 2007), 221.

15. "As this legal principle is overtaken by that toward which it points, so also is this hardness of heart. The OT prophets foretold a time when there would be a change of heart among God's people, living under a new covenant (Jer 31:31–34; 32:37–41; Ezek 36:26). Not only would the sins of the people be forgiven (Jer 31:34; Ezek 36:25), but obedience to God would spring from the heart (Jer 31:33; Ezek 36:27) as the eschatological age dawned. Thus Jesus' instruction on these matters is grounded in eschatology. In Jesus and the kingdom, fulfillment (even if partial) of the OT promises, the eschatological age that the Law and Prophets had prophesied (Mt 11:13) arrives; and the prophecies that curbed evil while pointing forward to the eschaton are now superseded by the new age and the new hearts it brings (cf. Piper, pp. 89–91)." Carson, *Matthew*, 156.

16. D. Martyn Lloyd-Jones, *Studies in the Sermon on the Mount*, vol. 1 (Grand Rapids, MI: Eerdmans, 1969), 279.

17. France, *Gospel of Matthew*, 223.

18. France, *Gospel of Matthew*, 224.

19. France, *Gospel of Matthew*, 224.

20. Skinner died in 1994 of leukemia. "Tom Skinner, 52, Minister and Trainer," *The New York Times*, June 26, 1994, www.nytimes.com/1994/06/26/obituaries/tom-skinner

-52-minister-and-trainer.html#:~:text=Tom%20Skinner%2C%20the%20son
%20of,before%20that%20in%20midtown%20Manhattan.

21. Tom Skinner, *Black and Free* (Grand Rapids, MI: Zondervan, 1970), 88.

22. Skinner, *Black and Free*, 89.

CHAPTER 8: OUR NEED FOR FORGIVENESS

1. Wilfred M. McClay, "The Strange Persistence of Guilt," *Hedgehog Review* 19, no. 1 (Spring 2017).

2. Over the past twenty years, it has become routine to say that guilt is feeling bad about what you've done and shame is feeling bad about who you are. This idea, while popular, is contested. A better and more justifiable distinction is one that sees guilt as more individual and shame as corporate. That is, when I do wrong, I feel guilt and a sense that I need to be punished. But wrongdoing can also bring shame on my family, my people, and that is an additional burden. Non-Western people are more likely to interpret their wrongdoing as bringing shame on their community. For our purposes, I will talk about shame and guilt as virtually the same thing—a sense that we have failed and deserve punishment.

3. McClay, "Strange Persistence of Guilt."

4. McClay, "Strange Persistence of Guilt."

5. McClay, "Strange Persistence of Guilt."

6. John Updike, foreword to *Franz Kafka: The Complete Stories* (New York: Schocken, 1995), xx.

7. Some readers will notice a similarity between "fig leaves" and "idols"—things that play the role of pseudogods in our lives. It is true that they are essentially the same thing, but to call them fig leaves here helps us see the particular way they help us control how others see us and even how we see ourselves. For more on the spiritual phenomenon of idolatry, see my *Counterfeit Gods: The Empty Promises of Money, Sex, and Power and the Only Hope That Matters* (New York: Penguin, 2011).

8. Derek Kidner, *Genesis: An Introduction and Commentary* (Downers Grove, IL: Inter-Varsity Press, 1972), 199.

CHAPTER 9: RECEIVING GOD'S FORGIVENESS

1. Charles Wesley, "And Can It Be?" (hymn, 1739). This hymn recounts its author's conversion.

2. For a mainstream example of an internal/horizontal-only approach to self-forgiveness, see Keir Brady, "7 Tips For Practicing Self-Forgiveness," Keir Brady Counseling Services, undated, www.keirbradycounseling.com/self-forgiveness.

3. Gail Sheehy, *Passages: Predictable Crises of Adult Life* (New York: E. P. Dutton, 1976).

4. Colin Tipping, *Radical Self-Forgiveness: The Direct Path to True Self-Acceptance* (Boulder, CO: Sounds True, 2011), 133. "I am a spiritual being having a human experience. . . . What happens during my life are my lessons. I have come into the life experience with the desire to fully grasp what oneness is by experiencing the opposite of it—separation. I had made agreements with souls prior to my incarnation that they would do things not so much *to me*, though it will feel that way while I am in a body, but *for* me. I also enroll others while I'm here to give me opportunities to learn. . . . While I remain accountable for what I do in the human world, in purely spiritual terms nothing wrong ever happens."

5. Darrell L. Bock, *Luke 9:51–24:53*, Baker Exegetical Commentary on the New Testament (Grand Rapids, MI: Baker, 1996), 1118–19.

6. Throughout church history pastoral caregivers have identified the spiritual problem of the "overscrupulous conscience." See, for example, Charles Hodge, "Diseased Conscience," in *Princeton Sermons* (1879; repr., Edinburgh: Banner of Truth, 2011), 122; William Bridge, "A Lifting Up in the Case of Lack of Assurance," in *A Lifting Up of the Downcast* (1649; repr., Edinburgh: Banner of Truth, 1961), 128–51; Thomas Brooks, "Precious Remedies against Satan's Devices" (1652), in *The Works of Thomas Brooks*, vol. 1 (Edinburgh: Banner of Truth, 1980), 91–117.

7. Brooks, *Works of Thomas Brooks*, vol. 1, 16.

8. *Broadchurch*, episode 6, directed by James Strong, written by Chris Chibnall, aired April 8, 2013 on BBC.

9. Richard Sibbes, *The Bruised Reed* (1630; repr., Edinburgh: Banner of Truth, 1998), 12.

10. Stephen Charnock, *The Works of Stephen Charnock*, vol. 4, *The Knowledge of God* (Edinburgh: Banner of Truth, 1985), 199.

11. John Newton, "Let.11 to Rev.Mr.S," in *Works of John Newton*, vol. 6 (Edinburgh: Banner of Truth, 1985), 185–86.

12. All three of these acts of repentance are found in Psalm 51 as well, but for the sake of clarity and brevity we will look at them only through studying Proverbs 28:13.

13. Johann Christoph Arnold, *Why Forgive?* (Walden, NY: Plough, 2010), 175–76.

14. From C. John Miller, "Completely Forgiven," self-published pamphlet, 1987, 10.

15. Bruce K. Waltke, *The Book of Proverbs, Chapters 15–31*, The New International Commentary on the Old Testament (Grand Rapids, MI: Wm. B. Eerdmans, 2005), 417–18.

16. William Cowper, "Sometimes a Light Surprises," *Olney Hymns* (1779).

17. Stuart K. Hine, "How Great Thou Art" (1949).

18. Charles Hodge, *Princeton Sermons* (1879; repr., Edinburgh: Banner of Truth, 2011), 48–49.

19. Thomas R. Schreiner, "Luke," in *ESV Expository Commentary*, vol. 8, ed. I. Duguid, J. M. Hamilton, and J. Sklar (Wheaton, IL: Crossway, 2021), 838.

20. There has been much discussion over whether God's dealing with David was just.

David had wronged both Uriah and Bathsheba and had broken the laws of God, the covenant that was the basis for his kingship. Should there be no just penalty for his actions? The Bible shows us that there was. Unlike Saul, who did not truly repent, David did. And so God allowed him to remain king. But the death of David's son was a direct execution of God's justice on David for his wrongdoing. Here, then, we see again God as both forgiving and just.

21. This paragraph summarizes Billy Graham's account in *Just As I Am: The Autobiography of Billy Graham* (New York: HarperCollins, 1997), 254–59.

22. Dick Lucas, "Romans 3:9–31," sermon, January 6, 1970, St Helen's Bishopsgate, https://www.st-helens.org.uk/resources/talk/3027.

CHAPTER 10: GRANTING OUR FORGIVENESS

1. Charlotte Brontë, *Jane Eyre* (1847; repr., Vancouver: Engage Books, 2020), 386.

2. Lewis Smedes, *Love within Limits: Realizing Selfless Love in a Selfish World* (Grand Rapids, MI: Eerdmans, 1978), 75.

3. Miroslav Volf, *Exclusion and Embrace* (Nashville: Abingdon, 1996), 124.

4. Rudolf Bultmann, "Ἀφίημι, Ἄφεσις, Παρίημι, Πάρεσις," in *Theological Dictionary of the New Testament*, ed. Gerhard Kittel, Geoffrey W. Bromiley, and Gerhard Friedrich (Grand Rapids, MI: Eerdmans, 1964), 509.

5. Dan Hamilton, *Forgiveness* (Madison, WI: Inter-Varsity Christian Fellowship, 1980), 10.

6. Hamilton, *Forgiveness*, 10.

7. Hamilton, *Forgiveness*, 11–13.

8. Brontë, *Jane Eyre*, 386.

9. It may be helpful to observe that sometimes the perpetrator's wrong was less deliberate or even essentially accidental. Forgiveness—and repentance—is still necessary if harm was done, even if the sin was a matter of thoughtless behavior or even just inattentiveness.

10. Doris Kearns Goodwin, *Team of Rivals: The Political Genius of Abraham Lincoln* (New York: Simon & Schuster, 2005), 679–80, cited in David Powlison, *Good and Angry: Redeeming Anger, Irritation, Complaining, and Bitterness* (Greensboro, NC: New Growth Press, 2016), 93.

11. Corrie ten Boom with John and Elizabeth Sherrill, *The Hiding Place* (Grand Rapids, MI: Baker, 2006).

12. Corrie ten Boom, "Guideposts Classics: Corrie ten Boom on Forgiveness," Guideposts, undated, www.guideposts.org/better-living/positive-living/guideposts-classics-corrie-ten-boom-forgiveness.

13. Ten Boom, "Guideposts Classics."

14. Joel B. Green, *The Gospel of Luke* (Grand Rapids, MI: Eerdmans, 1997), 613.

15. Green, *Gospel of Luke*, 624.

CHAPTER 11: EXTENDING FORGIVENESS

1. *Ted Lasso*, season 1, episode 9, "All Apologies," directed by M. J. Delaney, written by Jason Sudeikis, Bill Lawrence, Brendan Hunt, first aired on September 25, 2020, on Apple TV.

2. The Greek word usually translated in English Bibles as "deeply moved" means to bellow or snort with anger. Jesus was filled with rage. See the discussion by D. A. Carson, *The Gospel According to John* (Grand Rapids, MI: Eerdmans, 1990), 415–16.

3. D. A. Carson, "Matthew," in *The Expositor's Bible Commentary*, vol. 8, ed. Frank E. Gaebelein (Grand Rapids, MI: Zondervan, 1995), 150.

4. R. T. France, *The Gospel of Matthew*, The New International Commentary on the New Testament (Grand Rapids, MI: Wm. B. Eerdmans, 2007), 692.

5. France, *Gospel of Matthew*, 692.

6. France, *Gospel of Matthew*, 693.

7. Michael Green, *Matthew: The Bible Speaks Today* (London: Hodder and Stoughton, 1988), 174.

8. Green, *Matthew*, 174. It must be added that Green's counsel that we not "always do things behind closed doors" is especially crucial when there has been abuse or assault and the civil law is broken. In such cases the sin must not only be taken to the church but to the civil authorities.

9. It should be remembered that a particularly divisive and very hostile person may need to be subject to greater distancing. See 2 Thessalonians 3:14. As just noted in the previous endnote, when the civil law is being broken, the church should report the perpetrator to courts and police.

10. On the topic of how this text relates to formal church discipline, see Edmund Clowney, "The Marks of the Church," in *The Church: Contours of Christian Theology* (Downers Grove, IL: InterVarsity Press, 1995), 99–115; Daniel E. Wray, *Biblical Church Discipline* (Edinburgh: Banner of Truth, 1978); Jay E. Adams, *Handbook of Church Discipline* (Grand Rapids, MI: Zondervan, 1986); D. A. Carson, *Love in Hard Places* (Wheaton, IL: Crossway Books, 2002).

11. Many people are puzzled or troubled by the exhortation to "pour burning coals on their heads." Most commentators and scholars admit that there is no consensus on the meaning of the metaphor. Some think it means that being kind to your enemies will be tormenting to them emotionally or might increase their judgment from God. The problem with this idea is that it does not fit the context at all—everything else in the passage is against harming or retaliation. Most modern commentators think it means that meeting evil with good is far more likely to prick the conscience and bring a conviction of sin and repentance than retaliation will. See Douglas Moo, *The Epistle to the Romans*, New International Commentary, 1st edition (Grand Rapids, MI: Eerdmans, 1996), 788–89.

12. Barry Bearak, "Forgiving Her Family's Killers, but Not Their Sins," *The New York Times*, September 3, 1999.

13. D. Martyn Lloyd-Jones, *Romans: Exposition of Chapter 12—Christian Conduct* (Edinburgh: Banner of Truth, 2000), 489.
14. Lloyd-Jones, *Romans*, 489.
15. Lloyd-Jones, *Romans*.

EPILOGUE

1. Aljean Harmetz, "How Endings Have Affected Two Recent Movies," *The New York Times*, October 8, 1984.

APPENDIX B: BIBLICAL TEXTS ON GOD'S FORGIVENESS

1. All these verses are quoted from the English Standard Version translation of the Bible.

APPENDIX C: FORGIVENESS PRACTICES

1. D. A. Carson, *Love in Hard Places* (Wheaton, IL: Crossway Books, 2002), 83.

APPENDIX D: RECONCILIATION PRACTICES

1. Derek Kidner, *Proverbs: An Introduction and Commentary* (Downers Grove, IL: Inter-Varsity Press, 1964), 157.